Means to Message:

A Treatise on Truth

By the same author

(continued on p. [234])

Means to Message

A Treatise on Truth

Stanley L. Jaki

WILLIAM B. EERDMANS PUBLISHING COMPANY
GRAND RAPIDS, MICHIGAN / CAMBRIDGE, U.K.

© 1999 Stanley L. Jaki

Published 1999 by Wm. B. Eerdmans Publishing Co.

255 Jefferson Ave. S.E., Grand Rapids, Michigan 49503 /

P.O. Box 163, Cambridge CB3 9PU U.K.

Printed in the United States of America

03 02 01 00 99   7 6 5 4 3 2 1

Library of Congress Cataloging-in-Data

Jaki, Stanley L.

Means to message : a treatise on truth / Stanley L. Jaki.

p.   cm.

Includes bibliographical references and indexes.

ISBN 0-8028-4651-3 (pbk. : alk. paper)

1. Philosophy.   2. Knowledge, Theory of.   3. Christianity —
Philosophy.   4. Knowledge, Theory of (Religion)   I. Title.

BD21.J35   1999

121 — dc21   98-53408

CIP

Table of Contents

Introduction

Approaches to philosophy are almost as many as are philosophers. This does not mean that relativism, an absolutism in disguise, is the gist of philosophical truth. It rather suggests the vastness of the conceptual riches that can be mined by the philosopher. Such riches turn into penury whenever a philosopher takes for his ideal the linear pattern along which the propositions of Euclidean geometry are unfolded. There the advance is straightforward from the parallel postulate to all the theorems Euclid set forth in Fourteen Books. If one transposes the parallel postulate to a spherical, or hyperbolical surface, one still posits a starting point from which all the theorems of this or that non-Euclidean geometry can be derived as if they formed a straight track.

The ideal of a straight, indeed a single-track advance, so dear to mathematicians and also to some physicists, is a mirage in philosophy. The reason for this lies with philosophy itself, which, if it is truly a love of wisdom, must deal above all with reality. Is it not in one's dealing with the real, especially in dealing with real thinking beings, so much more than mere minds, that wisdom proves itself? A wisdom that fails to be communicated is the hallmark of self-declared wrestling champions who never enter the ring. When one hears a world renowned astronomer-cosmologist boast of his solipsism, one's reaction is rightly a mixture of amusement and pity. The matter is much more serious when philosophers market their ware, presumably some form of love of wisdom, without seeing that their presuppositions forbid them to talk about it to anyone except themselves.

Philosophy has to be the love of reality all across the spectrum, which is, however, complexity incarnate. The real nowhere resembles an ideally simple point such as the one from which a geometer can derive, by juxtaposing many such points, a line, and a surface from lines, and from surfaces all conceivable volumes or forms of space, without as much as jotting anything on a sheet of paper. Moreover, in the real one finds simultaneously the test of what is true, as well as the expression of the good and the beautiful. It is up to the philosopher's predilections which of these aspects of the real will be central in his discourse.

If the philosopher focuses on truth, he will have to face up to the realm of objects. There alone can a truth proposition, insofar as it is more than a mere logical relation among concepts, be verified. If the philosopher focuses on the good, questions about the right purpose freely pursued would immediately arise. Advance in philosophy therefore resembles the continual enlarging of an area, with its confines being extended now in this, now in that direction. This may in part justify the order of topics adopted in this treatise on truth. It deals with truth insofar as truth reveals itself in real messages, which as such must make use of means of communication.

Different as they may be in their respective directions of advance, philosophy and geometry (or exact science) are very much alike in one basic respect. Insofar as they are a message addressed to others, philosophy and science depend on a means, an object, some physical reality, which even spoken words are, as the carrier of their message. That this dependence of the message on the means gives priority to the means over the message, will be recalled again and again throughout this book. The means, usually a book, raises, however, questions about much more than an object's reality as if this were not momentous enough. A book is an object produced freely and for a purpose, which is to make an impact on others. In other words, a book is a tool made by man and only by man in order to extend man's range of causation and achieve thereby a purpose.

This sequence is not pursued immediately after Chapter 1. Instead, right after that Chapter attention is drawn to the baneful influence of science on philosophy, a point which is again often recalled in this book. The influence in question started with Descartes, who at least was a first-rate geometer. Rather meager, at times vanishingly small was the scientific expertise of most of those philosophers who continued in the direction set by Descartes. Some, such as Kant in particular, cashed in on the second-rate philosophy which Galileo and Newton grafted onto science. Others, such as Hegel, turned with fury on good science which they were unable to disentangle from its pseudo-philosophical cocoon spun in part by leading scientists.

Lately, philosophy has been increasingly expropriated by philosophers of science and cultivators of cognitive psychology. These two professions claim to themselves the study of all the psychological and cultural conditions of empirical knowledge. They would leave philosophers with logic, which in turn is increasingly claimed by mathematicians. Being particularly adept in manipulating phrases, students of linguistics are apt to claim "modal logic," if it is still left at all in the domain of philosophers. Philosophy can indeed appear a meaningless enterprise if students of semiotics are right to claim to themselves the study of meaning.

Philosophers, who for some time turned lackadaisical about considering their subject matter as love of wisdom should only blame themselves if they see it being stolen from them. Most philosophers have for some time ceased to see any merit in basic considerations that alone could help them reclaim their own profession. One such consideration is that man can know only by knowing something, the only way to know, before he can do anything with his act of knowing even in the form of a mere conceptual analysis.

Neglect of such and other basic and very philosophical considerations by many philosophers is the cause of the fact that knowledge, as something severed from its philosophical matrix, has become a suspiciously marketable item. A most recent illustration of this is the creating of a richly endowed chair for philosophy in a business school in a prestigious American university. This is not to suggest that it would necessarily hurt a businessman to be a lover of wisdom as distinct from being a clever manipulator of customers or something even less reputable. But, tellingly enough, the first appointee to that chair earned international repute by co-authoring the book, *The Knowledge-Creating Company*. Even more expressive is the book's subtitle: *How Japanese Companies Create the Dynamics of Innovation*.[1] All this prompted one professor of philosophy to quip: "I couldn't understand what he could be a professor of. I was sort of baffled by what kind of truth it involves."[2] One wonders whether this was not the case of the kettle being jealous of the pot for its having turned into a jackpot.

Revealingly, the book deals with knowledge only in its first thirty or so pages, and even there it offers only a pedestrian survey of the major problems raised within philosophy since its inception. Beyond that, the book is a complicated oversystematization of exchange of information among people working in various sectors of the same company. Heads of great industrial establishments, who worked themselves up from the factory floor to the board-room, will not lose much by not joining this or that "knowledge-creating company." As to philosophers, only those will not be overawed by that book (leaving aside the problem of envy) who notice in its title a rank abuse of the word "creating."

Readers of my previous books, now almost forty in number, will easily recall that this is not the first time that I have deplored the increasingly facile handling of the word "creation," once a chief glory of Western culture. They will also find familiar some paragraphs and arguments in this book. A reason for this is that although a principal interest of mine is the history of science, I have always considered the study of history to be a branch of philosophy. All history either teaches by examples, which are such only if they serve as so many mirrors in which one can take a proper measure of oneself and of society. Otherwise, history will teach but dates, places, and names. One of the most profound statements a modern philosopher can make in defense of his subject is that only by saying nothing can one avoid becoming a philosopher, indeed a metaphysician.[3] This, however, means that in writing on philosophy one willy-nilly has to write a treatise on truth. For if anything, it is then the consideration and love of truth that puts one beyond the realm known as physical.

In writing such a treatise, one's primary attention has to be on the content of what one says. Contrary to the program set by logical positivists, philosophy is not a Post Office where what counts is not the content of letters but only whether they are properly formatted, addressed, and stamped. Philosophy is not "talk about talk" but a concern for the message that has been conveyed either by word or in print. Philosophy has therefore to be about something and inevitably also about the thing too that delivered that something (message) to philosophers and lesser mortals.

That thing or means should indeed be a first concern for any and all philosophers. In the measure in which such a concern is generally shared, one comes also a step closer to a long cherished ideal, namely, the bringing together of whatever there is valuable in the most varied philosophical systems. The ideal may seem unattainable in view of the attachment of any philosopher of some consequence to the initial direction he takes in extending the domain of philosophy. All too often this attachment takes the form of a rigid adherence that allows no compromise, not even some latitude, or liberality of mind. The entire history of philosophy is a proof that no philosopher has ever considered the initial direction or step taken by him to be negotiable.

The same history also shows the futility of attempts made at synthesizing or unifying often very disparate systems. That failure would easily reveal the ineptitude of trying to put the superstructure together without paying thorough attention to the fundamentals. But in focusing on those fundamentals one must do something different from reviewing those initial steps that had been offered so far. Not that all of them are equally good or bad. But perhaps there is something common to all those steps which as such would not prejudge the choice among them, although ultimately mean a very definite choice.

Now, for all their differences, philosophers are at one in a crucial and fundamental respect, be they skeptics, dogmatists, realists, idealists, rationalists, empiricists, positivists, phenomenologists, deconstructionists, materialists or what not. They all use tangible means for the delivery of their respective messages. The means may be the spoken word, a clay tablet, a scroll, a parchment, a codex, a broadsheet, a book, an E-mail projected on the monitor, or whatever even fancier, but it has to be a means, that is, something tangible. Therefore, if philosophers are logical, their strictly primary concern should be about the extent to which their particular philosophy justifies the use of any such means, indeed its very reality and all the consequences, both numerous and momentous, that follow from this.

There seems to be some originality in this approach to philosophy. I would not have started or continued writing this book, if my recollection of the history of philosophy had not assured me that I am not treading on a well-worn path. The perusal of representative selections from the works of modern or pre-modern philosophers hardly reveals on their part a sense of the need to justify thematically the means that carries their message.[4] Yet only in the measure in which that justification is done, implicitly or, what is far better, explicitly, may the philosopher's message become truly about truth.

Concern for that justification is therefore much more than a matter of logic, logical as the concern itself may appear. Concern for anything serious cannot be taught in a straightforward manner, if it can be taught at all. And since concern is a form of love, philosophy too, insofar as it is a love of wisdom, is not entirely teachable. Together with painting, sculpting, and composing, philosophizing is among the academic subjects that can least be taught. For just as art is in a good part a matter of inspiration, so is philosophy. Without being inspired by the love of truth, the philosopher at most becomes a logician, a glorified woodcutter, even when he does something better in the way of doing philosophy than just chopping logic. Philosophy can only be taught to one ready to be impressed by the mere reality of objects, inclined to marvel at their specificity, and disposed to savor the question that can be raised about any object, however trivial: why such and not something else?

Any sensitive pondering of this question may suggest that in ultimate analysis philosophy is about the peculiarity or specificity of the means that carries the message. In that sense the means anticipates the message which, if it is philosophy, must at least contain the full justification of the means used. The question— why such and not something else?—propels the search for truth, for all forms of truth. Since of the various forms of truth the scientific one has today an overweening significance, something is to be pointed out right at the outset about the difference between philosophy and science. While both philosophy and science begin with the question—why such and not something else?—they pose it in a different light already at the very start. Ideally speaking, the scientist singles out what is quantitative in reality and therefore he deals only with matter and only insofar as matter embodies quantitative features. From there the scientist proceeds along a straight track which conceptually is also an extremely narrow track, whatever the universal presence of quantities in the material world. The scientist need not probe into the deeper origin of matter as quantitatively patterned. It is enough for him to assume the validity of that patterning on the basis of common sense, which may or may not be the most widely shared sense, let alone a sense supported by ever-fickle opinion polls.

The philosopher must probe into the deeper reasons for all that and into many other aspects of reality in which the true, the good, and the beautiful are intertwined as they reveal ever greater depths that cannot be fathomed quantitatively. Moreover, the philosopher has to advance along a broad front, pushing forward now in this, now in that direction. For unlike the scientific truth, always sharp because narrow, the philosophical truth is always broad, because comprehensive, no matter how particular, and in fact how trivial, it may appear.

Being comprehensive, philosophical truth calls for embracing it, that is, to love it and turn it thereby into wisdom, which is an attitude that allows no parcelling. Dividing philosophy into topics is merely a practical necessity. The act of dividing presupposes, however, something that can be divided, not merely as so many concepts that can be analyzed but as a reality that alone yields real parts. Therein lies a logical first step for philosophy if it is not to become a solipsist's talk about talking to oneself even in the guise of an idealist's discourse in which philosophy becomes a series of mere ideas about ideas. Empiricists do not fare much better if they cannot find in the means something which can truly carry their message. Philosophy, which is a message addressed to others by some means, has therefore to be, before anything else, about objects, the very first topic in this book.

[1] New York: Oxford University Press, 1995. The authors are Ikujiro Nonaka and Hirotaka Takeuchi.

[2] See *The New York Times,* June 5, 1997, p. E5.

[3] A. E. Burtt, *In Search of Philosophic Understanding* (1965; New York: New American Library, 1967), p. 26.

[4] A case in point is the anthology, *American Philosophers at Work,* edited by S. Hook (New York: Criterion Books, 1956), consisting of two dozen selections from the writings of about as many American philosophers. I mention this book merely because it fell in my hands shortly after the completion of this book.

1

Objects

A book with the subtitle, "a treatise on truth," must, from its inception on, convey its author's resolve to face up to the question: What is truth? The question evokes Pilate's skepticism as well as Francis Bacon's observation: "'What is truth?' said jesting Pilate and would not stay for an answer."[1] The reader is asked to stay for the length of a few paragraphs to see the first intimations of the answer to be unfolded in this treatise which is emphatically meant to be on truth and not on a set of opinions about it. Those who find this dogmatic may very well reflect for a moment whether it is not some dogmatism that motivates their reaction. An apparently detached but actually unswerving, that is, dogmatic adherence to this or that "opinion" or even to one's "considered view" should seem less commendable than an undisguised presentation of this or that statement as truth, even if this passes for dogmatism.

Opinions about truth are legion and invariably have a dogmatic touch to them. All the hundred fifty or so dicta on truth in Mencken's *New Dictionary of Quotations* lay down something very definite. It is affirmed that the value of truth is priceless, that truth is universal, that ultimately truth would triumph, that children and fools are alike prompt with it, that truth and roses are equally endowed with thorns, that truth is naked as well as tough. Among these dicta there is, however, only one that would qualify as an answer to the question, What is Truth? Even Shakespeare's answer, "Truth is truth, until the end of reckoning,"[2] is in part an apparent tautology and in part an assertion of truth's exacting nature. Shakespeare, to whom we owe many pithy statements, full of philosophical depth, could, of course, very well suggest that truth was truth because it was irreducible to anything else and the reckoning merely separated truth from falsehood.

In Mencken's list, which is chronological, three scores of names are from Antiquity, Tertullian being the last of them. The next in the list is Wyclif. The two are separated by twelve centuries, most of them medieval centuries, all apparently void of quotable remarks about truth. Yet to that age belongs a definition of truth which would certainly pass for a straight answer to the plain question, What is Truth? The answer, "adaequatio rei ad intellectum," is Aquinas' definition of truth. It often turns up in modern reflections on philosophy in proof of the universally shared conviction that truth somehow must be connected with reality.[3]

Instead of reality it may be better to speak of objects. The immediate and pressing reason for speaking of objects rather than of reality, does not lie in the incredibly vast extent and variety of meanings that can and have been attached to the word *truth*. The reason relates to the title of this book, "means to message." Whenever a philosopher offers the kind of message which is philosophy, it must contain, at the very minimum, a justification of the means used to convey the message to beings no less real than the author himself. The means therefore is not a medium, or a tool contrived for the purpose of making the message indistinguishable from its packaging or even subordinate to it. Whereas Marshall McLuhan of "the medium is the message" fame helped focus on this widespread abuse in communication, he did not care to disentangle the means from the medium. As a result he unwittingly fueled an abuse already reaching crisis proportions in public discourse, where what counts is no longer the message but the manner in which it is perceived. This sinister trend has not spared discourse about philosophy. In the "publish or perish" syndrome the book counts more than its message, which, to make all this worse, hardly ever contains even a fleeting reflection of the truth of the book itself.

A book is certainly an object, except perhaps for a solipsist. Even Kantians would spiritedly protest the objection (already made to their very master, and in full class) that their principles prohibit them from speaking of any object at all. At the very least, utter honesty should prevail concerning the reality of the means or object, or the book. Utter honesty is a quality which in general all philosophers claim, though all too often with no specific reference to even that object which is the means or book that carries their message. With honesty or not, philosophers have been prime breeders of skepticism. One need not be a philosopher to be bewildered by the endless infighting among philosophers, or at least schools of philosophy. There is a jarring contrast between the claim that important questions have been definitively clarified as philosophical systems followed one another, and the observation offered in the same breath that those systems do the same kind of service to one another that a lamb does to a lion.[4] For if such is the case, can one be sure of the survival of any lamb, or of the lion's lasting satisfaction?

Such a question is unsettling even when it arises in the context of a firm commitment to truth as different from a transient consensus about mere opinions. When such a context is absent, scoffing at philosophy may run rampant. The edge of the claim that philosophy is "a route of many roads leading from nowhere to nothing" may seem blunted somewhat if one recalls its provenance, *The Devil's Dictionary*.[5] No such saving grace is attached to Strindberg's declaration, that "the history of philosophy is a history of falsehood, the history of lying." Strindberg merely rubbed salt into wounds by saying that this was so because "nearly all philosophers are disguised rebels against God" and that therefore "all professorships of philosophy should be abolished."[6] Philosophers at most could point out that one became a philosopher when one denounced philosophy as "a systematic abuse of a terminology invented for that very purpose."[7]

Philosophers who readily handed down sharp indictments on their predecessors have some of the responsibility to bear. Philosophy hardly inspired confidence when William James portrayed it as "a collective name for questions that have not yet been

answered to the satisfaction of all."[8] The same is true of Wittgenstein's dictum, "most propositions and questions that have been
written about philosophical matters are not false, but senseless."[9]
Far fewer among philosophers took the more cautious stance of
Frederic Rauh, one of Etienne Gilson's teachers at the Sorbonne,
who used to muse in class: "There are times when one feels almost
ashamed to call himself a philosopher."[10] Only philosophers with
pantheistic proclivities could take comfort on being told that "a
philosophy may indeed be the most momentous reaction of the
universe upon itself."[11] But no pantheist can feel flattered on
being reminded, as Joshua Royce was by William James, of the
fun which the Almighty would feel of being part of him.

Yet, while indictments and dubious praises of philosophy
gained ever wider audience, attention to what is at the bottom of
the malaise of philosophy rarely became specific, let alone
conspicuous. Wittgenstein, for one, felt keenly that some sort of
cheating had become part of professional philosophizing. Otherwise he would not have addressed to a student who had just
received his Ph. D. in philosophy these sobering words: "May you
make good use of it! By that I mean: may you not cheat either
yourself or your students. Because, unless I'm very much mistaken,
that's what will be expected of you."[12] But Wittgenstein did not
preach this from the housetops. True, even if he had done so in
his *Tractatus,* it would have hardly provoked a significant echo.

Not that Wittgenstein had charged his fellow philosophers
with intentional cheating. He seems to have referred to a facile
acceptance of phrases and perspectives, which are imposed by the
consensus as starting points with no further questions asked. In
particular he deplored what he saw to be a chronic carelessness
on the part of philosophers about being as clear as possible. This
could only mean, as was indeed the case, that for Wittgenstein
clarity was the primary desideratum in philosophy. He did not
notice that in order to put across this desideratum he had to use
a concrete means, an object, a book, or even that still very concrete
though less tangible means which is human speech.

Indeed before any talk about clarity there comes the object or
the means that carries the philosopher's message about clarity.

For that reason alone objects that serve as the means of the philosophical message should be given the primary consideration. Otherwise philosophy is bound to degenerate into talk about talk even when that talk takes on the form of arcane discourses about doubt, certainty, habit, custom, probability, sensations, induction, testability, falsifiability, and even about clarity as such. The first step should be the registering of objects, or else the philosopher will be guilty of a sleight of hand, however sophisticated. He will have to bring in through the back door the very objects the use of which his starting point failed to justify. In fact, some starting points may have prohibited the philosopher from referring to any object at all, which, let it be noted, are not the same as mere ideas about them. If objects are not presented as a primary datum, some other factors will expropriate that role. As a result cheating, or at least some clever maneuvers, will be taken for the vindication of objects and for profundity in philosophy. For objects shall not cease claiming their rights to be recognized for what they are: objects and not their disembodied conceptual shadows.

Objects cannot be vindicated in terms of something else. The registering of objects cannot be reduced to any other proposition which is still addressed to others. The use of means, of any means, obligates the philosopher to recognize the objective truth of means, so many objects. This is a truth, the very first to be unfolded from among the steps that allow one to go from means to messages. This truth cannot be evaded, let alone be refuted, because the refutation itself is an act of communication, an implicit falling back on objective means whereby alone can other philosophers be reached.

The radical primacy of registering objects or, in general, tangible reality has other considerations as well to recommend it. Foremost of these is that it enables one to raise logically the question, What is an object, what is reality?—a question which is all too often taken for the first step even by philosophers who have a penchant for realism but fail to see their being captive to idealism. The registering of objects alone makes possible the improvement of one's knowledge of objects standing for reality. Ordinary, everyday direct knowledge of material objects may be incomplete or even outright faulty at times. But only by making use of another act of registering such objects can the process of improvement start and be continued.

This is even true in the arcane world of reality investigated by particle physics. All knowledge about those particles and all improvement on that knowledge ultimately depends on register-ing, again and again, the reality of objects called instruments, whose massive size does not demand arcane ways of observation. Something of this was suspected even by that foremost idealist among modern physicists, Eddington, when he remarked that "molar physics always has the last word in observation, for the observer himself is molar."[13] He would have zeroed in on the truth, had he spoken of instruments of observations, rather than of observers. But for an inveterate idealist even the moment of truth becomes elusive. Being an idealist, Eddington could not put his teeth into his fumbling grasp of the primacy of real objects over mere ideas about them, even if the ideas in questions are dressed in arcane mathematics.

The sole apparent disadvantage of according primacy to the immediate registering of objects is the circumstance that such an act cannot be rendered in terms of symbolic logic, which has increasingly become the sole accepted currency of philosophical transactions. Strange as it may seem, no logic can cope with the relation of the knower to the object registered by him. That relation is emphatically *sui generis* in the strictest sense, not comparable to any other relation. And certainly, the "adequation" of the thing to the knower is not an equation in the mathematical sense of the word. The equation is not an equalizing of the knower with the thing known, or vice versa, as either the idealist or the empiricist might be forced to suggest. In the former case, the equation means the dilution of the object into ideas, be they called categories that originate independently of things. In the case of empiricism, the equation prohibits the thing to reveal what is intelligible in it. The equation has therefore to be between a thing embodying intelligibility and a mind capable of responding to it, an equation best called adequation.

Anchoring therefore the truth in that adequation as rooted in the registering of objects, should commend itself as a most reasonable, primary act in philosophy, irreducible to anything else in the process of understanding. Its reasonableness can easily be tested by the results if one tries to substitute anything else for it. Indeed, vain substitutions to that primary act pockmark the entire history of philosophy, especially its modern part, which may indeed be called its skid row section, if a laboratory can be called such. For the history of philosophy plays for the latter the role of what a laboratory plays in science. History does not fail to test the message of philosophers. What a given generation of philosophers overlooked is mercilessly exposed by the next generation of philosophers and often even sooner. That history shows that in the measure in which a philosopher refused to turn the act of registering objects into the cornerstone of his system of truth, his system displayed more and more of its inability to cope with the truthfulness of reality, with the real world. For in philosophical discourse too the truth of the pudding is in the eating. A philosopher makes a good account of himself in the measure in which he can eat his words and prove in this way to his readers that they won't be in to an intellectual discomfort if they feast on those words. Were they served a healthy fare, they might ask, when presented with an increasingly contorted phraseology, or were they simply cheated?

Apart from questions of style, the cheating is detectable in the very first assertion of an otherwise unpretentiously phrased philosophical treatise. Wittgenstein did not suspect that he put himself, however unintentionally, into the camp of cheating philosophers when right at the start of the *Tractatus* he declared: "The world is everything that is the case." For this statement to be true, or at least that it may not be a gratuitous assumption, it had to be true that the world, or the universe itself, was no less a real thing than copies of the *Tractatus,* or the very means that carried that message about the world, which is supposedly everything. Unconditional registering of particular things, including copies of the *Tractatus*, merely transpires in its very first sentence. The rest of the *Tractatus* contains no justification of any talk of things or objects. This once celebrated work reveals a far greater concern about the clarity of propositions than about the propositions being about objects in the first place. But neither Wittgenstein nor any other philosopher can assert the totality of things, or the world, that is, the Universe, unless he has first accounted for the reality of that mere object, a book, or at least emphatically declared his intellectual surrender to it. For unless he does so, he will have no right to use that object as the means that carries his message about the world or even about anything far less comprehensive.

Whatever else a treatise on truth must account for, it first must do full justice to that most immediate reality which any object is. If not, the treatise becomes an illusory march, the like of which Chairman Mao parodied in his once famous "little red book" where he claimed that it is not possible to take the second or third steps without having taken the first. Poking fun at such homespun wisdom, another Chairman, Krushov, did not reveal philosophical acumen. He failed to see that all Marxists missed the boat of sound economics precisely because they took a second or third step for the first. Recurring upheavals in the capitalist economies have a similar moral, valid for philosophy as well: It is not recommended that one should borrow first before having deposited something at least in the form of some collateral and go on covering further debts with further borrowing, against no deposits at all. Like finances, truth too has its day of reckoning.

In this age of the cult of sport, including the sport of merely being its spectator (without counting stamp collecting as a form of athletics), the words of a famous cricketer might do even better. I mean Bob Simpson, captain of the Australian cricket team which, in 1989, dealt England its worst defeat ever. On being asked about the key to his team's phenomenal success, he said: "All of sport is about the initial movement and if you interfere with that you are in trouble."[14] Those who take philosophy for a mere game in logic, and their number is not small, have here much more food for thought than their logic chopping could turn into palatable pieces, so that their cleverness may go on digesting.

It may seem wholly trivial to insist that the first duty of a philosopher is to endorse the reality of the book (or the physical reality of a discourse) which is the means making his message available. Common sense, strengthened with keen attention to elementary logic, would demand this. Yet that very sense, if not sufficiently alert and not carefully distinguished from mere common opinion, may serve as an excuse to overlook that duty, because common sense seems to assure automatically that there are such realities as books. Once in the grip of that oversight, the philosopher may all the more readily indulge in patently self-defeating claims.

A case in point is Auguste Comte's favorite statement (a logical implication of his positivism) that everything is relative and this is the only absolute truth. Comte certainly did not take the heavy tomes of his *Cours de philosophie positive* for something which were only relatively positive. Had skeptics reflected on the means that carried their skepticism, they might have realized that there was nothing skeptical in their use of such means. Instead they have all too often tried to remedy matters by lame warnings that one should not be dogmatic about one's skepticism. Was not the warning covertly dogmatic? Materialists may have been in a logically advantageous position to lay claim to reality from the very start, had not their materialism forbidden them to see in their claims acts that were so many genuinely mental as well as free registering of objects.

Obvious as it may be that the first step is of crucial significance in discoursing about the real to real people, failure to pay heed to this is responsible for the fact that the history of philosophy may appear to be a chain of errors. A recent link in that chain was laid bare by none other than Ayer. At the end of a long career and in the wake of much popularity, he admitted that "the most important of the defects [of logical positivism] was that nearly all of it was false."[15] Such failure often derives from the philosopher's readiness to take easy cover with a reference to an earlier philosophical school. This became a pattern soon after philosophers began to describe themselves as Platonists, Aristotelians, Stoics, and Sophists or what not. The pattern, which has become an overweening academic pastime, certainly proves that the pasting of labels is a skill which is all too often taken for a dispensation from the duty of looking beneath the surface.

Platonists as a rule have not shown more concern than Plato did to justify the concrete means—scrolls, parchments, and books—that carried their discourses about ideas. They still have to show convincingly that the mere idea, however perfect, of a book can give reality to the book itself. They are still to show what is far less, namely, that mere ideas can set rules for the structure and action of tangible matter. Reliance on the five perfect Platonic bodies—floating in the metaphysical stratosphere—was a mere fluke in Kepler's case in determining the relative distances of the planets. It took him some time to digest the fact that the orbits of planets were not perfect circles *à la* Plato, but ellipses. Ideas were not to dictate to reality, except through some transparent verbalizations. Only those with no knowledge of what had happened in physics could be overawed by Hegel's claim that the elliptical orbit of planets necessarily followed from his dialectic. This trick, aimed at circumventing Newton, was part of the encyclopedic mess which Hegel's idea of the Absolute made of physics and other branches of experimental science.

The debacle of Platonist idealism can be further illustrated in the efforts of some 20th-century mathematical physicists who love to take mere numbers for things whose measures they skillfully count and co-ordinate. In fact, in a truly Platonist fashion they claim, as will be seen later, to have thereby the means not only to predict things but also to predetermine them in the sense of literally creating them. Such physicists do not take the trouble to study the history of the difficulties that have not ceased plaguing Platonists. They seem to think that some old errors are rectified by being served up again and again as if they were fresh truths just because dressed up in a new garb.

Rationalists did not give a better account of themselves in coming to terms with objects. Descartes' *cogito ergo sum* is a case in point. It assured him only of talking to himself about himself. He remained trapped in his *own* ideas as he tried to proceed to real things, but he could never reach them in terms of his own presuppositions. Instead of starting with objects that happen to be extended, he started with extension, a mere idea. This starting point could appear all the more promising as Descartes was the great inventor of analytical geometry. And since common sense could furtively be relied upon to assure the reality of things, all of which happen to be extended, Descartes did not feel it imperative to justify, in terms of his own presuppositions, the use of very extended realities, books, that carried his philosophical message.

Herein lies the ultimate source of the futility of the attempt of Descartes and of all Cartesians to discourse sensibly about physical reality on both the small and the large scale. Extension, taken abstractly, could not divert attention from concrete physical things. These would reveal their physics only if experimented with, a procedure which primarily demands the registering of physical objects. The rationalist Descartes' physics thus became a not too rational sidespur in the history of science. His scenario of cosmogony, which he thought God himself might have as well followed, turned out to be a mere novel, to recall an acid remark of Huygens.

No less instructive is the case of Spinoza, the most resolute Cartesian of them all. No sensible reader of Spinoza's great treatise, *Ethica more geometrico demonstrata*, could overlook the fact that he meant it to be about much more than abstract ethical principles. But that much more, which should have included real things, did not follow from Spinoza's typically Cartesian syllogisms. The airing of this was done swiftly, though as gently as this could be done by a gentleman philosopher, Tschirnhausen, from Heidelberg. In a letter he asked Spinoza about how particular, specific objects followed from the abstract considerations that Spinoza fashioned and marshalled along the pattern of Euclidean geometry. Spinoza promised an answer, which, however, never came.

Another memorable illustration of the consequences of positing a starting point other than the unconditional registering of objects or reality relates to the misfortunes of Kant's philosophy, another rationalist product. Such a registering was impossible once the thing, or object had been turned into a *noumenon* and became thereby radically severed even from its phenomena. The object has become unknown and unknowable because, severed from its object, the phenomena inevitably became mere sensations in the subject. No wonder that subjectivism, in fact of a very willful kind, marks every page of Kant's *Opus postumum* in which he applied the precepts of the *Critique* to the task of setting forth, indeed of legislating, about the various branches of physical science. The book, almost two thousand quarto pages in manuscript, written during Kant's last seven or so years, filled Neo-Kantians with dismay when it came to light seventy years after Kant's death, at the height of his Neo-Kantian glory. One wonders what Kant would have said had he cared to ponder the problem whether books exist as things even when they are not read or seen or are not in the focus of one's consciousness.

Realists of the Aristotelian tradition were in a far better position to posit reality as a first step in philosophy and avoid thereby resorting to subsequent illogicalities. Yet already with Aristotle attention shifted to what can be built on a reliable starting point rather than to have one's attention riveted on it for a while at least. Raphael's *Disputazione* rendered well the thrust of Aristotelian realism as he let the Philosopher pose with a finger pointed at the good old ground. Taking a stance on that ground he could argue that it was possible to justify ideas, though not Plato's ideas, and to resolve the dilemma set by Heracleitus and Parmenides, whether all was change or whether there was no change at all. Against Heracleitus it was possible to say that he wanted to communicate to others an unchangeable truth about change. Parmenides could be turned back by observing that his plea about no change at all, meant to bring about some change in some beings no less real than he himself.

On that realist basis it was also possible to refute Zeno's sophistries, among them the alleged impossibility to cover any distance, be it so short as the one stretching from one end of a room to the other. Zeno made sense only if one could be sure about things at a distance, even if at a leisurely walk, and if one could make one real step. But Zeno was forbidden by his own sophistry to refer to any real object that lay even at arm's length from him. Diogenes did certainly contradict his cynicism, when in a truly realist fashion he walked that distance and in doing so he provided the first recorded use of the proof called *solvitur ambulando*, a philosophical principle, which only thoroughbred realists can invoke consistently.

One would only wish that Aristotle had pointed in a more sustained and articulate manner at the primary status of the reality of objects around anyone who discoursed about having understood them. But even in philosophy as in life in general not every need can be fully anticipated, let alone in an emphatic way. Thus it happened that Aristotelians all too often got bogged down in secondary tasks such as the clarifications needed about the relation of substantial form and prime matter. Both were indispensable postulates to assure rational understanding of change as different from an incoherent succession of events across time. But once those postulates were taken for objects of empirical knowledge, a process started that sparked skepticism about the Aristotelian doctrine of substance. This happened even among Aristotelians, although their recent variety, Transcendental Thomists, who should be rather called Aquikantists for their egregious miscegenation of Aquinas and Kant, can only blame themselves for the skepticism, in the guise of subjectivism, they so effectively promote.

Tellingly, they formulated their program after the late-19th-century return to Kant made clear the appalling measure of skepticism which Kant's thought could generate. The measure could be best gauged by Vaihinger's imperious effort, the famed *als ob*, of escaping from it. But it was a cheating or at least a game in self-deception to claim, as he did, that although one does not know things and how they operate, it was best to assume that they function *as if* they should, at least for the sake of our convenience.

Not to start with things is to make things subservient to one's learned whim and fancy. Starting with the ideas of things instead of the very things is a form of cheating as inadmissible as would be a rewriting of the rules whereby baseball is played. There it is not possible to rush or slide to second base without first having reached first base. In fact no runner is allowed to first base, unless he has first successfully hit the ball thrown at him. The analogy can be further extended: The pitcher is the philosopher, the ball he throws is the book in which his treatise on truth is literally embodied. And since he throws that book (the legal nuance is not to be missed) at his fellow philosophers, his treatise on truth must be such as to assure rigorously the reality of that book or ball.

Unfortunately, much of philosophy, especially in modern times, has come to resemble more and more a spurious baseball game: There the opposing teams (schools of philosophy) assume without further ado, that one can get to first base without first really hitting a real ball, which in the case of philosophy is a book, in the first place. Yet nobody cares to press philosophers sitting in prestigious academic chairs (so many coveted pitcher's mounds in professional philosophy), whether they consider the grave implications of the fact that they are throwing real books at real readers and they do this all too often in utter disregard of what is allowed to them by their philosophies.

Therefore back to the book, that is, to the reality of the book itself! It is in that far from trivial sense that a sound philosophy, or any treatise on truth, must be a "bookish" philosophy. That reality cannot be convincingly reached by empiricism. Empiricism, apart from its willful restrictions on what reality is, does not begin with a categorical registration of reality, but with a characterization of it. Reality is declared to be empirical in the sense that it can be somehow sensed and that all knowledge not only must begin, but should also end in the sensory real. Empiricists overlook the fact that there is nothing sensory about empiricism as such. Empiricism is, of course, closer to reality than is mere sensationism, to which it logically leads. Sensationism begins with one's sensations that are strictly located within one's body being taken for the sensing self. Sensationism does indeed lock its consistent protagonists within their own selves. In espousing Buddhism Ernst Mach certainly testified to the logic whereby empiricism leads to sensationism, which in turn may make one simply exit from philosophy as a communicable set of propositions.

Rational discourse has to start with objects in order to be fully logical and consistent in its being addressed to others, who, persons as they are, are still objects. Talking directly to pure spirits may very well be possible and exceedingly fruitful. Mystics are taken lightly only by philistines. Mystical communing with pure spirits such as God or angels, can, however, be related only if one starts with the registering of objects. Only through the primordial registering of objects can anything, be it the highest form of mystical experience, be consistently asserted, articulated, and communicated to others.

In fact, even that act of registering of objects needs to be specified, lest it turn out to be idealism in disguise. A brief reflection on the etymology of the word *object* may help clarify this point. A mere reference to the Latin *ob-jicere* (to throw at one) from which the English *to object* derives, may make abundantly clear that an object is something which throws itself at one and therefore "objects." The object activates the mind, instead of being activated by the mind in any sense. It is therefore not enough to speak of the registering of reality as a program or method that reminds the philosopher to return continually to his primary contact with reality. One should think rather of the ability of objects to impose themselves on the mind, by constantly objecting to it and challenging it. The media, let us not forget this, would not be able to bombard the public round the clock, if objects, be they mere scintillations on the screen, would not be objecting.

An object or reality that can perform this function—regardless of the momentary or protracted diversions or deactivations of the mind—must exist independently not only of one's thinking but also of one's sensations. A case in point is a book when not held in one's hands and not beheld with one's eyes. Such an object alone can object to the mind and force it to perform that simplest of all recognitions which is carried by the apparently most trivial of all trivial phrases: "It is there." The phrase does not mean the happening of something there as its "emergence" at a particular point and moment. The phrase denotes the status of something insofar as it keeps existing and is *existential* in this sense.

The thrust of the phrase, "It is there," bears on the *existence* of the "it" or the thing or object. Heidegger, this master of squeezing unnoticed nuances of meaning from words, never came close to Chesterton's great philosophical and linguistic tour de force: "There *is* an is!"[16] The Sage of Beaconsfield did not mean to endorse thereby ontologism in which the "it" or the thing is primary. He simply asserted in an inimitable way that objects or things *are* before they do anything else. Indeed that phrase, "It *is* there!" may serve as the fulcrum that sustains and moves all the weight of philosophy, while discarding its vastly accumulated deadweight.

Logicism, which is a principal part of that deadweight, will be further discussed in connection with the topic of the mind, which is also a self. Here let it be stated that to register objects that "object" to the mind's subjectivity, is *to know,* and that it is impossible to know without knowing *something*, which in the first place has to be an object. Reflection on such an act of knowledge that registers reality is consciousness. The *cogito ergo sum* of Descartes merely reversed the right order, which may be phrased as follows: Objects prompt my knowledge of them; this I know, and in that knowledge I perceive that I exist. The starting point is the very object which by its existence is able to "object" to the mind or to alert it. Herein, in the object's "objecting," lies the source of all objectivity. Nothing can be clearer than this, or more immediately obvious. Indeed the obviousness is fundamental also in the sense that it cannot be traced to anything else. Reality (or objects) cannot be explained in terms of the unreal. Objects as directly known by man can only be traced to other objects and from there to something which is even more fundamentally real or objective, opening up thereby metaphysical depths.

On sighting those depths some would cry wolf and urge that mysteries be banished forever from philosophy. In trying to implement a mystery-free philosophizing, so attractive to rationalists of all sorts, one may, however, end up in banishing any firm foothold from philosophy. If the recognition that there is something that cannot be explained in terms of something else is equated with invitation to mystery mongering, such a use of the word "mystery" can be readily unmasked as a verbal confusion. The source of that confusion is simply an inordinate dissatisfaction with the fact that one has to start somewhere and be certain about this as well as utterly honest. Such is merely the reverse of the fact that somewhere even the buck must stop. Refusal to accept that certainty leads to the kind of mystery mongering which finally engulfs even the reality of one's very self. A classic case of this stultifying result is the statement of H. Reichenbach, a logical positivist, that we cannot be absolutely sure even of our own existence.[17]

Reichenbach was hankering after the kind of absolute certainty of which the equation sign (=) is a parody, because it does not deal with the real but only with ideas of some of its aspects. Absolute certainty about the real can certainly be had in the spiritual state called heaven, a prospect Reichenbach was not known to relish. His kind of hankering after absolute certainty could only be satisfied in the physical state known as absolute zero temperature. There even the mind would absolutely freeze into abstract logical propositions that are tautologies and never a tie to the tangibly real. In that state there will be no objects left capable of "objecting," because this act demands expendable energy, which is available only at temperatures above absolute zero. The only comfort that seems to remain for logical positivists, who are often grim physicalists as well, is that the absolute zero point is unattainable on the temperature scale. They can therefore forever repeat their specious claim that there is no such a thing as absolute certainty. In saying this they merely propose an absolute verity which they profess with no trace of uncertainty. To crown the comedy, they sin not only against logic, but, what should be a far greater crime in their eyes, against science. Does not Nernst's law state it as absolute verity that the absolute zero temperature is unattainable in a *real* world?

Hankering after a certainty which is so absolute that it causes one to cast doubt on the certainty of one's own existence leaves one with no starting point which is safe from wholesale doubt. That kind of certainty is the mirage of sheer tautologies. Their classic case is the class of mathematical definitions or in general of quantities. These can indeed cast a blindingly sharp light but only on quantities. To try to locate anything else in things, let alone the very reality of these, by *that* light so that one may *clearly* grasp them, only causes them to slip through one's mental fingers, an outcome to which we must now turn.

[1] The opening remark of Essay I in Bacon's *Essays*.

[2] *Measure for Measure*, Act V, Scene 1.

[3] See, for instance, E. A. Burtt, *In Search for Philosophic Understanding* (1965: Mentor Books, 1967), p. 26.

[4] J. Maritain, *On the Use of Philosophy: Three Essays* (1961; New York: Athenaeum, 1965), p. 25.

[5] A. Bierce, *The Devil's Dictionary* (1906; Cleveland: The World Publishing Co., n. d.), p. 251.

[6] A. Strindberg, *Zones of the Spirit: A Book of Thoughts*, tr. C. Field (New York: Haskell House, 1974), p. 255.

[7] The phrase seems to have originated in German academic circles in the late 19th century and ran as follows: "Philosophie ist die systematische Misbrauch einer eigens zu diesem Zwecke erfundenen Terminologie."

[8] W. James, "Philosophy and Its Critics," in his *Some Problems in Philosophy: A Beginning of an Introduction to Philosophy* (New York: Longmans, Green and Co., 1911), p. 23. Tellingly, James laid the blame for this on the fact that all too often the answers were expected to come from science.

[9] *Tractatus logico-philosophicus*, proposition 4.0003.

[10] E. Gilson, *The Philosopher and Theology*, tr. Cécile Gilson (New York: Random House, 1952), p. 37.

[11] W. James, *A Pluralistic Universe* (New York: Longmans, Green and Co., 1909), p. 317.

[12] Quoted in A. Kenny, *Wittgenstein* (London: Allen Lane, The Penguin Press, 1973), p. 12.

[13] A. S. Eddington, *The Philosophy of Physical Science* (1939; Ann Arbor: The University of Michigan Press, 1958), p. 77.

[14] "Why England Failed?" *The Times* (London), Aug. 31, 1989.

[15] Quoted in B. Magee, *Men of Ideas: Some Creators of Contemporary Philosophy* (London: British Broadcasting Corporation, 1978), p. 131.

[16] G. K. Chesterton, *St. Thomas Aquinas* (New York: Sheed & Ward, 1933), p. 206.

[17] H. Reichenbach, *The Rise of Scientific Philosophy* (Berkeley: University of California Press, 1951), p. 268.

2

Clarity

The reality of objects should be a truth clearer than daylight. What can be clearer than what is immediately evident? Can anything be more evident than an object, such as a book, held in hand, though the book's content may be anything but clear? What can be more obvious than the fact that any argument against the reality of objects must make use of objects in order to be conveyed? Yet the great majority of philosophers, or at least of their modern brand, would not hold high that obviousness. In its place they want clear ideas, before they will consider the question of whether any object can be clear at all, let alone admitting that there are clearly existing things. Yet, the more a philosopher refuses to surrender to the clarity of immediate reality, the less clarity he is able to pack into his books about reality or in fact even about ideas. This is especially the case when the ideal of clear ideas is taken from the exact sciences, increasingly heavy with mathematics. The philosopher who yields to the lure of that ideal will produce books that, like *The Critique of Pure Reason*, are void of mathematics but full of obscure passages especially at critical junctures.

Kant compounded his mistake of starting from ideas with trying to emulate the clarity of Newtonian physics. Worse, in physics Kant was a poor amateur, which not one of his contemporaries suspected, although it should have been obvious. Descartes, who instead of physics chose mathematics (geometry) to imitate, was the creator of analytical geometry and therefore not guilty of

27

incompetence. But he clearly meant to shut out all clarity except
that of geometry as he jotted down his memorable resolution: "To
accept nothing more than what was presented to my mind so
clearly and distinctly that I could have no occasion to doubt it."[1]
This went hand in hand with his having indicted all other
philosophers for having marketed obscurities.

    This may not have been altogether his fault. He referred to
the Jesuit College in La Flèche as he reminisced: "I had been
taught . . . that there is nothing imaginable so strange or so little
credible that it has not been maintained by one philosopher or
other."[2] If this was indeed done at La Flèche, it was a cheap way
of creating interest in the subject. Voltaire's leering at philosophy
may have had similarly doubtful pedagogical sources. Yet
Descartes should have remembered that he had been taught at
La Flèche some most credible things about reality. It was not
his teachers' fault that he became so taken up by his idea of
clarity that he ended up by urging all who experimented to
send him their results because he alone could interpret them
properly. Apparently, the clarity Descartes found was not entirely
communicable.

    The aggressiveness with which logical positivists demanded
that others obey their type of utter clarity, is now history. But the
deconstructionists, who replaced them as the imperialists of the
departments of philosophy and of editorial boards of journals of
philosophy, are actually operating with the tools sharpened by
logical positivists. The difference is merely this. The logical
positivists hoped to construct. Memorable examples are Carnap's
Logische Aufbau der Welt, and various productions of members of
the Wiener Kreis. Such among the latter who transplanted
themselves to the United States, inspired the University of
Chicago Press series, "Encyclopedia of Unified Knowledge." Its
professed program aimed at eliminating anything that could not
pass for knowledge according to their precepts. The unification of
knowledge thereby achieved was blinding indeed by its restrictive
clarity. But the price to be paid for this was that a vast amount of
knowledge had to be eliminated as unworthy of rigorous minds
and unsuited for survival. The procedure, that can be conveniently

studied in Herbert Feigl's program of "scientific philosophy," was even more radical than the triage practiced in military hospitals close to battlefields. However, the aim was still to construct.

The deconstructionists did not even care to suggest that, as they put their analytical crowbar and jackhammer into anything within their reach, they wanted to construct something. Of course, they could not help having some idea of construction in mind. Whatever the conceptual problems of utter negativism, it certainly contradicts ineradicable human purposiveness. Even suicide is committed for something positive, however misconceived. Refuse heaps are constructs, although responsible builders are not eager to use them for developments.

Sometime before the deconstructionists began to ride the crest of the wave, the one-dimensional clarity of logical positivism had prompted some notable reactions. Heidegger's Nazi sympathies should not distract from his basically romantic efforts to gain, with forceful twisting of old words and phrases, some new grip on reality. He suggested a great deal, without proving much. In particular he forgot that one must first have things before there can be on hand aspects to turn and twist. No romanticism seemed to animate the group that broke away from the American Philosophical Association in 1987. They could no longer tolerate the rank intolerance displayed, for instance, by the editorial boards of leading journals of philosophy. These seemed to accept only such papers for publications whose authors worked along the lines set by Quine's dictum that "to be is to be the value of a variable." This dictum Quine himself held, to quote his very word, "persistently."[3]

Had Shakespeare, who thrived on stories, old and new, lived to see such tyranny at work, he would have found inspiration for at least a tragicomedy in the story which is too good to be a mere invention. The story is about an engineering major who, in order to enlarge his mind, took a survey course in English literature. On being asked to evaluate Hamlet, he described him as a low efficiency internal combustion engine, who destroyed six people although he could have resolved the problem by killing only one, his mother. Whatever the merit of this as a piece of literary criticism, it is unobjectionable if "to be" is merely the value of a variable, and not the alternative to "not to be."

The true instructiveness of Quine's definition of "to be" lies not so much in his persistence in preaching it, suggestive as this can be of intellectual imperialism. The words, "the value of a variable," are much more instructive in that they evoke mathematical physics to anyone even vaguely instructed in it. This is why those words are seductive as well as blinding. Mathematics is the *par excellence* study of quantities, and what can be clearer than a quantity? Quantities seem to be self-evident. Anyone who knows the unit number will have a clear idea of the numbers two, three and so forth. Any integer number beyond one can be obtained by mere addition, which in turn can be represented by a mere juxtaposition of any number of the same clear geometrical unit, a square for instance. Subtraction is merely the reverse of the same. Multiplication readily follows from addition, and division again is the reverse of the former.

Of course, problems arose already at the dawn of mathematics and seemed to pose a threat to its very rationality. It is no accident that certain kind of numbers came to be called irrational. The recognition that the length of the hypotenuse of a right-angled equilateral triangle cannot be measured in terms of integers or of their fractions made it clear that complete quantitative clarity was not to be had even in mathematics. Then there followed the recognition that one could not square the circle. The exact calculation of the ratio of a circle's circumference to its radius also proved to be unattainable. Had those who first noted this spoken English, they might have perceived that by calling that ratio π they put a pie in the mathematical sky.

Other perplexities emerged in the measure in which mathematics developed and became applied in physics. Some of these perplexities were eliminated in the long run. The imprecision in the definition of the limit in calculus was banished by Cauchy in 1821, but only after generations of physicists and mathematicians had to satisfy themselves with the faith that a solution would eventually come. The imprecision of imaginary numbers that play a fundamental role in electromagnetics was not to be eliminated. Mathematicians were to face even deeper imprecisions. Bertrand Russell was only half joking when in 1901 he described mathematics as "the subject in which we never know what we are talking about, nor whether what we are saying is true."[4]

A generation later a fundamental lack of clarity was disclosed about mathematics, when Gödel presented his incompleteness theorems. They render futile any effort to construct a mathematical system with built-in consistency. But a still more basic lack of clarity in mathematics resides in a circumstance which is as obvious as is all too often forgotten, especially by philosophers. Yet, their entire *raison d'être* depends on making the most of that lack of clarity in this age when almost everything is given attention, provided it is couched in references to science and especially if it comes from the mouth of a prominent scientist.

Certainly prominent was Hermann Weyl among mathematicians of this century. No less prominent was the forum, the bicentennial celebration of Columbia University in 1951, where he was one of a score of distinguished speakers to emphasize the convergence, indeed the unity of the various branches of human knowledge. In speaking of his own field and its relation to other areas of inquiry, Weyl made a remark, which, trivial as it may appear, conjured up the most fundamental point that can be made about mathematics: "One must understand directives given in words on how to handle the symbols and formulae."[5] To note that symbols—such as +, -, x, :, Σ, $\int$, and many others—must be explained in words before they can be used, did go a long way in the right direction, but not far enough. Weyl should have added that integers themselves, or the very basis of all mathematics, must first be verbalized before they can be given their standard notation, or any notation at all.

Weyl's failure, of which more shortly, related to the fact that if what he said and intimated was true, he should not have spoken of the convergence of the various branches of knowledge. Rather,

he should have held high the truth that all branches of
knowledge are rooted in philosophy, or the thematic study of
what all messages are and of the means they cannot dispense
with. But he should have also warned that this common root,
however profoundly philosophical, cannot mean a conceptual
homogeneization. Convergence is not reduction.

Of course, even today, after several millennia of mathematics,
it is words that explain that the figure 1 stands for the number
one, an integer. Leaving aside the unfathomable problem of how
that explanation was first given by humans, the concept of a
number is inseparable from its verbalization. To communicate
anything one needs words, a point already touched upon in the
preceding chapter. In view of this, insufficiently deep should
seem Kronecker's often quoted dictum: "God made the integers,
and everything else is the work of man."[6] He should have added
that the words of the Bible, "In the beginning was the word," are
a starting point indispensable even in mathematics.

The phrase formed by those words is theology at its best, but
it still rests ultimately on a purely human understanding of what
words are. Words, of course, cannot be understood except in
terms of words. Tacit knowledge needs to be vocalized in order to
become knowable even for the one who has it. Instead of coming
to grips right away with this apparent circularity, it may be useful
to consider first the various classes of words, a topic almost as old
as philosophy. The ten categories into which Aristotle classed all
words have been the object of many commentaries, contentions,
and disputes. Whether there is a thing, which he called
substance, is, as was already hinted at, hardly an idle question,
but it need not be of concern at this juncture. One may say the
same about the Aristotelian notion of accidents, another in his list
of categories. The rise of modern science has been taken by
many—Galileo was among the first to do so—for a proof that
taste, color, warmth, cold and so forth are but secondary qualities
because they seem to be reducible to the primary quality, or
extension. Reductionism was waiting in the wings.

Regardless of how one chooses to resolve these problems, one cannot disagree with what is merely implicit in a remark of Aristotle. In speaking of the ten categories, he noted that "the category of quantity does not admit of variation of degree,"[7] whereas notions that belong to the other nine categories all admit such variations. This should be clear of all the categories other than quantity, such as quality, relation, place, time position, state, action or affection. The quality known as the color red can be more or less red; goodness too can be realized more or less; conscience can be more or less upright. But no given number can be more or less than that very number. Thus Aristotle might have said that instead of ten categories one may speak only of two: quantities and everything else, or, inversely, everything except quantities. He should have also stated emphatically that between those two domains of categories, the difference was such as to render inane any attempt of reducing one to the other.

Had he done so, he would have anticipated insights which some prominent interpreters of modern physics voiced again and again, although with some notable one-sidedness. Thus Eddington rightly emphasized the cleavage which the difference "between the metrical and the non-metrical" (measurable versus non-measurable) introduces into our dealing with material reality. But for him the difference related not to that between the quantitative and non-quantitative properties of the same reality, but to the difference between concrete and transcendental (or metaphysical) realities. He further emphasized the same by his claim that only a part of the entire realm of "experience" lends itself to "exact metrical representation which is the requisite for development by the scientific method."[8] Eddington failed to note that metaphysical and spiritual realities are not to be brought in when a scientist speaks of experience. The latter, for a scientist, must refer to that matter of which no part is lacking in quantitative properties.

By comparison, rather crude was a similar reflection on the difference between the metrical and the non-metrical as offered by Bertrand Russell. According to him, "Physics is mathematical not because we know so much about the physical world, but because we know so little: it is only its mathematical [quantitative] properties that we can discover."[9] Here the source of the trouble lay with the vague use of the word "discover." It reflected Bertrand Russell's thematic restriction of knowledge to ascertaining something scientifically, an operation certainly confined to the determination of quantitative properties. It escaped him that by holding high that restriction as the domain of true knowledge, he unwittingly lined himself up with Plato, the very last thing he meant to do.

Aristotle, who explicitly said in the same context that we perceive any object primarily through its quantitative size, did not want, however, to slight the significance of the other categories even in respect to the physical status of things. On the contrary, he saw the force that drives things physical in some qualitative aspect of theirs. It was the urge of their nature, so Aristotle claimed, that propelled all things toward their "natural place." This teleological idea underlies all Aristotelian physics. This is why qualitative notions dominate in that physics at practically the total exclusion of that beam of light, a very sharp beam to be sure, which is the exclusive peculiarity of quantities.

In other words, Aristotle himself dimmed the profound instructiveness inherent in that section of the *Categories*. Aristotelians followed suit, which in part explains why that section is still to be mined by philosophers. Failure to do so fuels the discredit which overshadows philosophy. Philosophy is in the process of being swallowed up by science, or what is just as disastrous, philosophy is being confused with the discourse of non-scientists who try to ape science. Worse, scientists in their old age are apt to wax philosophical. A generation ago, Feynman deplored the symptom that physicists, on reaching middle-age, take up philosophizing. Today some physicists wax philosophical already when still young. The prospect of fat royalties seems to be irresistible because few things sell so well as the philosophoumena of scientists. Rarely ever was the warning, *caveat emptor*, more appropriate.

In saying that the so-called secondary qualities can be realized more or less, one does not necessarily speak of quantitatively ascertainable degrees. To be sure, degrees of sensations of warmth and cold can be rendered quantitatively. But a given degree, say 18°C, falls very short of rendering the fullness of experience that can be attached to such a temperature. Moreover, quantities have nothing to do with degrees of moral goodness, unless the relative proportions of pain and pleasure are taken for virtue and vice. That this misguided approach was first attempted during the Enlightenment proved once more that brilliance always shines better when some dark patches are also on hand.

Actually, it is not even possible to come up with quantitatively exact standards when one defines tangible objects, to say nothing of intangible and abstract entities. Take the object, called bench, for instance. It is defined in the *Random House Dictionary* as "a long seat for several persons." The definition does not give the exact measure where a seat becomes a bench. The word "several" leaves matters no less undefined. Whereas a love seat is for two, on most such seats three can comfortably sit without turning it into a bench. Definitional problems arise with every tangible object. No measure, unless it is rather arbitrary, can be given of the point where a stick turns into a pole, a knife into a sword, a hut into a house, a lake into a sea, a hill into a mountain, a path into a road. Bibliographers set an arbitrary measure when they take a pamphlet, with more than sixty pages, for a book. In other words, no things, no notions other than integers can have a spatially, that is, measurably clear representation of the range of their meanings.

This is far from being the entire problem of the clarity of words, understood in terms of a clarity patterned on measurability. In the definition of a bench as "a long seat for several persons" already the indefinite pronoun bespeaks the impossibility of a strictly defined area of meaning. This has to be the case if that pronoun stands for something truly indefinite. Further, no exact measure can be given to the word "long," which, let it be recalled, is purely relative. What is long in one respect can be extremely short in comparison with something else. As regards the word "person," all the tools of psychometry can skim only the surface. The philosopher who claimed that "all psychology is an integral part of physics,"[10] is not known to have sought counseling by locking himself up in a bubble chamber or by hurling himself around in an accelerator. Nothing can be measured about those "inalienable rights" which are part and parcel of what constitutes an individual taken for a person. Incidentally, no one knows the exact point where a part is not basically a whole and where a parcel becomes a crate.

The next step of unfolding the lack of measurable clarity in words relates to the functioning of, say, half a dozen words, as they define the meaning of another word. Their function is the partial overlapping of the range or extent of their respective meanings. Since none of those ranges are definite, the area defined by their partial overlapping remains no less indefinite.

It would be tempting to render those respective areas with irregular shapes circumscribed by dotted lines. But this would suggest something definite which those areas cannot have. It would perhaps be better to compare those areas to patches of fog that do not have distinct edges. As any air traveler knows, clouds appear to have distinct edges only from a distance. On flying closer to a cloud bank, one has a sensation different from the one which is on hand when one walks to the edge of a river. One enters a cloud bank imperceptibly, whereas the act of entering a river is a fairly definite act, although one never knows whether just standing up to one's ankles in the river is really entering it.

Undoubtedly several patches of fog, when partially superimposed on one another, would produce a darker patch somewhere in the center. But that central area will lack sharp edges no less than the individual patches do. Such an indefinite dark patch is the area of the meaning of any word, defined in terms of other words insofar as they are given a spatial representation of the extent of their meaning. In sum, efforts to render the extent of meaning in terms of mathematical clarity produce but patches of that kind.

Nothing of this was suspected by Hobbes, who late in life came across Euclidean geometry and took it for the only kind of clarity worth considering. Present-day devotees of artificial intelligence may well ponder the inanity of Hobbes' dictum that where "addition and subtraction have no place, there reason has nothing at all to do."[11] It should not seem promising to subject patches of fog to such mathematical operations unless, of course, one makes the arbitrary decision about the shade that should stand for the confines of the fog. It would therefore be utterly counter-productive to take, with Hobbes, "words for wise men's counters" and take all wisdom for counting. But this is what Hobbes himself did by adding that wise men "do but reckon by them, but they are the money of the fools."[12] Fortunate are the "fools" who do not take all words for numbers in order to gain in wisdom.

Words present one with more perplexity than that, as if this were not enough. The darkness of that central patch must be seen as subject to variations. To define a word better, one has to use more words than the ones making up the already existing definition. Redefinition of words constantly goes on as shown by ever new editions of dictionaries. They usually include more words and more nuances of meaning, while at the same time they no longer carry some words and some meanings, because they longer seem to be in sufficiently wide use. The compilers of the Oxford English Dictionary can go on registering all the nuances of all English words, partly because its two dozen thick volumes can now be unloaded on a few thin plates called CDROMs. Further, the meaning of words can take on radically new hues as well. The process can be dramatic and even shocking. A century ago the word "intercourse" principally meant conversation, and its more refined form at that. As everybody knows, for the last fifty years or so the same word has increasingly lost the refined nuances formerly attached to it.

In sum, words that are not numbers have meanings that are not to be compared to squares or blocks, unless one is to barter clarity for glitter. Within that area-type representation of the meaning of words meanings appear to change as so many amoebas, though with one big difference. Any amoeba is held together by a membrane; the meanings of words have no such boundaries around them. The respective ranges of meaning are best described as so many patches of fog, if their clarity is to be found along the lines set by mathematics. The fact that many words have homonyms—suffice it to think of the word "bit"—turns them into far less definable entities than are chameleons. These, change as they may their color and even shape, remain the same animal. But a bit put into a horse's mouth belongs to a class totally different from the bit which is a unit of "information" in computer programming. Of course, this kind of bit may eventually prove no less restraining for brave lips thriving on the subject of artificial intelligence than bits used to refrain horses.

So far only words relating to concrete objects have been considered. In coming to abstract words the picture becomes outright fuzzy within that perspective of mathematical clarity. The word "abstract" can as a noun mean "the concentrated essence of a larger whole." Each of these words is a mine field ready to explode under the feet of anyone, who looks for clear meaning by taking the world "clear" indicative of measurability alone. The word "concentrated," which appears at first sight truly measurable, is not in fact. Even in chemistry the measures of concentration vary from substance to substance and are arbitrary in each case. One may also rightly ask whether a whole can be really larger if it is truly a whole. Finally, those who have already declared with Kant that the essence of things is unknowable, should disqualify themselves from coming to grips with the word "abstract" as given in that definition.

But even numbers do not fail to rebuff those who model their search for clarity on the presumed clarity of numbers. The proof of this is the definition of integers, which are the *par excellence* numbers: "An integer is a member of the set of positive whole numbers (1, 2, 3,...), negative whole numbers (-1, -2, -3, ...) and zero." First, the general notion of integers is not a number. Second, can zero, another word for nothing, be really anything, even if so abstract as a mere number? And if the word "negative" is taken strictly for negation, does not this take away the very reality, however abstract, of a number?

To break through the fog enveloping even the definition of integers one needs an intellectual resolve to appreciate a kind of clarity which is unmistakably non-mathematical. The resolve may appear dictatorial to some, who see in it a recourse to the linguistic *fiat* of Humpty Dumpty: "When *I* use a word, it means just what I choose it to mean—neither more nor less." Had Humpty Dumpty referred to mathematics, the reference to "neither more nor less" would have been appropriate, although even there the foundations are not so clear cut. But Humpty Dumpty referred to matters very different from mathematics as he said: "There is glory for you," by which he meant a "knock-down argument."[13] Taken in that sense, there are no knock-down arguments outside mathematics, where, let it be noted again, such arguments are mere tautologies. Arguments makes sense only if they are about meanings that relate to the real world and are addressed to real minds. Arguments therefore must rest on an act of the intellect that does not hesitate to do the obvious, namely, to register concrete reality as its very first act. In doing so the mind registers in the sensory a meaning for which no better word has so far been invented than the word "universal."

Surprising as it may appear, the very ability of the human mind to abstract from the sensory and form thereby abstract notions, undermines Plato's approach to knowledge right in its presumed appeal to clarity. Knowledge for Plato was the contemplation of ideas, which—it should be enough to recall the Greek word *idein*, the origin of our "idea"—implies visualizability. The Platonic heaven is supposed to be full of images of ideal objects, such as an ideal table, an ideal pebble, an ideal teacher, and so forth. Actually no such images can be pictured and be assigned therefore to that heaven. It can at best can accommodate the ideas of geometrical figures, such as a triangle, a square, a circle, or perhaps the five perfect bodies. No real object can reside there even in its ideal form, because the latter eludes an ideal definition. To see this it is enough to recall that the meanings of words,

when cast into the perspective of mathematical clarity, resemble
so many patches of fog which show at least that Plato's claim is
a resplendent fuzziness at best. All this can be understood with
perfect clarity, even the fact that a meaning, if sought in terms of
mathematical clarity, becomes an elusive patch of fog, with no
clear edges whatever.

This may appear to be the kind of paradox that signals a blind
alley. However, paradoxes have a better use as well. As
Chesterton once put it, paradoxes serve the purpose of
awakening the mind.[14] Since one can understand the paradox,
even if it indicates a blind alley, one should awaken to the fact
that the trouble is not with understanding. The trouble lies in
putting a specific brand of clarity first and understanding second.
Once this is done the evidence of elementary truths becomes
befogged. Such a truth is that concepts other than quantities have
a clarity of their own that cannot be properly rendered in terms of
a clarity which quantities alone possess.

On the crucial importance of that truth one cannot insist
enough in this age of science. For the confusion between these
two, and mutually irreducible types of conceptual clarity is being
powerfully fomented by the effectiveness of science to promote
its own, truly indispensable type of clarity. Too many are then
inclined to take any other type of clarity for obfuscation if not for
plain darkness. What suffers is the quest for truth. To make
matters worse, it has become highly recommendable to look at
science as a newly opened potent source for philosophical
enlightenment—a perfect case, as will now be seen, of perverting
a splendid means by tagging a murky message on it.

[1] *Discourse on the Method*, Part II, see *The Philosophical Works of Descartes*, tr.
E. S. Haldane and G. R. T. Ross (1911; New York: Dover, 1931), vol. 1, p. 92.

[2] Ibid., p. 90.

[3] W. V. Quine, "Ontology and Ideology Revisited," *The Journal of Philosophy*
80 (September 1983), p. 499.

[4] "Recent Work on the Principles of Mathematics," *The International Monthly*
4 (1901), p. 84.

[5] H. Weyl, "Knowledge as Unity," in L. Leary (ed.), *The Unity of Knowledge* (Garden City, NY: Doubleday, 1955), p. 22.

[6] About this statement of Kronecker, made in 1866 at the Naturforscher Versammlung in Berlin, see his obituary by H. Weber, "Leopold von Kronecker," *Jahresbericht der Deutschen Mathematiker Vereinigung* 2 (1891-92), p. 194.

[7] *Categories*, Section 6a.

[8] A. S. Eddington, *The Nature of the Physical World* (1928; Ann Arbor, MI., The University of Michigan Press, 1958), p. 275.

[9] B. Russell, *Philosophy* (New York: Norton, 1927), p. 157.

[10] I mean G. Hempel. See his "Analyse logique de la psychologie," in *Revue de synthèse* 10 (1935), pp. 27-42.

[11] *Leviathan*, Part I, ch. v. in W. Molesworth (ed.), *The English Works of Thomas Hobbes* (London: John Bohn, 1839), vol. 3, p. 30.

[12] *Leviathan*, Part I, ch. iv; ibid., vol. 3, p. 25.

[13] L. Carrol, *Through the Looking Glass*, ch. 6.

[14] G. K. Chesterton, *St. Thomas Aquinas* (New York: Sheed & Ward, 1933), p. 176.

3

Science

Whatever else it may be, science is a means and a most powerful one. If one disregards such inventions as the making of fire, the planting of seeds, the domestication of animals, the art of writing and printing, one may safely take science for the most momentous means ever invented by man. Science is a tool that unfolds its potentialities at an explosive rate under our very eyes. Science is also a message, indeed a message that seems to drown out all other messages, including the message known as philosophy. In spite of the harrowing abuses that are being made of the means which is science, there are still some who prominently echo Herbert Spencer's unqualified panegyrics of science. He made a habit of extolling science as the *only* source of information worth consulting in any area of concern, including politics, family life, and philosophy to boot.

If this was true of classical physics which Spencer took for the ideally perfect science, it had to be even more so with the coming of modern physics that gave man an incomparably greater hold on matter. It has indeed become a fashion to claim that a vast philosophical message is deposited in science, a fashion rampant among those who knew physics only by hearsay. Early in this century Adolph Harnack, whose words commanded attention far beyond his field of historical theology, singled out Einstein and Planck as the true philosophers of modern times.

Einstein's warning that "the man of science is a poor philosopher,"[1] did not make enough impression in his own time nor later. Einstein himself did not take his own words seriously. Otherwise he would not have produced a good number of philosophical essays on a variety of subjects, many of them thoroughly philosophical, during his last thirty years. His warning certainly fell upon deaf ears among philosophers, who began to feel that their credibility increased in the measure in which their references to science became more numerous.

Conversely, one's renown as a physicist (or astrophysicist or biochemist) quickly became a warranty that his philosophical reflections were not only worth studying but simply indispensable. When scientific prowess was coupled with superb literary style and with a prestigious platform, such as a Gifford Lectureship, the philosophical message took on a special significance. A classic example of this is Eddington's *The Nature of the Physical World*, reprinted again and again since its first publication in 1928. Planck, Einstein, Heisenberg, Bohr, Born, Schrödinger, and Compton all produced books that gave further credence to the perception that exact science is a potent source of philosophical insight.

This perception greatly fueled the runaway commercial success of Jacques Monod's *Chance and Necessity* (1970) and Steven Hawking's *A Short History of Time* (1990). Undoubtedly some of the more than five million buyers (and still many more readers) of that Hawking's book saw merit in its last chapter that had little to do with science but almost everything with philosophy. There Hawking called for nothing less than for a synthesis of the philosophies of Aristotle and Kant. One wonders whether more than a handful of Hawking's readers suspected that those (known as transcendental Thomists) who really tried their hands on that synthesis, certainly succeeded in shortchanging Aristotle as well as Thomas. Others, and certainly the Neo-Kantians, could not care less about reconciling Kant with Aristotle. Still some others, such as Hegel and some Hegelians, took only the volitional aspects of Aristotle's physics, ignoring all his ontology. At any rate, one could only wish that Hawking had indicated the exact *scientific* grounds that necessitated such a philosophical synthesis, regardless of whether it was feasible or not.

It is, of course, true that many distinctly philosophical assumptions go into the making of science, including its most exact kind which is physics. Such an assumption is that matter is uniform throughout the universe, that the reactions of matter are consistent, that matter cannot come into existence or go out of it at will. Philosophy is at play in the assumption that separate human minds operate along essentially same lines. Thoroughly philosophical is the assumption that nature works in the simplest way and therefore the simplicity of a scientific theory should be a vote in its favor.

More aesthetic in character is the principle of symmetry that proved its heuristic value in physics time and again. It greatly motivated Faraday in his work on electromagnetic induction. Symmetry considerations led Dirac to postulating what later became known as antimatter. Dreams too may help, such as the one about snakes that led Kekulé to surmise the ring structure of benzene molecules. Diversions too may be a godsend. Pauli hit upon the exclusion principle while relaxing in a cabaret. The idea of the bubble chamber, a powerful tool for tracing fundamental particle reactions, occurred to Glaser as he was sitting in a bar with his eyes fixed on the bubbles moving upward in his glass of beer.

The very limited value of some of these factors should be obvious. Steady attendance in cabarets is hardly necessary for making progress in physics. Drinking too much beer can but dull the mind. Poets' imaginations may be stimulated by opium, but the handling of equations demands sober minds. About some steps in the procedure known as renormalization, charity should brand them as being just bold instead of illogical. Even the principle of symmetry, hardly a hallucinogen by any stretch of imagination, cannot be resorted to indiscriminately. In a thoroughly balanced (symmetrical) universe nothing would happen at all. Actually, a universe of absolute symmetry is just as inconceivable as a universe of absolute chaos.

While logic may seem absolutely indispensable, it has led physicists time and again into a blind alley. The inference—if there are waves there ought to be something that undulates—was taken by generations of physicists for a strict proof of the existence of the ether. Maxwell, for one, held the ether to be the largest body of which we have direct knowledge. A perfect case it was of logic being the art of going wrong with confidence. Worse, it was confidently carried to the four corners of the globe in the pages of the famed ninth edition of the Encyclopedia Britannica.[2]

Speculations about how the ether worked in transmitting light waves and electromagnetic influences became the classic case of model making in the history of physics. A hundred years ago Lord Kelvin identified understanding in physics with the making of mechanical models. In that sense the making of science could be likened to the construction of an ever larger edifice, with all sorts of mechanical materials going into the project, all of them supposedly being the modifications of the same basic stuff. Classical physics was able to show that heat and mechanical work were two faces of the same kind of material reality; that electricity could induce magnetism and vice versa; and that light itself was a form of electromagnetism. In our times the weak force turned out to be a variety of the electromagnetic forces and of the strong force that keeps the atomic nucleus together. Only the force of gravitation remains in splendid isolation from the other forces.

Yet, what actually kept the edifice of classical physics together was not the assumed truth of one basic mechanism or kind of matter, but the fact that something quantitative could be said of all physical factors. The so-called philosophical presuppositions proved to be useful parts of the physical theory only insofar as they could somehow be given a quantitative cast. This recognition, already anticipated in Newton's work on gravitation, became acute when Maxwell's theory was subjected to experimental scrutiny. True, Maxwell himself had discarded all references to quaint mechanical details by the time he came out with the final form of his electromagnetic theory. But this was more a technical convenience on his part than a break with the conviction that ultimately all had to be mechanical in nature and therefore the science of physics revealed the very nature of physical reality as embodied in a world taken for a mechanism.

This conviction reflected the belief that there was an ontological connection between mathematical formalism and material mechanism. Had this belief been proven correct, philosophy would have become a mere appendage of science. Indeed this almost happened in spite of the fact that the supposed ontological connection kept eluding the grasp of physicists. Reflection on that elusiveness forced itself on the minds of some physicists, such as Kirchoff and others, from the mid-19th century on. It was enough to ponder the difficulty of retaining anything of Kepler's physical explanation of the elliptical orbit of planets. Quite naive had to appear by the mid-19th century the view that magnetic rays emanated from the Sun as if they were so many arms ending in cupped palms, so many snug nests for the planets. Nothing remained of Newton's "physical" speculations that filled the Queries of his *Optics*, speculations totally absent from the *Principia*. This epoch-making book, whose title page pointedly stated that it was about the mathematical principles of natural philosophy, was for that very reason rejected by most Cartesians as not being a treatise in physics, but a parade in mathematics.

But whereas Newton's *Principia* stood the test of times, nothing remained of the "physical" speculations that filled Descartes' *Principes de philosophie*. Of course, the assumption underlying Descartes' *Principes*, namely, that all was mechanical, held sway over most physicists, Newton not excepted. It did not matter that the ever more esoteric function and operators of classical physics, such as Fourier transforms, Lagrangians, Hamiltonians and so forth, could not be given a mechanical and material meaning. Matter itself poked fun at the physicists. This became first clear in thermodynamics. Its first law, the conservation of energy, could still be tied somehow to the energy carried by the motion of matter or of its particles. But the second law, the increase of entropy in all real processes, could in no way be thought of as the increase of something material, not even of something practically useless, such as the filings produced by a lathe or a bore. The increase of unusable energy within a closed system turned out to be an increasing equalization of the kinetic energy of all its parts. The parts were molecules or atoms, but as it turned out, the proponents of the statistical gas theory proved to be quite wrong in imagining them to be perfectly elastic bodies, so many billiard balls raised to physical perfection.

Still the mathematical formalism of gas theory worked, at least for monatomic gases insofar as it predicted some quantitative data of their specific heat. Similar was the case with the mathematics of Maxwell's equations that certainly worked while nothing could be verified about the ether which those equations seemed to control. Maxwell's calculations of the coefficients of the rigidity of the ether, and similar data offered by Lord Kelvin do not belong to the proud pages of physics. Hertz himself found that electromagnetic waves spread across space but he did not find the ether, the presumed material substratum which was supposed to undulate if there were waves. The gripping recognition of this failure prompted Hertz to coin what has become the most pithy phrase ever uttered in reference to physics: "Maxwell's theory is Maxwell's system of equations."[3]

The phrase summed up what should have been formulated about all earlier great laws of physics. Kepler's theory was the system of his three laws, all mathematical. Newton's theory of gravitation was indeed a set of mathematical formulas. All that Newton built lastingly around the idea of central field of force was mathematics. Mathematics alone remained of his explanation of colors. The urge to identify the mathematical laws of physics with some physical properties of matter could not, of course, be exorcised overnight. Hertz's insight will be even more appreciated if one compares it with Michelson's reluctance to see in a similar light the fact that his famous interferometer experiments could not detect the ether.

Hertz's dictum implies that to construct the edifice of exact science demands a readiness to demolish much that went into constructing it. This is what has been ignored by those who during the last half century have spent so much energy in probing into the psychological, sociological, economic and cultural components of scientific work. It is enough to recall such words as paradigm shifts, revolutions, research programs, images and the like to evoke shelves of book and papers full of at times interesting insights about *how* scientists work, though very rarely about *what* they are actually doing. Einstein's dictum, "when you want to know what physicists are doing watch their deeds not their words,"[4] were not specific enough. For physicists were doing much that proved to be so much grist for the mills of paradigmists and their like, and yet all that was not science but only some accompaniments to it, none of them intrinsically necessary for doing science.

In other words, physicists built the edifice of physics in a way very different from the manner in which an ordinary edifice is constructed. There for a while the scaffolding dominates with huge cranes hovering over the scene. This may also be true of the early phases of constructing a physical theory, with patently non-scientific considerations visible everywhere. In an ordinary construction, once the edifice is completed the scaffolding is removed and the cranes move elsewhere. Still there remains a vast set of tangible matter, from the foundations through the walls and interior outfitting to the very roof.

Quite the contrary happens once the construction of a major physical theory is completed. There remains nothing in it with explicit contact with anything material. The edifice becomes a complex of equations. As such it exists in full independence of all the philosophical and quasi-philosophical assumptions and factors that helped its erection in the first place. Even letters, wholly arbitrary signs of course, that stand, say for the electric charge, for mass, and so forth, are, within the theory, merely reference points to correlate quantitative data.

This is not to say that physicists are strictly consistent in recognizing the fact that their theory says nothing about what electricity is, what energy is, what a field is, if it is something at all. Discourse in a realist vein about purely mathematical factors, such as co-ordinate systems, four-dimensional space-time, world lines, wave-packets, and zero-point oscillations in the vacuum, has been contagious throughout the history of modern physics. In a sense this should seem all too understandable. Physical science has to be about the physical. But the question is whether it is the mathematical formalism that justifies this or whether the justification lies in something else.

The mathematical formalism seems to be wholly ambiguous as to what kind of matter is involved or whether matter is involved at all. The inverse square law is just as applicable to gravitating matter as to electricity. The weakening of the intensity of light is governed by the inverse square law as is the case with the spreading of any physical effect in a homogeneous manifold. (Statistical sociologists found that the spreading of rumors also obeys that law). The exponential law about the rate at which the temperature difference between two bodies disappears, is applicable to the rate of equalization in many other contexts. Fourier's equations can handle a large variety of the propagation of material effects in various mediums. This ambivalence of the mathematical formalism to physical reality obtained a particularly graphic illustration in the fact that Mathieu's equation is as applicable to the dynamics of a pulsating ellipsoidal surface as it is to the dynamics of an acrobat balancing himself on the top of a sphere. Those unable to savor that equation must settle with Feynman's remark that "two theories, although they may have deeply different ideas behind them, may be mathematically identical, and then there is no scientific way to distinguish them."[5]

In saying this Feynman merely echoed a Bohr and a Heisenberg, to mention only two prominent names, and was followed by others, among them Hawking. According to Bohr "it is wrong to think that the task of physics is to find out how nature is. . . . The mathematical formalism of quantum mechanics . . . merely offers rules of calculations."[6] Heisenberg admitted that the quantum mechanical representation of the objective world "is completely abstract and incomprehensible, since the various mathematical expressions $p(q)$, $p(p)$ [standing for conjugate variables] etc., do not refer to a real space or a real property" and therefore that representation "contains no physics at all."[7] Heisenberg could have just as well said that the edifice of physics was totally void of any reality, lacking even walls that could be called real. As to Hawking, he could not have put it more concisely: "Even if there is only one possible unified theory, it is just a set of rules and equations."[8]

Clearly, a physicist is saddled with a problem even deeper than to specify the kind of matter to be tagged to this or that equation. His basic problem is to argue that matter is indeed a basic part of the edifice about which he can predicate only an abstract structure, his set of equations. His basic problem is to give a positive answer to the question: Does the mathematical formalism assure, even if successful, its being embodied in physical reality? Only an unreconstructed Platonist would give an unhesitating answer in the affirmative. Even such an answer would fall short of coping with the touchstone of the truth of any physical theory, namely, experimental verification. During much of his career Einstein derived inspiration from the idea that the really true physical theory should be so perfect in its mathematical formalism that even the good Lord could not come up with anything better. Yet as a physicist he knew that ultimately experimental results, that is, quantitatively ascertained data, decide the fate of a physical theory. He took the view that the entire theory of general relativity would have to be discarded if only one of its predictions failed to agree with experimental results. Not even the mere possibility of such a discomfiture was hinted at by Penrose as he outlined a future and ultimate theory in which the general theory of relativity would be united with a still unknown form of statistical physics or quantum mechanics.

If physical theory is so profoundly an abstract complex of quantitative propositions, any consideration of it as a depository of profound philosophical insights, let alone the only safe depository of such insights, should seem most doubtful. Outsiders, such as Harnack, may indeed be forgiven to some extent for seeing something there where it was not. To some extent, because in ascribing philosophical depths to modern physics, Harnack gave away his lack of philosophical judiciousness which he, as a theologian, should have possessed. Other theologians followed suit. They merely proved that the poverty of theology nowhere shows up so strongly as in the fashionable effort to shore it up "scientifically." The effort involves them time and again in a conceptual contortionism that does not bear being translated from one language to another.

Of course, physicists were not eager to point out certain aspects of their theories that at least rebutted their reckless cultural exploitation. A case in point is the popularity of the shibboleth that Einstein proved everything to be relative. Einstein never denounced this shibboleth, although he must have known that relativity theory was the most absolutist theory ever proposed in the history of physics. Otherwise he would not have bemoaned, in 1922 and apparently for the first and the last time, that the theory of relativity should have been called the theory of invariance. Other specialists on relativity theory were equally remiss in stressing the absolutist character of relativity theory. It was indeed possible to create moderate astonishment, though not in circles that should have taken note, by pointing out as late as 1985 that even in relativity physics the absolute lay beneath the relative.[9] By then *TIME* had promoted its own relativization of everything with an advertisement half of which was taken up by Einstein's classic portrait, and the other began with the declaration: "Everything is relative. In the cool, beautiful language of mathematics Einstein demonstrated that we live in a world of relative values."[10]

Many a leading physicist enthusiastically promoted plain illogicalities by endorsing Bohr's convoluted formulations of the philosophy of complementarity. Without doubt some experiments in atomic physics demand an approach that takes matter for particles, while other experiments demand that matter be seen as a wave packet. But for the physicist the ultimate difference between the two perspectives lies in a mutual irreducibility or incommensurability of two mathematical formalisms. The situation is not at all different from the old recognition that a circle cannot be squared. From this, however, nobody concluded in saner times that everything was now a square and now a circle.

At any rate, it should still be demonstrated that the wave-particle duality, which is above all a duality of mathematical formalism, would justify the broader proposition, so dear to Bohr, that for a truth to be true its contrary also must be true. As one with profound sympathies for Stalin's Soviet Union, Bohr could not be expected to see that he thereby made democracy complementary to dictatorship and vice versa. Should this mean that in a democratically elected parliament half of the seats should be assigned to Party stalwarts or to those who in the safety of their professorial chairs still cherish their Marxist dreams? When a great physicist is found to be so shortsighted, as Bohr was, about the stupefying implications of the dubious philosophy he erected around his good science, then the claim that one should go to science for philosophical insights should seem suspect, to say the least.

Many non-scientists took the principle of complementarity for a liberating perspective in areas other than science. Their procedure should have seemed doubtful for the sole reason that it amounted to a systematic evasion of questions about reality itself, or the reality of objects. Any assertion of complementary aspects entail the question as to what they are the aspects of. However long one may discourse about the slight disparity between one's two cheeks, ultimately one must admit that cheeks make sense only if they inhere in a face. But in Bohr's philosophy of complementarity a similar inference is essentially forbidden. According to that philosophy meaningful discourse is restricted to aspects, in strict disregard to the question of whether they belong to anything at all. On that ground one could speak only of the aspects of atoms but not of atoms as such. Bohr never came even close to seeing this consequence. He preferred to stay impaled on the two horns of his complementarity and never ceased urging others to seek mental comfort in that logically tortuous posture.[11] Religion produced many tortures but the principle of complementarity, which Bohr expected to supplant all religion, can hardly be looked upon as the ultimate philosophical bed of roses.

The most important lesson to be drawn from all this does not, however, relate to the philosophical comeuppance of this or that great physicist, although such cases are obviously very instructive. Again, one cannot ponder enough the futility of the efforts of some prominent physicists to rehabilitate Platonism, let alone Pythagoreanism. No physicist has ever proved that mere ideas, not even the crisp ideas of numbers, can generate tangible reality. The edifice of exact science, or physics as a purely conceptual structure of quantitative ideas cannot provide the very material, tangible physical reality, on which its equations are supposed to work.

The difference which modern physics shows to exist between its abstract mathematical structure of equations and tangible reality should seem all the more telling because those equations enable the physicists to manipulate that reality in stunning ways. The extent to which this difference would ever dawn on Plato's latter-day scientist-admirers, let alone on those who know science only by hearsay or by popularizing presentations, is not something to be easily fathomed. But whether one has been infected by Platonizing idealism or not, one cannot ponder long enough one feature of science as a purely abstract edifice of quantitative propositions, from which all scaffolding has been removed.

The feature in question consists in an impossibility. No matter how heavily and specifically philosophical that scaffolding may have been, it is not possible to establish anything specific about it from considering that abstract edifice alone. That edifice is an edifice of mathematical propositions. Include as it may symmetries, it does not provide the exact measure to which symmetry assumptions are applicable. It does not tell anything about other minds, let alone about their essentially identical structure. It does not tell anything about real matter. Without minds, embedded in brains, the message of that structure is absolutely voiceless. It does not say that there is a truly coherent totality of things, or universe. Things not being part of that structure, the message cannot say that things behave consistently. It cannot even say that things, so many objects, cannot go in and out of existence at will, because neither existence nor non-existence is part of that structure. The nothing it denotes by the symbol zero is not the nothing contemplated by the philosophical mind.

The road that connects philosophy and exact science is a one-way road. One can travel from philosophy to science, but not from science to philosophy, unless one confuses science with the philosophy which scientists throw around their science. Moreover, the road is a very short one as a road common to both science and philosophy. At the start it is a very broad road, a broad area, an area all philosophy. But no sooner does one cast one's lot with the quantitative properties of things, the path of advance becomes increasingly specific and, in that sense, a very narrow one. Moreover as the correlation of quantities becomes more and more complex, the one-to-one correspondence between the terms of equations and physical reality becomes more and more elusive. Ultimately, this correlation is no longer possible to specify in detail, which means that the road cannot be traced backward. Nothing in that most general application of the equivalence of all accelerated reference systems, which is Einstein's cosmology, indicates that its remote start, or special relativity, there loomed large (*pace* Einstein himself) a presumed physical reality, called the ether, with its contradictory physical properties.

To those who find all this too abstract or abstruse or forced, telling cases are available from the pages of the history of philosophy. Nobody can deny that René Descartes was a philosopher, or that John Locke was one, and so were Immanuel Kant, Auguste Comte, and Herbert Spencer. Perplexities begin only when one asks what proved to be of lasting value in Descartes's assertions about clarity, in Locke's "moderate realism," in Hume's skepticism about everything save his own habits and longing for comfort, in Kant's critical theory of knowledge, in Comte's positivism, in Spencer's theory of increasing heterogeneity. Similar perplexities arise in reference to Dewey's empiricism, to Whitehead's process philosophy, to Popper's principle of falsifiability. Time and again they were found right only in details that could not be justified by their general principles. Tellingly, such was the basic fault which even the far from philosophical *Economist* could spot in Popper's philosophy, following his death.[12] For all their diversities, all those philosophers were at one in trying to go from science to philosophy as if science contained the philosopher's stone.

One would merely touch the surface by saying that all these great names in modern philosophy failed because they did not pay sustained attention to the quantitative properties of empirical reality. Such a remark may not only prove very superficial (in the literal sense of the word), but may also miss the issue. In fact, it would prove self-defeating for the purposes of this book, which is to vindicate philosophy by vindicating truth. It is not the purpose of this book to suggest that to be a great philosopher is necessarily equivalent to articulating error or even half-truths on a grandiose scale. That, unfortunately, this is all too often the case, remains, of course, full of instructiveness. The purpose of this book is precisely to hold high philosophy by indicating what the philosopher can and should do and what the philosopher should avoid.

The philosopher should avoid at any cost to play the part of the scientist, especially of the exact scientist. But this is what all those "great" philosophers tried to do, however partially. Their stated intentions suggested exactly the opposite. In trying to escape abstract scholastic subtleties, leading to uncertainties, Descartes seized on what alone seemed to be indisputably true. He specified it as the extension of matter. In doing so he set out on a philosophical march that began with the second step, or the quantitative properties of matter. Had he noted that one had to have matter so that one could discourse about its quantitative properties rooted in matter which is extended, he would have also raised a set of questions very different from the ones he had raised. The set of questions he raised did not constitute philosophy but a mere camouflage of science, though not amenable to scientific treatment. He tried to do philosophy by doing physics without dealing in quantities, except their semblance. In the end he lost out on physics as well as philosophy.

Locke decided to become a Newtonian philosopher on the meager ground of having been assured by Huygens that the physics of the *Principia* was reliable. There was nothing Newtonian in the pragmatism which Locke's "moderate realism" consisted of. Newton, the scientist, had nothing to do with what has become Locke's most enduring contribution, namely, that the State's *raison d'être* consisted in protecting the use and accumulation of private property. Capitalism is certainly a philosophy, among other things, but neither Newtonian, nor fundamental. Hume, whose familiarity with Newton amounted to some trivial remarks, was not obeyed to the point where all books that contained no quantities or matters of fact are committed to flames. Kant never retracted his preposterous claim that he could have set forth, if required, his theory of the formation of the planetary system in full mathematical formalism, although Newton himself recoiled from the task, a point never recalled by his philosophical admirers. Scientists, Gauss was one of them, who read Kant carefully, saw that what he bequeathed amounted to trivialities. Comte's ultimate philosophical offering was Catholicism minus Christianity, a system of no more worth than physics, astronomy and chemistry would have become if cultivated, in obedience to his precepts, without mathematics. Herbert Spencer, whom Darwin admired as one of the greatest philosophers ever, certainly proved himself as a fluent prosewriter.

Dewey's empiricism quickly became a period piece precisely because he tried to get around that most empirical feature of empirical reality which is its measurability. The total lack of impact of Carnap's logical construction of the world is to be sought in the same direction. Wittgenstein, who set so much store by clarity, neglected to consider that nothing is so sharply clear as the quantitative contours of things. Popper might have escaped the circularity of his principle of falsifiability had he considered that quantitative results, such as the inverse square law, can be proven false only in terms of not at all false quantitative measures and relations.

If philosophy is not to become pseudo-mathematics, it must not take its starting point in mathematics even in its being part of physical theory. Philosophy must begin with the physical and in its pristine form, which is not yet put through the mould of science. Consequently the initial step has to consist in an unconditional assertion of material reality, embodied in objects. Second, no opportunity should be left aside to disclaim any affinity with Platonism, where ideas, including their quantitative or geometrical kind, represent the starting point in existence and all dicta about it, in rank disregard of the right order between means and message. Moreover under no circumstance should the philosopher let himself be blinded by the clarity of quantities even though things are primarily "objects" through their quantitative properties, such as size and weight. The principal domain of philosopher relates to categories other than the category of quantities.

What is further asserted here, and asserted as truth, is that science, ultimately a set of quantitative correlations of quantitatively specified data of observation, presupposes philosophy instead of providing it. It is also asserted as truth that the chronic failures of great philosophers can be traced to their illusion that science can be done as a form of philosophy. All this is, of course, exactly the opposite of what positivism, either in its logical or in its empirical form, stands for. Positivism is a denial, covert or open, of the legitimacy of philosophy which does not end with "positive" data, cast or not yet cast into the mould of mathematics. It is the validity of that denial which is denied here. It therefore follows that philosophy has to be positive in a far more positive sense than positivists could ever dream of. Philosophy has to be positive from the very first step it takes which is to register the existence of objects. Positivist positivism could not care less about existence. Such a positivism is merely a parasite on the tree of existence that pushes its branches infinitely broader than the entire realm of positive data useful for science.

It was not the science of special and general relativity that forced Einstein to take a realist stance, which he could never articulate, but which he forcefully asserted time and again. The factor that drove Einstein away from Mach's positivism to a realism, which was not empiricism but something even metaphysical, was his keen perception that science made sense only as the study of an aspect of a material reality which it could not provide. One could only wish that the one who said that he had never derived a single moral insight from science, would have also realized that science, including his superb physics, was not the source of any philosophical proposition. The science itself was all mathematics, which anyone who worked himself through the arcane formulas of general relativity, knows all too well. The theory is so mathematical that Einstein himself needed accomplished mathematicians to work it out. Standing by itself that mathematical construct said nothing of physical reality. This is why it could be seized upon by idealists, relationists, paradigmists, operationists etc, so many scoffers at realism.

Quantum mechanics brought out no less strongly the mathematical character of exact science by which much more is meant than that it relies heavily on mathematics. That much more is nothing less than that quantum mechanics is Schrödinger's wave equation or Heisenberg's and Born's matrices, all purely mathematical formalisms, in line with Hertz's dictum that Maxwell's theory is Maxwell's system of equations. Quantum mechanics is a statistical method, utterly void of philosophical propositions. The expression, the philosophy of quantum mechanics, is a glorified oxymoron.

Those who are strangers to quantum mechanics *and* philosophy may be impressed by claims, such as that "We live in a remarkable era in which experimental results are beginning to elucidate philosophical questions."[13] The topic of "experimental metaphysics" grows in attractiveness[14] and may eventually give respectability to symposia on, say the physics of the intangible, the chemistry of abstract forms, and the biology of the lifeless. Unfortunately not much better is the philosophy of those who invented quantum mechanics. The claim made by Heisenberg, that the wave function reveals something of the Aristotelian potency, certainly proved a rank unfamiliarity on Heisenberg's part with what Aristotle said on the transition from potency to act. In general, such forays of scientists into philosophy evidence the wishful thinking that science can validate philosophy and that nothing is more desirable than such a validation.[15]

Among such victims of wishful thinking are those who listen in awe to reports about the consensus of quantum cosmologists concerning the ability of their *métier* to deal with the transition from non-being to being. Some quantum cosmologists notwithstanding, one can only say that the transition will forever remain a topic for metaphysics and for metaphysics alone. To those educated in the best graduate schools, where they learn that quantum mechanics proved that the nothing is also something and the something is also nothing, one may just as well give the advice that they should transfer to places where such brainwashing is not yet *de rigueur*.

There they may glimpse something of the fact that physics, as the model of exact science, is the quantitative study of the quantitative aspects of things in motion. Being precisely such study, it does not produce things and it does not even put them in motion. Science does not even unveil new things. It merely shows, for instance, that material reality exists in highly concentrated forms (called atoms and nuclei) at very small orders of magnitudes. Common sense, for want of a better term, is the only source of giving access to reality. Something else and indeed very misleading is attributed to that term in Huxley's dictum that "science is nothing but *trained and organized common sense*,"[16] and even more so in Santayana's version of it: "Science is the attentive consideration of common experience; it is common knowledge extended and refined."[17]

Santayana largely missed the point that it was through quantitative procedures, and by them alone, that science performed that function of it on a reality which it owed to common sense in the first place. Of that reality science ever unveils new aspects but only in the sense of measuring material reality ever more globally and ever more minutely. Thus physics unveiled ever larger masses of matter (stars and galaxies) and ever smaller concentrations of it, such as atoms and nuclei and parts of nuclei. In this process, which seems to know no limits in either direction, science comes up ever more convincingly with quantitative data about matter rather than with information about its nature, let alone about its existence as such. Those data appear to be more and more about energy, a most generic name of material reality. Physics, as an exact science, appears to be the art of measuring of what seems to hide behind the word energy and may one day become spoken of not so much as physics as energetics, to recall a penetrating observation, now almost a century old, of Pierre Duhem.

Physics is indeed a system of equations relating to purely quantitative data gathered about material reality. This proposition is offered here as a truth, the validity of which is brought out by the futility of applying consistently any other definition of physics. The truth in question was valid already in classical physics, but full recognition of it could come only with modern physics. In the former, the role of mechanical models still could create the illusion that they provided reality for the equations. In modern physics, where the satisfaction of making mechanical models of physical processes had to be renounced, in principle at least, the mathematical structure need not at least be overshadowed by pseudo-ontology, garbed in mechanism.

Those who suggest that in order to gain philosophical insights one should go to physicists confuse physics with the thinking of physicists. What is truly of lasting value in physics is independent of that thinking, independent even of that reality which is constantly in change. For physics change means either acceleration or deceleration, although change means immensely much more. And so does causality that brings about change. The topic of change and the topic of cause remain thoroughly philosophical, in spite of their being mixed up nowadays with a thorough misinterpretation of quantum mechanics. Those topics were not to be taken up before cutting science to size which is about sizes and ultimately about nothing else. In particular, science has nothing basic to say about two other topics, free will and purpose, although both are indispensable to its practice. Science (including prestigious awards for scientists) makes sense only if it is done freely and for a purpose. The same holds true of a treatise on truth inasmuch as it centers on the correlation of means and message. These two are made freely and for a purpose, topics to which we must now turn.

[1] A. Einstein, "Physics and Reality" (1936), in *Out of My Later Years* (New York: Philosophical Library, 1950), p. 59.

[2] Reprinted in *The Scientific Papers of James Clerk Maxwell*, ed. W. D. Niven (Cambridge: University Press, 1890), vol. 2, pp. 763-75.

[3] H. Hertz, *Electric Waves*, tr. D. E. Jones (London: Macmillan, 1893), p. 21.

[4] This dictum of Einstein is the initial salvo in his Herbert Spencer Lecture (1933); in *The World as I See it* (New York: Covici-Friede, 1934), p. 30.

[5] R. Feynman, *The Character of Physical Law* (Penguin: 1992), p. 168.

[6] N. Bohr, *Atomic Theory and the Description of Nature* (Cambridge: University Press, 1934), p. 60.

[7] W. Heisenberg, "Development of the Interpretation of Quantum Theory," in *Niels Bohr and the Development of Physics*, ed. W. Pauli (New York: McGraw Hill, 1955), p. 26.

[8] S. Hawking, *A Brief History of Time: From the Big Bang to Black Holes* (Toronto: Bantam Books, 1988), p. 174.

[9] I did this in my essay, "The Absolute beneath the Relative: Reflections on Einstein's Theories" (1985); reprinted in my *The Absolute beneath the Relative and Other Essays* (Lanham MD: The University Press of America, 1988), pp. 1-17.

[10] Sept. 24, 1979.

[11] For details, see ch. 13, "The Horns of Complementarity," in my Gifford Lectures, *The Road of Science and the Ways to God* (Chicago: University of Chicago Press, 1978).

[12] *The Economist*, Sept. 24, 1994, p. 92.

[13] A remark of the physicist A. Shimony in his "The Reality of the Quantum World," *Scientific American*, January 1988, p. 46.

[14] As shown, for instance, by the publication of *Experimental Metaphysics: Quantum Mechanical Studies for Abner Shimony. Volume One*, ed. R. S. Cohen *et al* (Boston: Kluwer Academic, 1997).

[15] For further discussion, see my *God and the Cosmologists* (Edinburgh: Scottish Academic Press, 1989), pp. 155-56.

[16] T. H. Huxley, "On the Educational Value of the Natural History Sciences," (1854) in T. H. Huxley, *Science and Education*, (New York: The Citadel Press, 1964), p. 46.

[17] G. Santayana, *The Life of Reason or the Phases of Human Progress* (New York: Charles Scribner's Sons, 1906), p. 37.

4

Free Will

Clarity and science were taken up early in this treatise merely as a means for clearing the air. Intellectual pollution has for some time been powerfully fueled by the illusion that a very narrow type of clarity and it alone can clarify everything. To be sure, quantities are on hand wherever anything tangible is encountered as it happens in any encounter whatsoever which is more than mere shadow boxing. But, as was shown in the second chapter, even the notions of tangible things escape our conceptual grasp whenever we aim at "exact" definitions. The sharp light of quantitative clarity, which is already dimmed when we define tangible things, turns more and more into diffuse fogginess as we define matters intangible, such as abstract notions. Definitions have a way of becoming less and less definite.

As to science, it is, of course, a superb tool for handling things, because they all have quantitative properties, but is of no help in understanding anything else about things, let alone what things are. Still fully valid is the remark which Lord Kelvin addressed to a young man who guided him, without knowing who he was, through a plant of electrical appliances. After he listened patiently to the young man explaining such elementary notions in electricity as voltage and resistance, Lord Kelvin expressed his wish to be informed as to what electricity was. The young man fell silent. The great scientist patted his back and said: "No matter, that is the only thing about electricity which you and I do not know."[1]

Perhaps the most trivial, yet most fundamental aspect of that exchange of information was that both sides acted it out freely. In this respect it mattered not that one knew enormously much and the other very little. With respect to their acting freely, they were equals, and certainly so on the scale of mathematical physics. On the reality of free will a clarity which is patterned on mathematics and theoretical physics can shed no light whatsoever. This is true regardless of whether the free human act is "extended," that is, elaborate and protracted such as the persistent resolve of writing a treatise on truth, or shorter, such as a visit through a plant, or something momentary, say a sudden decision. After all, even the resolve to go on with a lengthy project is made up of many acts of the moment. But the free act carries an even greater philosophical weight with it than does the registering of reality. Already the philosopher's attention to the act of registering the reality of objects as a primary datum can serve, as was shown, as a litmus test for the reliability and consistency of his message about truth. This is even more true of the intensity of a philosopher's attention to free human acts as so many primary data. The more intense is that attention, the more assurance is on hand that the philosopher's message is truly about truth and not a clever footwork about it.

Of course, here too, attention can be carried to self-defeating lengths, such as in Sartre's existentialism in which only momentary acts are recognized. He did not care to explain why some of those acts were free. Much less did he explain how those acts could cohere into a protracted resolve of his to go on writing his at times very long books. Yet that resolve had to be propelled by an intense exercise of free will. A Nobel Prize in literature, which Sartre gladly accepted, could hardly be given to a mere robot churning out fascinating phrases, if there is such a robot at all. The problem is all the more serious because in the end Sartre emphatically dismissed the reality of free acts. In doing so he denied himself the right to qualify as truthful his discourse about anything, including the fullness of momentary events on which his existentialism rested.

Truth is a relevance of notions to objects that transcend the moment, including the always momentary registering of their reality. Insofar as that registering is limited to its being subjectively experienced, it is void of communicability and therefore may be left aside as a variant of solipsism. But truth is far more than what empiricists and physicalists can dream of, although they stake their case with the reality of physical objects. The truth of physical reality takes one beyond physics to a realm that can be designated only by the word "metaphysical," chronically abused as that word may be. Exposure to the realm of the metaphysical will be felt keenly only by such who have developed sensitivity to what is "beyond" the physical though never severed from it. No such specially developed sense is needed for grasping the metaphysical bearing of any free act. What is needed is merely an intimation that freedom or rather free will belies mere material existence. Once that intimation is reflected upon, nothing prevents that one should be seized by a sense of metaphysics. Appreciation of that sense may more than anything else help one see a philosophical system for what it really is. The sense in question is elementary, though it will help only in the measure in which it is elemental.

For, in the final analysis, the elemental registering of free will almost exhausts whatever can be said about its reality. Everything else is embellishment, very useful and informative as it may be, because it is irrelevant unless achieved and articulated freely. In a sense the philosophy of free will amounts to a declaration similar to the immediacy of kicking a stone, or Samuel Johnson's famed demonstration of external reality. The one-liner, "Sir (said he), we *know* our will is free, and *there's* an end on't,"[2] with which he brushed aside Boswell who wanted to discuss free will, capsulized all that can be said in essence about free will as a reality. As in connection with one's immediate registering of external reality, here too the additional and most valuable information comes from considering the philosophical landscape insofar as it is dominated by a studied slighting, let alone outright denial of free will.

The first sketches of the modern rendition of that landscape were drawn by Descartes. Apart from occasional declarations of the obviousness of free will,[3] Descartes was tight-lipped on the subject. He did not find much food for thought on a felicitous note dating from his early years, in which he declared free will as one of the three great miracles, the other two being the creation of all and the Incarnation. In his later years he hesitated to ascribe freedom to God himself. Free will became the stepchild of philosophy in its Cartesian tradition, indeed its chief outcast. No wonder. Free will is hardly something to be measured with a yardstick that enables one to size up extended objects.

Spinoza, the most consistent of Cartesians, did not hesitate to expel free will from among topics worthy of philosophical considerations. In his chief work, the *Ethica more geometrico demonstrata*, Spinoza declared indeed that "there is no absolute or free will." In speaking of "absolute or free will" he came, as will be seen, close to the central issue, but then he barred himself from reaching the nerve center of the question. This happened when he declared that the will was not different from the mind which he took for a machine: The mind "is determined to wish this or that by a cause, which has also been determined by another cause, and this last by another cause, and so on to infinity."[4] The one who excoriated orthodox Jewish dogmatism and its resistance to free inquiry was unwilling to justify his own freedom to criticize any and all, though he did it liberally. It was not the first time that minds keen on a one-track type of logic and disdainful of reality, forgot about the illogicality of their first step, to say nothing of their cavorting in regress to infinity. Such is a penalty to be paid when the first step towards the infinite, or indeed towards anything else, is not pondered carefully, whether it is truly a first.

The rationalist boasting of the idea of extension as distinct from and prior to objects that are extended, was such an extreme stance (even apart from the questionable character of the boasting itself) as to invite inevitably its very opposite. Matter became everything in De la Mettrie's *L'homme machine* (1749). There all manifestations of the human psyche, all forms of reasoning, all emotions, all morality were made equivalent to mechanical processes in the body. But the most telling detail in that notorious work was not the identification of the soul as "an enlightened machine,"[5] but the utter silence of its author about free will. Like all materialists before and after him, De la Mettrie could not be consistent enough to face up to the question of whether he wrote that book freely or whether he reasoned freely about its message. The latter was the denial of free will, although not by a means which could be taken for a necessary outcome.

Among the imitators of this illogicality was Baron d'Holbach, author of *Système de la nature*. But it was not the book's trite reasoning about matter as being all Nature that provoked the revulsion of young Goethe as he read it at the tender age of eighteen. The book evoked for him a "Cimmerian darkness" through its portrayal of virtuous behavior as the quiet humming of a well-oiled machine. His solution was to cast overboard the mechanistic view of nature and with it the science of Newtonian mechanics. Neither then, nor much later could he understand that materialism and Newtonian mechanics have precious little to do with one another. For all his penchant for poetizing, Goethe failed to see that instead of the poetry of nature, he promoted a nature worship of nature in all his poetical work. The pantheistic idea of God, so different from a Creator, could not even justify his musing in old age: "If we grant freedom to man, there is an end to the omniscience of God, for if the Divinity knows how I shall act, I must so act perforce." For indeed if man was a piece of deity, he had to share its omniscience and there remained no room for Goethe's advice: Man was born merely "to find out where the problem begins, and then to restrain himself within the limits of the comprehensible."[6] The task of finding out where the problem begins was important enough, but, as will be seen, in a far more logical sense than Goethe could suspect.

Whereas it is easy to throw free will overboard and ignore whether the ship of philosophy had not lost thereby its rudder, it is not so easy to dispose of sheer willfulness. Its clutches are lethal even when couched in charming sophistication, such as William James' dictum that "the question of free will is insoluble on psychologic grounds." Did not those grounds, as James saw them, imply willfulness? Was it not willful to treat contemptuously whatever could not be handled by science, just because science was limited to establishing measurable correlations? James was not alone in resting his case with a willful paradox. Most psychologists, as James admitted in the same breath, saw in that distinction a justification for "denying that free will exists."[7] Yet any psychologist can see, if he or she wants to, and by mere introspection, that free will is immensely more than the consciousness of "feeling" free, let alone a sequence of "feelings" that may appear to form a causal chain. In not seeing this William James committed a methodological bungle not so much in psychology as in philosophy. Even greater was his bungling in logic. He failed to consider that his discourse on psychology made no sense unless it was a free discourse.

William James saw an agonizing dilemma where there was none, and agonized where he should have kept calm. His pragmatism, a philosophical transposition of his psychologism, could not cope with the most practical and elemental reality, which is the free human act. As one whose first training was medicine, William James should have realized that healing aimed at more than at a replacing of one sickness with another. The curing of sickness makes sense only if there is such a thing as health. Further, all clinical approaches to the psychic impairments of one's use of free will had to be free. Otherwise medicine could not even live up to the dictum, "medice, cure te ipsum," a prescription which James declined to accept for himself.

The mere similarity of the title of William James' most mature work, *The Will to Power*, to Nietzsche's *Die Wille zur Macht*, suggests that his pragmatism was but a muted form of the rank willfulness preached by Nietzsche and all his admirers, among them the Nazis. For both the ultimate target to demolish was what transcends the merely physical. Tellingly, William James took the doctrine of creation out of nothing for the worst aberration of the human mind. Little did he suspect that this idea alone could resolve the problem posed by old Goethe, or the very beginning of all problems. Once that idea is discarded nothing can be seen as transcending mere matter, although this is what every free act does. Within that materialistic outlook, each exercise of the free will degenerates into an act of sheer willfulness.

The Western World quickly forgot the lessons which two world upheavals, especially World War II, provided about the indiscriminate use of the will to power. The will of the people may express truth, especially if done freely. Yet this is increasingly less the case when the people are exposed to daily brainwashing by the media that are interested not so much in reality as in the manner in which reality is perceived, or rather with the mannerism prescribed by the gods of the antenna. Indeed during the post-War decades the Western world found itself less and less capable of countering totalitarian Marxist regimes that brazenly controlled the will of the people by glorifying the will to power of the "oppressed." The propaganda machine of those regimes found its most supine allies in that Western academic world that for centuries now has taken it for a sign of sophistication to talk around the existentially metaphysical depths of man's ability to act freely.

Circles boasting of their prowess in logic took it in a stride that Kant laid a mine field against his own system of critical reason when he cast radical doubt on free will. He did so in one of the four antinomies of the *Critique of Pure Reason,* where the free will was set up as no more evident than ironclad determinism and therefore intrinsically doubtful. Nowhere did that famed critique of pure reason appear more impure and uncritical than in that unreasonable and in fact very willful procedure, whereby its author tried to make it appear that it was unreasonable to talk about the soul as the agent that alone can be free. With that he set in train the academic fad according to which if one talked of free will, one could do it only uncritically and willfully.

That discourse on free will would move in that direction was very clear when Fichte took the will for the keystone of critical philosophy. Kant was displeased, but he could not deny that very Kantian was the antinomy as formulated by Fichte: "In my immediate consciousness I appear to myself to be free, but through reflection upon the whole of nature I find that freedom is utterly impossible." And still partly Kantian (it is enough to think of Kant's saving of free will in terms of practical reason) was Fichte's resolution of the dilemma: "The former [nature] must be subordinated to the latter [will], for it is to be explained only through the latter."[8] No wonder that when Fichte took up the task of that explanation, all nature began to appear as driven by some will and the genuine science of nature was driven out by Naturphilosophie.

The futility of explaining in such a manner either free will or
of securing the explanation of mere natural processes could dawn
at least momentarily on anyone attracted to it. A case in point is
Tennyson's musing: "Our wills are ours, we know not how." It
was not resolved by his conjuring up the help of divinity to make
the will right: "Our wills are ours, to make them thine."[9]
Tennyson was not enough of a philosopher to realize that
preachers he used to hear readily ignored the crucial point: One
could talk of making the will right only if there was already a will,
able to act freely. Being an entity, a free act, even inasmuch as it
was free, had to be made ultimately by the Maker of all, or else it
would not exist.

It was precisely the perception of this that was blocked by
Tennyson's use of the word *how*. His use of that word was
expressive of the inanity of much of the modern approach to the
reality of free will. By trying to understand free will by finding out
the manner in which it operates, one simply undermines the
significance of one's immediate grasp of being able to act freely,
a grasp which is ontological. Every effort to specify that *how* is a
free act and therefore begs the question. This holds true also of all
"critical" reflections on free will. They are so many unwitting
votes cast on behalf of the absolute priority, indeed primordial
quality, of free will. All arguments against free will are so many
proofs of it. Poincaré's now century-old dictum, "no determinist
argues deterministically,"[10] sums up it all.

But all determinists, from the rude mechanists of the 18th
century through the behavioral psychologists of the early 20th
century down to the latest reformulators of psychoanalysis are
one in their resolve not to face up to the reality of free will. They
largely ignore the lessons of concentration camps, so grippingly set
forth by Victor Frankl, that survival there rested on the will to
survive. But that will in Frankl's case too could deliver its utmost
only by reliance on "faith," a shorthand for giving religion its
due.[11] Severed from such transcendental ties, the fact of doing
anything freely elicits, even more than the act of registering reality,
the worst imaginable nightmares in the world of those who are

determined to know only matter, whether crudely or with the veneer of "scientific" refinement.

In the strategy of avoiding the need of facing up to the truth of the monumentally metaphysical reality of free will few tactics proved to be so palliative as the one proposed by David Hume. He proposed it as the very basis of human reasoning, indeed its very first step. As one whose chief aim was to remove the specter of anything transcendental, he singled out the subjective emotive custom as the factor that held together man's sensations into something apparently coherent. The irony was all the greater because the specter of the transcendental, which Hume tried to ward off at any price, was the specter of Calvinist divines, heirs to the radical subjectivism bequeathed to them by the Reformers. But this was not the sole irony. Hume came to represent in the Western world (Einstein held him high on that score) the cause of radical skepticism, which in turn served as the justification of free inquiry and of the free propagation of ideas, whether true or not, right or wrong. Hume, who in his *An Enquiry concerning Human Understanding* (1748) touched on the freedom to circulate ideas, kept mum there whether that freedom was exercised by truly free acts or not. Hume's failure to raise the question of free will tells more than anything else about the true value of his *An Enquiry concerning the Principles of Morals* (1751).

Many followed him in this unphilosophical march where everything appeared progressive, but only the first step was lacking. Today's "ethicists" represent the latest step in that dubious march farther and farther away from the task of facing up to the meaning of their free cashing in on their increasingly rich emoluments. The modern world is all too ready to reward generously its ethical haruspices who readily chart a convenient course around even the greatest ethical issues, such as late-term abortion, euthanasia, and now cloning. Their ease of doing so is dependent on their studied and therefore free avoidance of what it means to be free. This inconsistency enables them to act as the supreme masters in the art of satisfying the two opposing camps in the medical world of organ transplants. One camp, still conscious of the Hippocratic oath, is resolved to stretch the time needed to declare brain death. The other is eager to reduce that time so that other lives may be prolonged and an already flourishing business in organ transplants may become even more lucrative. Our ethicists, so insensitive to what free will means, will find "ethical" formulas to let that business flourish as another branch of "free" enterprise, an enterprise increasingly free of ethical grounds and justification.

In doing so they merely follow Freudian and other psychoanalysts. Sigmund Freud never pondered whether he arrived freely at his conclusion that libido drives everything in man. Freud's disciples never cared to ponder whether their own libido made them adopt their master's theories. The psychoanalysis to which each psychoanalyst should submit himself or herself before submitting others to it, should include something even more basic than a mere probing into suppressed sexual fantasies. As is well known, although caught almost *in flagranti*, Freud resisted taking the medicine which he prescribed as the cure-all for any and all. The primary fantasy to be unmasked is the unconscionable pretension of being free while slighting and even implicitly denying that there is such a reality as free will.

After having been taught for now over two centuries to think lightly about his free will, late-20th-century man shows far less sensitivity than Diderot did. To be sure, modern man is no different from Diderot in having a mistress or two, but he shows even less concern than Diderot did about the possibility that his love may not be less foreordained than a comet's blind obedience to the inexorable laws of gravity. Viewing the Hale-Bopp comet did not prompt modern man to write to his paramour as Diderot wrote to Mme de Vaux: "It makes me wild to be entangled in a devil of philosophy that my mind cannot deny and my heart gives the lie to."[12] Diderot was not, of course, the kind of thinker desirous to see to the bottom of Pascal's famous dictum: "The heart has its reasons of which the reason knows nothing."[13] Tellingly, Condorcet, a comrade in arms of Diderot, urged the publication of a garbled edition of Pascal's *Pensées* in order to dim their light. The age of the Enlightenment could indeed act in a way which would have been abhorrent to those centuries it contemptuously called the Dark Ages.

Voltaire, another libertine, was too hardened to let something grave show through the facile witticism he poured on the subject of free will. In doing so he was much more modern than Diderot. It was Voltaire who made quite modish the art which takes one's musing on the apparent contradiction between physical laws and free will for an excuse not to face up to some momentous implications. Voltaire's leery smile shone through as he cautioned his readers against being proud of one's freedom to implement some of one's wishes. Huge bodies, like stars, do not have even this meager measure of freedom, so Voltaire preached his version of humility. Worse, he recommended this "humble" approach, so modern in many ways, in a book that carried the title, the principles of philosophy.[14]

The book was an unprincipled approach to that most basic principle, which is man's ability to know. "Intellect annuls Fate. So far as a man thinks, he is free," as Emerson put concisely a truth, which should be within the ken of anyone who reflects, however briefly. To think is an act, an act no less free than any act made deliberately, because the deliberation itself is an act of thought, before it issues in a decision. In this sense alone can one see the constructive side of the paradox which Emerson added in the next breath: "To hazard the contradiction—freedom is necessary."[15]

The destructive side of the paradox is tied to Emerson's pantheism. Emerson, the pantheist, had no justification to see something special in man's thinking as expressive of his being free. For in a divinized nature, either all is free or there is no freedom at all. The price of pantheism is to ascribe free quality to every natural, in fact, even to forced motion. Yet even an Aristotle, who said that bodies fall because they are propelled by some love toward the center of the earth, would not have ascribed such freedom to stones. He remembered that his god, the Prime Mover, was not free and therefore nothing else, including man, could be really free.

Emerson, together with most other pantheists, including Spinoza and his fanciers, was under the dictate of his clearly non-divine humaneness as he expressed his perplexity over the presence of free will in nature: "The one serious and formidable thing in nature is a will."[16]   Emerson was, of course, also misled by the mechanistic philosophy grafted on the good science of Newtonian mechanics. He ignored that most leading physicists at that time— yes, even in the middle of that materialistic 19th century—would have told him that the science of physics has nothing to do with free will,[17] partly because it cannot be observed and measured. Free will is experienced personally and in that sense is subjectivity itself. This is one's innermost testimony, as well as the testimony of anyone else. But any and all can only infer its existence in others. A capital point of which more shortly.

A century later Emerson would have received a different report from leading physicists. These, however, merely displayed their very shallow understanding of what they were doing in physics. Particularly instructive is the case of Einstein who time and again offered ringing endorsements on behalf of an external reality independent of the mind. But he also confessed, though not publicly, that the free will was not an objective reality for him. Whereas he did the former even at the risk of being considered by others to be "guilty of the original sin of metaphysics,"[18] with respect to free will he lost his metaphysical nerve. He clearly wanted to escape the force of logic already mentioned: far more grippingly than one's immediate grasp of reality does one's registering of the reality of one's free will bring one face to face with that realm of metaphysical reality which hangs in mid-air unless suspended from that Ultimate Reality, best called God, the Creator. But as an avowed pantheist, Einstein preferred not to admit that reason justified one's encounter with that supreme metaphysical reality. He therefore had no choice but to write that "objectively, there is, after all, no free will."[19] Tellingly he said this only in private. There alone did he also discount any talk of meaningful purpose. He failed to consider a purely pragmatic point, which should seem paramount in this age when all fundamental issues become the prey of sheer legalese. If free will is declared to be subjective, as opposed to the real, identified with the "objective," legal procedures lose their *raison d'être*, because no purely subjective evidence can be allowed in courts.

To his credit Einstein, a determinist in physics, did not, unlike many other prominent physicists, see rhyme and reason in saving freedom through the alleged loopholes which quantum mechanics seemed to find in the chain of physical causality. One of those physicists, Eddington, even computed the extent of free will granted to humans by quantum mechanics. Yet within a year or two he perceived that the computation was sheer nonsense. Others became more and more entangled in the task of saving free will by science. Most memorable in this respect was A. H. Compton. His case is all the more pathetic because he first declared that all of Newton's physics was to be discarded if it truly came into opposition with one's immediate experience that one could move freely one's little finger. Such an immediate experience did not really mean much to that distinguished physicist. Otherwise he would not have continued with the "good news" that the science of quantum mechanics provides a reliable ground for man to hold that he can indeed act freely.

The conceptual confusion that fills Monod's famed effort, his *Freedom and Necessity*, to save free will through quantum mechanics, is not worth delving into. Those who readily follow a scientist into a conceptual jungle should not complain about not seeing their way out and seeing wild beasts where there are none. Those who think that computers eventually will make free decisions, should first prove that a free act is nothing more than a given flow of electrical impulses. All actual and potential victims of taking such somersaults in logic for proofs might perhaps ponder what is purely pragmatic. Scientists readily accept awards for their scientific work, ordinary and extraordinary. Are Nobel Prizes given to robots, or are they rewards for a work freely done? Is it not strange that in an age when science, or rather scientific work, proves to be the most effective means of disposing of dictatorships, whether they be of the Party or of some individuals or of some religion, increasingly less attention is paid to the reality of free will, the only safe foundation of democracy. Political freedom without attention to free will invites rank irresponsibility, couched, of course, in convenient slogans about human fulfillment and economic prosperity.

It is therefore imperative to consider the question: What justifies the importance attached to freedom in the Western world? That justification must imply much more than freedom from constraints. Yet already that freedom makes sense, in the case of human beings, only if they are other than mere objects. As will be seen, all objects, all bits of matter are under total constraint, natural or man-made, all the time. For man, his freedom from constraints can make sense only if he and his fellow human beings can refrain themselves from posing constraints. This means that the freedom of society rests with the free will of individuals, regardless of the disdain in which philosophers, psychologists, and educators hold free will and of the callousness with which the media make fools of men by manipulating their will all the time.

But this societal reality of free will is not something for positivist and pragmatist philosophers to fathom. Neither kind can cope with that immediate metaphysical experience vibrant in anyone free of stimulants. The experience is metaphysical, because it defies all laws of physics. Neither positivists nor pragmatists can cope with the task of validating the existence of free will in others. That validation can only be an inference, again the kind of reasoning which is best called metaphysical. It certainly goes beyond the physique of the individual, including all his psychological make-up taken for physics.

Free will remains therefore a mysterious factor for positivist, pragmatist, and empiricist thinking. As was shown, neither pragmatism, nor other fashionable forms of modern philosophy give any meaningful support for thinking that man can truly act freely. One can but speculate about primitive man's reflections about having free will. But it is not a matter of speculation to find the very first and robust appearance of the conviction that man is indeed free. The first unequivocal and sustained assertion of free will has little to do with Greek philosophers, but enormously much with the perspective registered in the Bible, which here is taken for just another cultural document. There the idea of an eternal moral responsibility gave rise to the assertion that man is freely the maker of a fortune which moth and rust do not devour. There it was realized that Commandments, be they Ten or Two in number, make sense only if man is free to comply with them or disregard them. The conviction that man is free was born out of the perspective that man was given freedom not in order to do anything he wants to but that he should be able to do what he is supposed to do. The Western World lost its hold on the reality of free will in the measure in which it let some biblically inspired convictions fall into disrepute.

No that those convictions had not at times issued in sheer mockery of free will. Suffice to think of Luther's and Calvin's diatribes against free will in the name of Revelation which they wanted to reconstruct with rank disregard of fifteen hundred years of profound reflections on what Revelation teaches about free will. Those diatribes, in particular those of Luther, convinced an Erasmus at long last that instead of a reformation he was in the presence of a deformation which he refused to join, regardless of his profound dissatisfaction with the Church to be reformed. He, however, failed to probe into the fact that he was free to undertake a thorough (and much needed) self-reform. Much less was he ready to come to grips with that all-important task. His defense of free will anticipated much of that insipid diction about free will that comes from the pen of humanists. True to form they care to protect the flower and the fruit without caring for the soil and the roots.

This is not to suggest that all was fortunate in the quasi-official Catholic elaborations on free will, although they were far more credible than Erasmus' discourse on it. In all of them, riveted on the relation of free will and grace, it was overlooked that the mystery of free will does not begin with its relation to God's always gratuitous supernatural grace. Free will is a mystery already on the natural level before it becomes at times a most somber mystery on the supernatural level, because there it is intimately connected with the mystery of heaven and hell.

Free will is a mystery on the natural level in the sense that it cannot be reduced to anything else. It is a primary datum, a supreme, most immediately known reality. Insofar as it is a reality, it owes its existence in ultimate analysis to the Creator as nothing can exist without being created by Him. But insofar as the Creator is infinitely more than a demiurge or a cosmic designer, it is not a contradiction to assume that He and He alone can create something, an act of free will, which is both fully created and in that sense "physically," that is, fully determined, and yet genuinely free at the same time. The mystery of free will ceases to appear a contradiction in terms, or a wholly unmanageable conundrum only when seen in the context of the infinite power and goodness of God. He created man to be free so that man's service may have that merit which only a freely performed act can have. God therefore has to remain a subtly hidden God, lest man should find himself "constrained" to obey Him. This subtle hiddenness of God, demanded by man's freedom created by Him, has found its best characterization in a biblical context, chapters 12 and 13 of the Book of Wisdom, that abounds in phrases like, "You govern us with great reverence" (12:18), exuding unparalleled philosophical balance in correlating God's infinite power over and utmost respect for his free creatures. More of this in connection with miracles.

Those who do not relish the tracing of free will to its ultimate metaphysical source, whose thematic vindication is left to the chapter on God, still have to face up to the reality of free will, including the reality of their freedom to do or not to do so. Any denial of free will is a free act or else it is not a denial, but a blind reaction, a sort of reflex cop-out. Here too, utter negativism is the only logical alternative to truth which is always positive, and certainly so in that reality which is man's ability to act freely. A most positive aspect of free will is that its use is always for a purpose and that one must have a purpose to deny this. Some evolutionary biologists have attached a scientific aura to that strangely inconsistent procedure, which makes it all the more imperative to probe into the reality of purpose.

[1] About this story, whose provenance is *2500 Anecdotes for All Occasions,* ed. E. Fuller (New York: Avenel Books, 1978), p. 192, one may certainly say: se non è vero, è ben trovato.

[2] J. Boswell, *The Life of Samuel Johnson* (October 10, 1769; Everyman's Library, n. d.), vol. I, p. 363.

[3] Thus, for instance, in *Les principes de la philosophie,* I. 39, in *Oeuvres de Descartes,* ed. C. Adam and P. Tannery (Paris: J. Vrin, 1964), vol. 8, p. 41, where he said that "it is so evident that we have a free will . . . that it can be taken for one of our most common notions."

[4] *Ethica more geometrico demonstrata,* Part II, Prop. XLVIII. See *The Chief Works of Benedict de Spinoza,* tr. R. H. M. Elwes (1883; New York: Dover, n. d.), vol. 1, p. 119.

[5] J. O. de la Mettrie, *Man a Machine* (La Salle, IL: Open Court, 1961), p. 128.

[6] J. W. von Goethe, *Conversations with Eckermann* (Washington: M. Walter Dunne, 1901), p. 130 (October 15, 1825).

[7] W. James, *Psychology* (New York: Henry Holt, 1915), pp. 457-58.

[8] J. G. Fichte, *Die Bestimmung des Menschen* (1800), in *Sämmtliche Werke* (Berlin: von Veit, 1845), vol. 2, p. 184.

[9] A. Tennyson, *In Memoriam,* Introduction (London: Methuen, 1902), p. 24.

[10] H. Poincaré, "Sur la valeur objective des théories physiques," *Revue de métaphysique et de morale* 10 (1902), p. 288.

[11] Victor Frankl, *Man's Search for Meaning* (New York: Washington Square Press, 1963), pp. 104-06.

[12] Quoted in Arthur M. Wilson, *Diderot* (New York: Oxford University Press, 1972), p. 577.

[13] *Pascal. The Pensées,* tr. J. M. Cohen (Penguin Books, 1961), p. 164 (#477).

[14] *Les principes de la philosophie* in *Oeuvres complètes de Voltaire* (Paris: Garnier Frères, 1877-85) vol. IX, p. 27.

[15] R. W. Emerson, *The Conduct of Life and Other Essays* (London: J. M. Dent, n.d.), p. 161.

[16] Ibid. p. 165.

[17] For documentation, see my *The Relevance of Physics* (Chicago: University of Chicago Press, 1966), pp. 381-83.

[18] See his "Reply to Criticisms," in P. A. Schilpp (ed.), *Albert Einstein: Philosopher-Scientist* (Evanston: Library of Living Philosophers, 1949), p. 673.

[19] Letter of April 11, 1946, to O. Juliusburger in *Albert Einstein: The Human Side: New Glimpses from His Archives,* ed. H. Dukas and B. Hoffman (Princeton: University Press, 1979), p. 81.

5

Purpose

The means whereby a philosopher conveys his message imposes on him the duty of accounting for the reality of that very means, be it as trivial an object as a book. He has a similar duty with respect to free will or else his philosophy may become subject to a double jeopardy. Either his use of the means would not differ a whit from the inevitable working of an automaton, or his using it freely may not be justified by his philosophy. It is equally his duty to offer a philosophy which fully accounts for, or at least takes into full account, the fact that in writing the book he pursued a purpose, the purpose of activating other minds in order to bring them around to his own way of understanding. In doing so, the philosopher, by the means of writing a book, does what man has always done ever since his emergence as a man from his animal ancestry. He makes and uses tools, a performance that bespeaks consciousness acting for a purpose.

The actual step of man's emergence from his animal ancestry may forever remain shrouded in mystery in spite of the growing variety of fossil remains coming to light that point toward such a most momentous step. Yet paleontology sees no gradual transition from the absence of tools to their presence. For paleontologists man remains an animal very different from all others, none of whom are known to have made and used tools and an ever wider variety of them. Man is primarily a tool-making being. Man had to be first a tool-maker before he could display his symbol-making ability by covering with paintings of animals the walls of his caves.

For whatever paints and brushes he used, they were so many tools in his hands and he used them for a purpose, indeed, to express that purpose symbolically. To say, as Chesterton did, that "art is the signature of man,"[1] is to cast in the best light man's ability to make tools and become through this means a symbol-making animal, that is, a being with a message. Tools were and still are the most tangible and palpable means whereby man manifests his purposive being which is about much more than mere physical survival.

It should seem the height of cultural irony and philosophical obtuseness that machines, so many sophisticated tools, could be taken for evidence that everything was a mere machine in man. There is indeed a supreme irony in the fact that man, the tool-making animal, became so overwhelmed by the mechanism of evolution as to become oblivious to the loud testimony of the machines made by him that he has to be immensely more than a machine. This comedy of philosophical myopia was crowned by the matter-of-fact acceptance of the view that an evolutionary process, which is seemingly and allegedly purposeless, could produce a being whose very nature is to act for a purpose. The view implies a monumental *non-sequitur*, which remains the Achilles' heel of an evolutionary science turned into an ideology of evolutionism. The latter has no better foundation than the miscegenation of chance and necessity. Of these two, chance remains a glorious cover-up for ignorance. As to necessity, it is refuted by the very freedom whereby it is posited.

Within the context of such an ideology no room is left for speaking of man as a being with a purpose, unless this is done with a convenient sleight of hand. Here too, as was the case with plain reality, nothing is easier than to rely furtively on that common sense that naturally assumes the obvious, namely, that human acts are done with a purpose and for a purpose. Yet such a reliance on common sense is most illogical within the ideology in question. Within such an ideology there is no room for speaking of a being that can act for a purpose, including the purpose of cultivating evolutionary science in order to prove that there is no purpose.

This lack of logic is conveniently overlooked in "brave" but purposeful portrayals of man as a chance product all of whose beliefs, hopes, fears, and loves are but the "accidental collocations of atoms." The true repulsiveness of this picture is not its grimness, although it includes the inevitable burial of "the whole Temple of Man's achievements . . . beneath the debris of a Universe in ruins." The picture's real sadness lies in its inconsistency and in the fact that so egregious an inconsistency failed to be noticed by that very logician, Bertrand Russell who formulated it. No philosophy, he claimed, that rejects the details of that picture as not worthy of being called truths, "can hope to stand" and "only within the scaffolding of these truths, only on the firm foundation of unyielding despair, can the soul's habitation henceforth be safely built."[2] Standing as it does for one's inability to see any purpose, the word despair was certainly well chosen. Unintentionally telling was the word scaffolding. It could but evoke scaffolds which anyone agreeing with Bertrand Russell could retain as the sole instrument on which to snuff out human existence in a desperate flight from truths, among them the truth of purpose.

To heighten the irony, the foregoing passage appeared in an essay, which Bertrand Russell called a "A Free Man's Worship." It should have been his duty as a philosopher to face up to the fact of assigning himself the freedom to "worship" in this fashion or to do freely anything at all. He should have pondered that the sense of his being free was far deeper than just being free of external constraints, which, let it be noted, is in the first place a physical impossibility for a materialist. But once more it was convenient to start the game from the second base. Again, it would have been the same logician's duty to consider why "an accidental collocation of atoms" could coalesce into beings, not all of whose acts are accidental, that is, purposeless. For even if the chain of purposeful acts seemed to lead to a blind alley of utter purposelessness, the question remained of why there was a single purposeful action at all, such as Bertrand Russell's writing that essay obviously for a purpose. Does the reality of a brick become doubtful just because the height of an edifice that can be constructed from bricks may be very limited indeed? Does thereby the act of making bricks for a purpose become an act of no philosophical consequence?

Similar questions may be asked about another celebration of purposelessness, one that possibly reached even larger audiences than the very large ones interested in Bertrand Russell's varied messages. Surely, the reprintings of Russell's "Free Man's Worship" did not match the thirty printings in twice as many years of Carl L. Becker's *The Heavenly City of 18th-century Philosophers*. There man is described as "little more than a chance deposit on the surface of the world, carelessly thrown up between two ice ages by the same forces that rust iron and ripen corn, a sentient organism endowed by some happy or unhappy accident with intelligence indeed, but with an intelligence that is conditioned by the very forces which it seeks to understand and to control."[3]

Almost two generations later Jacques Monod painted a picture no less grim: "The ancient covenant is in pieces; man knows at last that he is alone in the universe's unfeeling immensity, out of which he emerged only by chance."[4] The picture became even more dispiriting when Richard Dawkins overpainted it with flippant sarcasm, epitomized in his phrase, "the blind watchmaker." He did not produce that phrase blindly, nor did Stephen Gould produce accidentally an equally hollow phrase, according to which man is a "happy accident," which like other hollow constructs resounded far and wide.

These gurus, and many other examples could be added, were one in a hapless tactic which takes cover in blithe references to chance. Chance is invoked as a cheap escape from recognizing the significance of the obvious, or the fact that to write this or that book is a free act done for a purpose. It is not at all so obvious, let alone demonstrated, that the tactic is legitimate science, and above all evolutionary science, which is the trump card in the claim that purpose is a mere accident, a sort of a noble illusion.

Whereas Becker spoke unqualifiedly of chance, Monod, with an eye on the greatly increased sophistication achieved in the study of stochastic variables, felt emboldened to speak of a "tamed chance," without specifying what he meant thereby. He said, of course, nothing new if he meant that there was no such a thing as a statistical method all of whose parameters were fully random, or chaotic. Absolute chaos is inconceivable and can certainly not be programmed into computers, all of which, in their hardwares as well as softwares, are the most unchaotic of all complex machines ever designed by man, and designed for very specific purposes. Those who try "to understand how patterns emerge from total randomness" do not seem to comprehend the meaning of the word *total*. That such claims are readily picked up by *Business Week*, merely shows some chaotic aspect of doing business nowadays, although it remains an activity very much for a very specific purpose and has to obey numerous patterns.[5]

No champion of evolutionary science who heavily banked on chance was consistent to the extent of recognizing the nonsensical character of devoting one's life to the purpose of proving that there was no purpose. By the time Becker came out with his once famous book, four years had already gone by since Whitehead spoofed all such preachers of no purpose as ones "who constitute an interesting subject for study."[6] His remark makes sense only as long as it is true that logic must be paid its due. Such an obligation is honored in the breach whenever one thinks that it is possible to set out with the second step, just because the road is paved with the latest in philosophically and scientifically sophisticated jargon.

This first step is hardly ever given its philosophical due by brave professions of faith in progress in the teeth of adversity. Only by taking into account the fact that the word "airy" could mean something really lofty in Samuel Johnson's time, can one see something substantial in his often quoted advice to someone who had just recovered from sickness: "We must always purpose to do more or better than in time past. The mind is enlarged and elevated by mere purposes," especially if "they end as they begin by airy contemplation."[7] No sound philosophy supported Tennyson's profession of faith that no matter what "thro' the ages one increasing purpose runs."[8] Then, we are in 1842, such confidence was in great part generated by a rather naive belief in progress. A few decades later, the idea of a great evolutionary process seemed to remedy the logical fallacies of such belief. These fallacies were not offset by Bergson's *élan vital*, or by a mythical process called "emergence," or by that *nisus* which Samuel Alexander conjured up to do the trick, or by Whitehead's setting up process as the ultimate reality, enveloping God himself. Such a process proceeded from nowhere to nowhere, whatever the merit of the claim of its being not so much a process at all as an allegedly rock bottom reality. A philosopher who casts his lot with the primacy of being over change, be it called process, may be wrong, but he is at least not guilty of a sleight of hand, that is, of the trick of taking something for a starting point that cannot be assigned that role as long as logic is respected.

The radical primacy of the purposeful human act in any and all reflections was not served any better by Teilhard de Chardin's vision of an irresistible upward surge toward the Omega point, which should have seemed suspect by the mere fact of his having said so little about the Alpha point. Literacy cannot be claimed without careful attention to all letters in the alphabet. It is, of course, not for grammarians to argue that the last letter of the alphabet makes no sense without the first, and much less that either A or Ω can stand for realities immensely more significant than mere letters.

Moreover, it is not for grammarians to argue that no letters can be produced by heaping numbers on numbers, except in that monumental wishful thinking which is the ideology of the Hegelian Right or Left. In both it is a basic dogma that quantities produce qualities in the broadest sense of this word. Heisenberg failed to see this when he saw in some quantum mechanical formalism a "scientific" version of the Aristotelian doctrine of transition from potency to act and thought that he had provided thereby a scientific justification for purpose. No better purpose was served by the pilot wave and even more recondite mathematical formalisms inasmuch as they were seized upon by some, egregiously uneducated in quantum mechanics, as scientific proofs of purpose. They should have at least reminded themselves of the elementary truth that a mill cannot produce something different from the stuff which it is made to grind. As long as numbers (or mathematical formulas) are fed into one's intellectual mill, only numbers come out of it even if they are mistaken for something else. The fact that the action of feeding the mill with numbers was purposeful does not amount to a proof that numbers produced the purpose, let alone the mill. Once this is ignored, one is caught up in fueling the process, known as "garbage in, garbage out."

In none of these dispiriting contexts is a reference made to the individual's purposeful action as the reality by which alone can any talk about purpose, whether in the individual or anywhere else, be justified. Of course, that action receives its most palpable public evidence in the individual's participation with other individuals in a purposeful exchange of ideas and sentiments. It is that communal reality, riveted in each individual's unshakable conviction that he or she acts for a purpose whenever the act is conscious, that supports the action whereby a philosopher works out a philosophical system about purpose at large. Whether that system is presented in a dry prose or in a soaring diction, it will hang in mid-air unless anchored in that basic reality which is one's unshakably sane conviction that every conscious act is an act with a purpose.

It should be easy to see that such a conviction is a truth even from the viewpoint of mere logical analysis. For whenever such a conviction is assailed by doubts that exist not merely in the doubter's mind but are conveyed to others, the assault on purpose, by being purposeful, testifies to purpose itself. As with reality, or with free will, so with purpose: only by granting its reality, and by doing this consciously and emphatically, can one improve one's intellectual grasp of it as an incontrovertible truth. As such, like reality, or free will, or causality, the reality of one' acting for a purpose is something irreducible to anything else. The truth of purpose is therefore "unexplainable" in the sense that it cannot be conceptually unfolded from something else or reduced to something else.

In other words, before one can raise with C. S. Lewis the question, "What is the Purpose of it all?", one has first to affirm that purposive act is a reality, an act inseparable from that conscious being which is man. Such an affirmation is indispensable if one is to consider the broader meaning of that question. It relates to much more than the purpose of the entire series of purposeful actions in an individual life. It implies even more than the purpose of all such series, that is, the purpose of mankind at large. It bears on the purpose of all living and of all that non-living material reality that makes life possible and is indeed an integral part of all life, non-conscious as well as conscious life.

To answer that question one has therefore to answer the question about the sense in which the reality of purposeful conscious action can serve as a justification for seeing some evidence of purpose in non-conscious living organisms. To see that evidence one needs eyes different from the ones used in science. There, in ultimate analysis, one can see only measurable data, their correlations and their succession. When a scientist claims to see more, he uses the eyes of philosophy whether he knows this or not, or whether he admits it or not. Further, his use of those philosophical eyes cannot be justified by his seeing, measuring, and correlating data. The predicament of the biologist as the one who, even more than a physicist, cannot think without philosophy, is well summed up in the now more than a century-old dictum: "Teleology is a lady without whom the biologist cannot live but with whom he would not appear in public."[9] In spite of its close resemblance to theology, teleology, or the study of purposive or goal-directed activities, is philosophy. Whatever the possibility of exorcising theology from teleology, the philo-sophical nature of teleology cannot be changed by, say, Monod's tactic of replacing it with the word teleonomy.

Monod should have paused. Words have their way of rebutting their misuse. Apart from the fact that *telos* remains a reminder of a goal that means much more than a mere terminus, the word *nomos* would still bespeak its original connotation, which was far from being a pointer to some impersonal regularity. On the contrary, *nomos* meant a rule, formulated and imposed by men, and very much for some purpose. They were imposed to save man and society from self destruction, whose physical variety can be most effectively be promoted by misconstructing the meaning of words. Lenin's instruction about using syntax to promote revolution should not be easily forgotten now when capitalism can proceed unhindered with its own sales tactics, or teleonomies.

The entire realm of the living is a vast set of indications that organisms, small and large, seem to be structured for the attainment of very definite ends as if seeking some specific goal. It should be enough to think of the immense variety and sophistication of mechanisms in animals. The name "bombardier beetle" received its full justification only after man constructed gun turrets that can be turned in various directions. Moreover, unlike manmade gun turrets, bombardier beetles produce their own ammunition in the form of lethal chemical sprays. The bombardier beetle does this with a skill that defies much of man's latest scientific know-how in molecular biology. Any of such mechanisms in two dozen or so species of beetles can, of course, strengthen the view that somehow they all are but variations on a proto-mechanism, and therefore purely evolutionary products. It is another problem to find the prototype of such protomechanisms in groups of other species. At any rate, such mechanisms will forever impose the perception that they are tools for a specific purpose. The same holds true of the great varieties of eyes. They all impose the view that, as L. Cuénot, the great French biologist, said earlier this century, eyes are obviously for the purpose of seeing.

One can just as fruitfully meditate on the ability of some sea slugs to eat little animals called coelenterates, whose defense mechanism is a set of coiled sting-cells that lash out at the slightest touch. Yet, those cells do not discharge as the coelenterates are digested by sea slugs, which implant those coils on their own backs as their own defense mechanism after they have consumed and digested other parts of the coelenterates. A similar topic for meditation should be the incredible complexity of the mechanism whereby the spinnerets' glands make possible the production of filaments of different kinds needed for web-making, which in turn implies the morphological conversion of legs and abdominal appendages into very different organs. Would any engineer expect such intricate mechanisms to come about through an incredibly long series of purposeless trials and errors?

Indeed with advances in biological science, ever more stunning details emerge about adaptations. A mere look, let alone a careful look at each of these can but strengthen the perception of the obvious, namely, that adaptations are for a purpose, or else they would not be adaptations but something else. Stones, precisely because they are not living, are not said to take on shapes of polished ellipsoids in riverbeds, are never said to adapt to the hydrodynamics of the current. And precisely because they are living, parasites have long been perceived to be classic cases of adaptation. A modest reflection on any detailed description of parasitism can be a shock treatment about a measure of adaptation that clamors for the recognition of purpose somehow being present. The details of any case can be gruesome, such as those graphically narrated by Sir Charles Sherrington in his famed Gifford Lectures *Man on His Nature* about the life cycles of Redia, that exploit the pond-snail, and about malaria that exploit both the dapple-wing gnat (*anopheles*) and human beings.[10] Here one can rightly say that the more gruesome, the more graphically true. One could only wish that Sherrington, who had piercing philo-sophical eyes, had also portrayed with similar vividness the intellectual life-cycles of those philosophers who thrive by deconstructing the intellectual scene, and do so, *à la* Derrida, by offering *texts* as if they were not so many *constructs*.

All these details are but particular aspects of what became recognized about a hundred years ago as "the fitness of environ-ment." This fitness has recently emerged as reacting far beyond planetary dimensions into truly cosmic range. For unless some physical constants, exceedingly specific quantities, were present from the very start of cosmic processes, the present system of chemical elements, without which there is no life, non-conscious or conscious, could not have evolved. This recognition sparked the trend to speak of an anthropic principle built into the universe from its very start.

This is not to suggest that the anthropic principle, either in its strong or in its weak form, would be equivalent to a consistent discourse about purpose. In its strong sense, the anthropic principle amounts to plain solipsism, well conveyed in the caption, "I am, therefore the Universe is," which is at best a rehash of Descartes' long discredited *cogito*. In its weak form, the anthropic principle simply means adaptation, a word that has been largely deprived of its purposive connotation. The process parallels what happened to the word "machine," a tool on a large scale. In its variant "mechanism" the word "machine" became a shibboleth for a philosophy grimly inattentive to the presence of purpose. Students of intellectual history may find in that process much more than meets the eye. Once this study is done, shackles may fall from eyes previously blind to the insight about the cosmic machine's adaptation to the task of producing purposive life and non-conscious variants of it, so many pointers to some factor at work which is not "mechanical," to recall a memorable statement of Newton's.

Search for that non-mechanical factor is as old as philosophy. Such a search was the Socratic reaction to the mechanistic science (and ideology) of the Ionians and the atomists. Socrates justified his heroic stance by a reasoning whose aim was to "save purpose," an aim far more influential in intellectual history than Plato's program "to save the phenomena." Unfortunately, Socrates threw out the baby (nascent mechanistic science) with the dirty bathwater (mechanistic ideology). He did so by claiming that unless one attributed purpose to anything that moved, one could not vindicate the soul's longing for something eternally true and therefore its existence beyond death as a truth. Such is the gist of *Phaedo* in which so many moderns can see only a political conflict, but not the profoundly moral reason that touched it off. Unlike Socrates, these moderns are the ones who "corrupt the youth" by making them believe that ethical norms are mere social conveniences, none with unconditional validity, rooted in the soul's immortality.

Aristotle's natural philosophy was but a huge elaboration of the Socratic attribution of purpose to all things and processes. Thus, in Aristotle's science, the more ample nature (mass) a stone had, the faster it was attracted to its "natural" place, the center of the earth. The nonsensical character of the quantitative example given by Aristotle (of two bodies, of which one has twice the mass of the other, the one with the larger mass would fall twice as fast)[11] did not prevent the adoption of his physics for two thousand years. This merely proved the elemental urge in man to vindicate his own purposeful nature, an urge that could not be stifled by the coming of modern science. The success of that science, as worked out by Galileo and Newton, rested on the systematic elimination of all considerations other than quantitative.

Neither Galileo nor Newton cared to reflect on what this was doing to man's radical sense of acting for purpose and to his no less radical need to have purpose. Some more ample minds than Galileo and Newton, and no less scientific than they, did care. Leibniz, the co-discoverer of infinitesimal calculus, was one such mind. Tellingly, he referred to *Phaedo* as he pleaded for a new physics that would give purpose its due. Already the intention was misplaced. Purpose was not to be found through physics for the simple reason that physics deals only with measurable parameters, that is, quantities. Leibniz's illustration of what that new physics would contain brought out all too well its futility. The curve called brachystron, along which a body reaches in the shortest time a lower point not directly under it, was just geometry and nothing else. One needed a reasoning other than mathematical to read purpose into moving along such a curve, even apart from the fact that such a reading of mere geometry could not be justified. But at least Leibniz recognized the legitimacy of thinking about purpose and made a try, however misguided.

In spite of all the achievements that physiologists have made with a reliance on physics and chemistry, they have not been able to stifle the urge to do justice to the apparent goal-seeking which is displayed by countless organisms. Again and again reputable biologists raised the idea of some vital force, though in a way which defeats the purpose. For as long as they assign some material reality to that force, they invite the search for its detection, which invariably ends in failure. A scientist cannot even see life itself, to recall a famous remark of Claude Bertrand, although life stares us in the eyes, scientific or not.

The famous French physiologist was careful enough to warn that not only what can be seen by scientific eyes is worth registering. Had he not done this, he would have become a pitiful forerunner of that great modern investigator of the biochemistry of vision, the late George Wald, who complained that he "did not understand what it means to see."[12] Such was a pitiful example of restricting the act of understanding to procedures of measuring. Wald refused to consider even the fact that the eye, perhaps more palpably than any other organ, was made for the purpose of seeing. He should have reminded himself that next to the peacock's tail, it was the thought of the eye that brought home most effectively to Darwin the patently incomplete perspective which his science allowed.

For to see life, let alone to understand what it means to see, let alone to see for a purpose, eyes are needed that can see more than extension and mere empirical data. To be sure, as will be seen in the chapter about the mind, any datum, as understood, is much more than a mere datum, but a datum carrying a generalized meaning. That mind, which can see beyond the immediate, can be supposed to see nuances of the meaning of purpose that are analogous, but not identical, to the purpose which the mind consciously knows to go with its own acts.

To make the mental effort to see purpose in this broader light is all the more necessary because to fall back on vitalism to explain purposeful adaptations in biology (or evolution) is neither science nor philosophy. Vitalism is a sort of gnosticism, or at best a pseudometaphysical poetry, which cannot be subjected to observational verification, nor can it constitute a consistent discourse. There is another facet of man's purposeful action which in recent decades has invited considerations no less unsavory than vitalism. I mean that dilution into randomness of the fact that by any purposeful action of his man makes an impact, which is to cause something, the topic of the next chapter.

[1] G. K. Chesterton, *The Everlasting Man* (1925; Doubleday Image Books, 1962), p. 32.

[2] B. Russell, "Free Man's Worship" (1903), in *Mysticism and Logic, and Other Essays* (London: Longmans, Green and Co, 1921), pp. 47-48.

[3] First published in 1932 by Yale University Press. My reference is to the 27th printing in 1965. See pp. 14-15.

[4] J. Monod, *Chance and Necessity: An Essay on the Natural History of Modern Biology*, tr. A. Wainhouse (1971; New York: Vintage Books, n. d.), p. 180.

[5] See *Business Week*, June 23, 1997, p. 76, where the immunologist Ellen Goldberg is quoted.

[6] A. N. Whitehead, *The Function of Reason* (Princeton: Princeton University Press, 1929), p. 12.

[7] Letter to Hester Thrale, Nov. 29, 1783, in *Letters of Samuel Johnson*, ed. G. B. Hill (New York: Harper and Brothers, 1892), vol. 2, p. 361.

[8] A. Tennyson, *Locksley Hall* (1842; Boston: Tricknor and Fields, 1869), p. 57.

[9] A remark attributed to the German biologist, E. von Brücke.

[10] 1940; 2nd ed., Cambridge: University Press, 1951, pp. 264-66.

[11] In *On the Heavens*, I, 6.

[12] Quoted in J. P. Davies and R. Hersh, *Descartes' Dream: The World according to Mathematics* (New York: Harcourt, Brace, Jovanovich, 1986), p. 245.

6

Causality

Anyone who writes a book in order to generate doubt on causality refutes the message by the very means that carries it. To indulge in such an inconsistency is suggestive of mental perversion which is worse than mere deterioration. Lie is not merely something contrary to truth, it is also a sin. To outline the measure of that perversion will have to be left to the chapter on ethics. Here it should be enough to note that one displays at least a rank short-sightedness in overlooking the fact that one instances a cause-effect relationship in arguing against causality. Whenever one does this in a systematic way, one's shortsightedness turns into intellectual blindness. In defense of one's arguing against causality, one may refer to the fact that in any act of persuasion the "exact" proportion between cause and effect cannot be evaluated and therefore the cause-effect relation does not hold. Still there remains the fact that with each further step of arguing his case against causality, the philosopher deepens the impact he intends to make. In other words, he tries to be ever more effective in bringing about something that was not on hand previously.

The effect which a philosopher can actually achieve may at times appear to be out of proportion to the soundness or unsoundness of his message. Whatever one may think of the merit of the message of the *philosophes*, any slighting of their influence on history would be most unphilosophical. The influence may be exaggerated. The presence of the works of Fichte and Nietzsche in Nazi field libraries does not necessarily mean that they inspired all crimes committed against humanity in World War II. There can be no doubt that the classics of dialectical materialism served on a colossal level as tools of brainwashing, this most despicable form of that cause-effect relationship which is to influence people. Chairman Mao's Little Red Book became a means "red in tooth and claw," where the coloring issued from the blood of over twenty million massacred Chinese. So much in the way of a reminder to philosophers who try to convince people, another cause-effect relationship, that there is no such a thing as causality, just because instead of missiles (or instead of a simple bullet, such as the one that was fired in Sarajevo in 1914), they use missives as the means of their message.

Any means that carries a message is a proof that a cause-effect relationship is aimed at. Modern life, so heavily molded by advertising, is a continual reliance on means that serve the strategy of becoming successful by influencing people's decisions. The strategy is still the same as outlined more than half a century ago by Dale Carnegie in his runaway bestseller, *How to Make Friends and Influence People*, only the means have changed and are changing ever more rapidly. Newspapers take now second place behind television as means that show the overpowering measure to which people's thinking can be shaped by exposing them to a relentless impact of messages. Television's leadership is being challenged by a feverishly spreading network of entertainment, called internet and website.

Ironically, as society cavorts in implementing causality, say by affirmative action, ever more spirited defenses are put forward in support of most obnoxious influences, with simultaneous disclaimers of the power of advertisements on people's minds. Suffice it to think of the defense of displays that promote smoking or pander to sexual instincts. It is argued that it has not been established "scientifically" that the smoking of cigarettes causes lung cancer or that displays of nudity do promote promiscuity, multiply one-parent families, breed unisex cohabitation, and accelerate the spread of AIDS thrown in for good measure.

Insofar as those defenses are based on playing a game with statistics, these can indeed be the biggest form of lie. But there is a more seriously "scientific" form of casting doubt on causality and in fact on points that touch the very core of human identity. An egregious and very recent example of this was the effort to allay fears about the cloning of humans. One need not fear, so the argument went, the destruction of personal identity, because the neurons in each of the two brains would fire randomly and therefore the consciousness produced in one brain would not be strictly identical with the consciousness in the other.[1]

The word randomness rightly evokes quantum mechanics. Indeed the creators of that marvelous science claimed emphatically from the very start that their findings proved that basically all events were random events and causality was a mere illusion, at least on the "fundamental" level. Worse, by putting a thick scientific veneer on that patently non-scientific claim of theirs, they certainly proved the effectiveness of scientific packaging. Science, as a packaging, ranks now with sex and sports in effectiveness. In addition to (at times in place of) the three R's we have now the three S's, Sport, Sex, and Science, all writ large.

The thickness with which that scientific layer can be dispensed is well illustrated in a most considered remark of John Von Neumann. He claimed in one of the great classics on quantum mechanics that "there is at present no occasion and no reason to speak of causality in nature—because no experiment indicates its presence, since the macroscopic experiments are unsuitable in principle and the only known theory which is compatible with our experiences relative to elementary processes, quantum mechanics, contradicts it."[2]

The "present" takes us back to the middle of the century. By then a generation of scientists and cultural gurus had already consented to the claim which Heisenberg offered in the March 1927 issue of the *Physikalische Zeitschrift* as if it had been a periodical for philosophy and not for physics. The claim was carried in the grand conclusion of his paper, the first to contain the uncertainty principle or equation, or rather inequality. This principle, or inequality, soon became known in the form, $\Delta x . \Delta mv \geq \hbar$ and means nothing more than that the product of the margin of uncertainty in *measuring* simultaneously the position x and the momentum mv in a physical interaction cannot be smaller than $\hbar$ or Planck's quantum divided by 2π. But Heisenberg claimed something immensely more: "Since all experiments are subject to the laws of quantum mechanics and thereby to the equation $[p_1.q_1 \sim h]$, the invalidity of the law of causality is *definitely* proved by quantum mechanics"[3] (emphasis added).

Heisenberg's claim implied an elementary fallacy in reasoning, which matters in philosophy before it matters in physics. This is not to suggest that a professional philosopher was necessarily needed to expose the situation for what it was. Right there and then, or in late March 1927, physicists should have been in the vanguard of alerting Heisenberg to the fallacy he had just begun to preach. They could have thereby prevented what eventually became not so much a comedy of error in logic, but a first-rate intellectual tragedy of the twentieth century.

But by then, as will be seen, physicists had for some time joined a pseudophilosophical bandwagon against causality, a well documented fact which is still to sink into broader cultural consciousness. Von Neumann's claim, that no experiment indicates the presence of causality in nature is simply refuted by the fact that an array of first-rate physicists proved themselves past masters in making bombs that now could turn the earth into a global cemetery. Some others certainly implemented the principle of cause-effect by excelling as zealous containers of a possible nuclear conflagration. A few of them gloried in that situation which a US Secretary of State described half a century ago by poking fun at them as he remarked that "in this age it appears every man must have his own physicist."[4] In general physicists have displayed conspicuous ineptitude in fighting cultural brush fires. Often enough they themselves touched them off and fueled them. In either way they implemented the principle of causality.

Any consideration, however brief, of the message of most modern physicists about causality should therefore dispel at once any illusion as to modern physics being a potent and primary source of philosophical enlightenment. This is not to say that philosophers were any better in spotting and denouncing what should be branded as the Heisenberg fallacy. This fallacy undermines a fundamental recognition in man's search for truth, namely, that nothing happens without a cause, indeed a fully adequate cause. Those ready to fall right away into the trap posed by that word "adequate," so evocative of equations, quantities, and measurements, should first consider the principle of sufficient reason, taking reason for a factor, for a cause. The principle means that the factor should suffice for the effect registered. Oversight of this may place one's reasoning on the slippery rosepath of clever cheating. There the starting point is an innocent-looking petty theft and the end point can in theory be far bigger than the great train robbery.

Almost four years had to pass after Heisenberg issued his fallacy before a philosopher decided to speak up. Of course, philosophers cannot be expected to keep track of and peruse highly technical journals of physics, such as the one that carried Heisenberg's essay. All too often they have to rely on high-level popularizations written by physicists. Such was certainly *The Atom* written by the prominent British physicist, G. P. Thomson, a future Nobel laureate. In retrospect it should seem a blessing in disguise that Thomson did not restrict himself to setting forth in non-technical language the newly discovered world of the atom and its working. Indeed he felt called upon to bring some glad tidings to the broader educated public: "Physics," Thomson wrote, "is moving away from the rigid determinism of the older materialism into something vaguely approaching a conception of free will."[5] The phrase was a classic in vague reasoning in which leading modern physicists proved themselves enormously proficient.

The book fell in the hands of J. E. Turner, professor of philosophy at the University of Liverpool, who quickly saw that Thomson's dictum was a somersault in logic. He exposed the fallacy in a brief Letter to the Editor of *Nature* that was carried in its December 27, 1930 issue. Turner first pointed out that unless the word determinism meant unvarying causation, there was no point in bringing in free will. Further, and this was Turner's crucial observation, there was no justification for doing so, if determinism simply meant, as was the case in the context of Thomson's statement, the procedure to ascertain. From that it followed that "every argument that, since some change cannot be 'determined' in the sense of 'ascertained', it is therefore not 'determined' in the absolutely different sense of 'caused', is a fallacy of equivocation."[6]

Turner's phrase was probably the most concise of all penetrating remarks made about modern physics by a modern philosopher. Turner's use of the word "equivocation" had a further irony to it, hitherto unnoticed. Equivocation should seem particularly deplorable when carried on the wings of a beautiful equation of theoretical physics. In the history of physics Heisenberg and others were not, of course, the first to turn a beautiful equation of theoretical physics into an equivocation, although in their case the equivocation had colossal cultural proportions. They served another egregious example of what happens when physicists cannot distinguish their *métier* from philosophy.

In Turner's cogent argumentation only one point was missing, although it could be readily assumed. Everybody knows or should know that when a physicist ascertains, he measures. Turner's failure to say this explicitly does not therefore detract from the force of his observation and from the magnitude of its potential influence. The influence should have been global and certainly so in contrast to the smallness of the observation, a brief letter in the lower right corner of a page in a globally read scientific weekly. No reaction whatever ensued. Physicists, if they paid any attention at all to that letter, must have brushed it aside with the remark that once more a philosopher barged onto their turf. They would have been entitled to be indignant only if it was true that even patently philosophical statements by physicists could be settled only by mathematics and by the quantitative data of measurements.

In fact, even those physicists who, as will be seen shortly, disputed the abolition of causality by quantum mechanics, rose to the defense of causality by endorsing what they should have denounced in the first place as a fallacy. They hoped to vindicate causality in terms of a physics that allowed, in theory at least, perfectly accurate measurements. So much for efforts to formulate a quantum mechanics of hidden variables, with or without the help of constructing pilot waves. Meanwhile the alleged liberation of man from the shackles of determinism reached proportions which a perceptive physicist, though not perceptive enough to see the basic fallacy at issue, described as an orgy of reasoning: "No simple slogan save 'violation of causal reasoning' was deemed sufficiently dramatic to describe the revolutionary qualities of the new knowledge."[7]

The drama included prominent physicists contradicting themselves. One of these was Max Born. In his *Natural Philosophy of Cause and Chance*, one of the most highly regarded works written by a physicist on the subject, Born wrote: "The statement, frequently made, that modern physics has given up causality, is entirely unfounded."[8] This was in 1948 or a little over twenty years after Heisenberg had made his declaration about the definitive invalidation of causality by physics. But the full extent of Born's trapping himself in a contradiction went beyond his having implicitly countered Heisenberg's declaration. For about the same time Born felt impelled once more to bring Einstein around to the Copenhagen interpretation of quantum mechanics as if it had not included Heisenberg's radical dismissal of causality in the name of the uncertainty principle, a dismissal which Einstein staunchly refused to concede. Einstein, however, never achieved a clear idea why he resisted Born's efforts set forth in letters written over several decades.

On seeing that his letters to Einstein finally affected the latter's long-standing friendship for him, Born turned in despair to W. Pauli for comment and advice. Pauli's reply displayed profound perceptiveness for ontology as well as rank flippancy about its portent. He called Born's attention to the fact that he had repeatedly heard Einstein state that the word "determined" was not really the fundamental point at issue. Obviously the word "determined" stood for Einstein, as it did for countless other physicists, for "ascertained," or measured. That semantic nuance was, as noted above, the gist of Turner's observation. But Pauli called Born's attention to the fact that Otto Stern, a Nobel-laureate, had "said recently that one should no more wrack one's brains about the problem of whether something one cannot know anything about exists all the same, than about the ancient question of how many angels are able to sit on the point of a needle. But it seems to me that Einstein's questions ultimately are of this kind."[9]

Einstein's questions were certainly not of that kind, but Einstein himself did not know how to answer them. His philosophical vision may have been impaired from the moment when at the age of thirteen he read Kant's *Critique of Pure Reason* and felt that it made all clear to him. Einstein was not the only one on whom the reading of that book produced a permanent myopia about the real, whatever his increasingly elemental affirmation of it in his later years. Only with this in mind can one understand why Einstein spent so much energy and time in devising thought experiments in which perfectly accurate measurements were possible. The same explains why he disliked all attempts to quantize general relativity. He did not want statistical randomness to spoil the beauty of that theory, which rested on the idea of the geometrical continuum. Acceleration, the object of general relativity, meant continual infinitesimal increments in velocity, and not discontinuous jumps, however minute. This Einstein perfectly saw, but he never perceived clearly the difference between the geometrical continuum from the one which is ontological.

It never dawned on Einstein that in trying to save causality by trying to evade operationally the consequences of Heisenberg's uncertainty principle he merely endorsed the very fallacy which is at the root of the Copenhagen interpretation of quantum mechanics. I have already on numerous occasions rendered that fallacy as equivalent to the inference: an interaction that cannot be measured exactly, cannot take place exactly. The fallacy consists in taking the same word "exactly" in two different senses. The first sense is clearly operational as it refers to the operation whereby an interaction is measured with numerical exactitude, with no margin of numerical error whatever. The other sense is ontological, for the phrase "to take place" means to happen, to occur, to exist.

Sensitivity for ontology cannot be imparted in the space of a short chapter. No reasoning, however impeccable, about the real is equivalent to infusing in the reader a vivid sense for the real and a thirst for its study, ontology. No defense of reality, however dramatic, can wake one up from an antiontological slumber. Exceedingly small may seem the number of those physicists who threw away the pseudophilosophical straitjacket of the Copenhagen interpretation on reading A. Pais's report about a conversation he had with Einstein as they walked to his home in Princeton. Einstein suddenly stopped, pointed at the moon and asked Pais, many years his junior: Does the moon exist only when you look at it? The question brings out vividly the utter subjectivism to which that interpretation logically leads once one adopts its premise that things exist only insofar as they are being observed, which for a physicist also means the act of measuring.

At that time, or around 1947, still several decades were to pass before that fallacy obtained its full unfolding within quantum mechanics proper. Clearly, if the act of observation made things to exist, nothing stood in the way of arguing that there were as many worlds as there were observers. This inference certainly showed the radically philosophical and unscientific basis of the Copenhagen interpretation as well as the nature of the bargain when a realist look at causality is bartered for a subjectivist version of it, coated, naturally, with science. In fact, in the end even the act of observing had to yield to one's being merely conscious of the wave-function of the universe. Needless to say, that interpretation offered no clue as to why the acts of countless different observers or their states of consciousness had any coherence among them and provided a universe common for all to investigate. The absence of such a clue generated the pathetic talk about "passion-at-a-distance," in reference to certain coincidences on the level of fundamental particles.

There is a another consequence which shows just as well the pathetic results whenever the real is approached with a flippancy emboldened by science. The consequence is worth recalling because it has been developed in very technical forms by some physicists. They claim nothing less than that quantum mechanics enables them, in theory at least, to create entire universes literally out of nothing. Worse, they insist that the word *literally* should be taken literally. They claim that physics now can perform experiments in metaphysics, and indeed the kind of experiment which touches on the very depths of metaphysics. For nowhere else does metaphysics come into play than in understanding the transition from nothing into something, that is, from non-existence into existence. In line with this it now became customary to claim that physics can measure the power of nothing in a "foam," a word that stands, of course, for some most abstract mathematical construct.

Anyone moderately aware of the infinite "distance" between non-being and being should be struck by the disproportion between the cause, quantum mechanics, and the effect, entire universes. But the really instructive aspect of this for an appreciation of the principle of causality lies in the process that led to this supreme example of all the hubris ever displayed in the name of science. The process is the inevitability of moving from small thefts, once these have become habitually condoned, to thefts that are not simply colossal but simply cosmic. The legitimization consists in agreeing with the fallacious sense in which Heisenberg and after him countless physicists took the uncertainty principle.

Let us assume that the uncertainty relation means that there is no causality, because there is a margin of imprecision in measuring simultaneously the position and momentum of a particle. The relation can be recast in a form in which the imprecision will concern the mass of a particle, which is something far more "real" than its position and momentum. In other words, the relation $\Delta x.\Delta mv \geq \hbar$ is equivalent to $\Delta E.\Delta t \geq \hbar$ where E stands for energy and t for time. But since E can also be written as mc^2, one can write the uncertainty principle as $\Delta mc^2.\Delta t \geq \hbar$. This in turn can be rewritten as $\Delta mc^2 \geq \hbar/\Delta t$. Since, however, c or the speed of light is constant, Δm is the only factor in the left side that can have a margin of uncertainty. At any rate, even if the margin of error in measuring c is taken into account, Δm is still a factor in evaluating the total uncertainty.[10]

If therefore the uncertainty principle means the absence of causality or at least a partial absence of it, the causality defect becomes a true mass defect in the interaction. Consequently, whenever a physicist wants to ascertain the moment or time of say a particle emission from a radioactive atom, he cannot avoid concluding that in the emission, one has on hand an amount of mass which is missing without a cause.

Not that G. Gamow would have seen this kind of break in the chain of material causality when he used in 1928 the uncertainty principle to explain the emission of alpha particles from radium. As one who could make fun of everything, and even of most sacred things, Gamow was certainly not the kind of physicist with any concern for the ontologically real. Moreover, all in a typical alpha particle emission the amount of mass defect was perhaps of the order of 10^{-34} grams, an inconceivably small amount. To ignore such a minuscule quantity of mass was an inconceivably smaller matter than the items on hand in any petty theft. But a theft it was and could only invite further thefts or at least rank insensitivity to them.

Indeed that insensitivity was so widespread by 1948 or so that the proponents of the steady theory boldly claimed something until then unheard-of in the history of physics. They postulated that hydrogen atoms were being created out of nothing at a steady rate everywhere in cosmic spaces. Further, they claimed that the creation in question was a spontaneous emergence out of nothing and had nothing to do with a Creator. The disproportion between effect and cause could not have been greater. Compared with this gamble, the traditional doctrine according to which only a Creator can produce anything out of nothing should seem pure rationality. In the latter at least a cause is postulated which is adequate to the effect, whereas in the former the principle of proportionality is honored in the breech. In being faced with a choice between the two, one may profitably ponder the reaction of Stephen Daedalus, representing James Joyce in the latter autobiographical *A Portrait of the Artist as a Young Man*. He could not help wondering: "What kind of liberation would that be to forsake an absurdity which is logical and coherent and to embrace one which is illogical and incoherent?"[11]

Certainly indicative of insensitivity for ontology was the fact that the steady-state theorists were not taken to task on philosophical grounds, the only ground on which one can argue about causality. They were rather disputed on scientific grounds which, however, had nothing to do with the postulate itself. For even if an extra amount of radiation, characteristic of the hydrogen atom, had been observed in outer space, the observation itself could in no way be construed as a detection of a transition of hydrogen atoms from non-being into being.

So much in a way of background for the idea that quantum mechanics, with the uncertainty principle at its basis, enables the physicist to create universes literally out of nothing. The claim, as was pointed out, is a theft of matter on a cosmic scale, the ultimate stage of progressing from petty thefts to tricks of much greater proportion than the great train robbery. But when a gravy train is pulled by the locomotive of physics, apparently no semaphore can indicate some fatal derailment lying ahead.

The process of small thefts whetting the appetite for ever larger ones illustrates the logic of the game called "truth or consequences." Science is not immune to that logic. Science too has to pay the penalties for the wishful thinking that its books need not be balanced, the books that are about matter and energy, because the two are interchangeable. Those books deal, on the level of the atoms and on levels below it, with aggregates of events and not with individual events, because there no individual interactions can be measured with reasonable accuracy with the tools and methods now available for physicists. Fallacious reasoning can alone infer from this the claim that therefore on that level individual events cannot take place with precision. The claim is a *non sequitur* and lies at the root of the reasoning that begins with a reference to the (operational) impossibility of locating particles, continues with a disclaimer about truly causal interactions, and ends with the assertion that no distinct line can be drawn between existence and non-existence.

The foregoing claim is already dubious physics, independently of the fact that no physical theory contains so far the possibility of an eventual replacement of quantum mechanics with something even more sweepingly efficient in coping with the quantitative aspects of physical reality. Most importantly, the same claim is very bad philosophy, implying as it does a jump from the operational to the ontological level. If one allows himself to be overawed by the glitter of interpretations which prominent physicists give about physics, one may choose to ignore the level of ontology, but one does not thereby become the kind of lover of wisdom a philosopher is supposed to be. Wisdom is tested in its encounter with reality.

In this connection one need not even make much of the old observation that not all that glitters is gold. It is enough to recall a fact, well documented historically. Physicists, including Heisenberg himself, had for years rejected causality before the uncertainty principle appeared in print.[12] They did so on various philosophical grounds. Some rejected causality in the name of pragmatism, others in the name of empiricism, still others in the name of Kantian rationalism, and some did it, including Heisenberg himself, in terms of a cogitation evoking sheer romanticism. All such grounds were clearly antimetaphysical. On such grounds nothing is more logical than to think that causality amounts to mechanical determinism which, if valid, would hold in its ironclad grip man's very actions, because in an antimetaphysical perspective all reality is purely physical. In that perspective all reference to spiritual realities and values degenerates into mere estheticism, be it the praise of the beauty of young Beethoven's D Major Serenade, which brings to a close Heisenberg's *Physics and Beyond*, where nothing convincing is shown about anything truly beyond physics and the physical.

One need not explicitly entertain metaphysical considerations in order to see the truth of causality, a truth far broader and deeper than mere mechanical causality, let alone one that can be measured exactly with the tools of the physics of the day. To recognize causality one need not do more than recognize reality as something that exists independently of one's thinking, in fact as something which prompts or causes one to think. To know the real is already a recognition of causality, insofar as objects activate the mind, instead of minds activating objects. Therefore, on that ground alone, no act of knowledge should be construed as invested with the power to make or undo reality. Mere thought cannot even change that reality.

The recognition that, apart from shaping this or that bit of reality, man cannot create it, because man can know that it exists in utter independence of him, is the ultimate basis for asserting the *truth* of causality. Contrary to Hume's claim, man does not hold causality because it is a convenient habit to do so. Anyone from early childhood has a direct experience of being able to effect changes in one's immediate surroundings. Conversely, one also has from an early age the experience of being changed by outside impacts.[13] It is therefore fully logical for man to see a cause-effect relationship among objects as they change their respective positions and movements by impacting on one another. Such a set of considerations and experiences about causality underlies the well-tested scientific principle which for over three hundred years now has been known as the principle of the conservation of matter.

Had Heisenberg been led by such philosophical considerations and not by the ones that guided him in 1927 and for the rest of his life, he might have spoken not of an uncertainty principle, not even of a principle of indeterminacy, but simply of the principle of imprecision. He would have thereby put a semantic barrier in the way of what soon became a rush to an orgy of fallacious reasoning and a huge red herring thrown in the path of those in pursuit of truth. Science too would have been helped because it is never about causality, not even about reality as such. Science merely presupposes reality in order to make meaningful its special work about the quantitative aspects of reality. Science is not about ontologically exact laws, and may not even be about measurably exact laws. But science must assume a nature which is lawful, that is consistently causal, or else it would make no sense to investigate those aspects of it scientifically, which science alone can investigate.

It should seem telling that Bertrand Russell's reversing himself on causality parallelled his shift from a purely positivist approach to science to a realist epistemology. Not only causality, but the word "cause," Russell wrote in 1912, "may prove a relic of a bygone age."[14] Two years later, he repeated the same: "In a sufficiently advanced form of science, the word 'cause' will not occur in any statement of invariable laws."[15] The formulation of the uncertainty principle did not, however, prevent him from claiming in 1935 that "the discovery of causal laws is the essence of science . . . The maxim that men of science should seek causal laws is as obvious as the maxim that mushroom-gatherers should seek mushrooms."[16]

By then Bertrand Russell was a realist, desperately trying to ward off the specter of that deeper reality which is genuinely metaphysical. No less obvious should seem the fact that any implementation of any cause issues in changes, this most universal facet of the real world. Change is also the oldest problem in philosophy and its ever fresh challenge, a topic to be taken up next.

[1] As this was done by G. Johnson in an essay, "Don't Worry. A Brain Still Cannot Be Cloned," *The New York Times* March 2, 1997, Section 4, p. 1.

[2] *Mathematical Foundations of Quantum Mechanics* tr. R. T. Beyer (Princeton: Princeton University Press, 1955), p. 327.

[3] "Ueber den anschaulichen Inhalt der quantentheoretischen Kinematik und Mechanik," *Zeitschrift für Physik* 43 (1927), p. 197.

[4] J. F. Byrnes, *All in One Lifetime* (New York: Harper, 1958), p. 284.

[5] G. P. Thomson, *The Atom* (London: Thornton Butterworth, 1930), p. 190.

[6] *Nature,* December 27, 1930, p. 995.

[7] H. Margenau, *The Nature of Physical Reality* (New York:McGraw Hill, 1950), p. 418.

[8] Oxford: Oxford University Press, 1949, p. 4.

[9] *The Born-Einstein Letters: Correspondence between Albert Einstein and Max and Hedwig Born from 1916 to 1955 with Commentaries by Max Born,* tr. Irene Born (New York: Walker and Co., 1971), p. 223.

[10] For the first time I set forth this argument in my book, *God and the Cosmologists* (Edinburgh: Scottish Academic Press, 1989), pp. 125-26 and almost simultaneously in my essay, "Determinism and Reality," in *Great Ideas Today 1990* (Chicago: Encyclopedia Britannica, 1990), pp. 277-302.

[11] See Penguin Books edition, p. 244. Such is the reason Joyce specified for his refusal to exchange Catholicism for Protestantism even though he did not practice the former.

[12] P. Forman, "Weimar Culture, Causality and Quantum Theory 1918-1927. Adaptation by German Physicists and Mathematiciains to Hostile Intellectual Environment," *Historical Studies in Physical Science* 3 (1971), pp. 1-115.

[13] Studies of J. Piaget on child psychology left these considerations fully valid.

[14] "On the Notion of Cause," in *Mysticisim, Logic and Other Essays* (New York: Longmans, Green and Co., 1921), p. 180.

[15] *Our Knowledge of the External World* (New York: Norton, 1929), p. 223.

[16] *Religion and Science* (New York: Holt, 1935), p. 153.

7

Change

Means are instruments of change, this most obvious facet of existence, human and cosmic. The observation, that the times change and in the process we too change,[1] is valid for any and all. Attention to change ought to be the hallmark of that philosophy which is about knowing things, where the first step is to register objects. These, if they are to be registered, must absorb and re-emit photons, and thereby change, however slightly. The very act of registering objects makes in turn countless neurons fire in the brain. Even the most private self-reflection means a physical change in the nervous system.

Whether one likes it or not, it is not possible to escape from the grip of change. Even those, Buddha and his followers, who most resolutely tried to be enveloped in that state for which Nirvana has become the classic label had to find in change the very means to approximate the blessed state of changelessness. All ascetical practices, however monotonous, which have been devised for that purpose, are exercises that, of course, mean change.

Being a basic facet of personal and physical existence, change is therefore better confronted with all the courage and sincerity the mind can muster. John Henry Newman certainly did this in stating that "to live is to change, and to be perfect is to have changed often."[2] Not that he wanted thereby to advocate a cult of change. Nor could he prevent the emergence of that cult on a colossal scale. Already in his time, technology fueled that cult which in our times has become *l'art pour l'art* in a virtual world of technological

111

make-believe. Through the exploitation of the magic of feedback mechanism, man has a plethora of means at his disposal that are literally exploding in their varieties. Ever vaster waves of new gadgets are flooding the market place, although not without a paradox. Ever new sales tactics rest on the conviction that what is new will certainly sell as if this were an unchangeable verity. This conviction, it is only fair to note, is a further proof that change best thrives on something unchangeable.

At any rate, modern man is becoming addicted to change. He needs ever fresh forms of novelties to satisfy that addiction. Nothing satisfies him unless he finds it exciting, which merely subjects him to a change, though with some psychological qualification. He fails to perceive the extent to which he is caught in a rat race, an image which recalls a senseless repetition of acts apparently performed for no purpose. Instead of satisfaction, he reaps a sense of exhaustion. Yet few things upset him so much as moments, let alone hours, of quiet and peace. Moreover, his gurus make him believe that change is the only goal worth pursuing. He is not alerted to the contradictory character of this belief which actually is not supposed to be subject to change.

Modern man is told that by implementing more change he would implement reform, though hardly the kind of reform which is meant by the etymology of the word, the restoration of some form, indeed of an archetype. The Marxists preferred not to think of the fact that there was something contradictory in pushing for a classless society in terms of their own dialectic. Similar contradiction, precisely because of its Hegelian provenance, plagues the idea of an affluent global society, standing on the threshold of the end of progress taken for the end of history. Progress has, of course, proved itself a piece of circular reasoning. This does not prevent the pursuit of affluence from rushing on at a maddening rate. There is no end to catching up with the Joneses, which means ever more change through the acquisition of ever more means.

Part of this cultural atmosphere has penetrated the groves of philosophy. Philosophers in academia are in the throes of the publish-or-perish syndrome, which is a forced cultivation of the art of saying the same with a new slant. Nothing that has already been said or argued over seems to command intellectual respect-ability. Truth, if there is any, can never be old, and if new, because it is merely a novel phrase, it ages quickly. Yet, in order to obtain a hearing, one is increasingly compelled to forge something new, which all too often amounts to an ever more convoluted phraseology.

This academically hallowed fad is not really new. Already a hundred years ago it became recognized in Germany that Kant had made imperative the use of complicated style in which he was certainly a past master. Very recently the fad in question received a memorable spoof in an article, "Transgressing the Boundaries: Toward a Transformative Hermeneutics of Quantum Gravity," consisting of variations on ultra-arcane philosophizing by physi-cists.[3] Convoluted phraseology, often beyond the pale of compre-hension, is no longer a possible reason for dismissing academics from their jobs. Rather it earns them *kudos*, as for instance the dictum that anonymous multi-user domains "can give us uninhib-ited access to emotions, thoughts and behaviors that are closed to us in real life." Virtual reality then becomes a "safe space in which to confront disturbing feelings."[4] Perhaps, but those feelings can only be virtual, as long as logic is not honored in the breach.

Those who enjoy (and they are the great majority) such fruits of the rush for novelty can hardly be expected to pause for a moment. To pause is to renounce the excitement of change for at least a moment, but it is as painful to those feeding on novelties as the mere idea of withdrawal from drugs is to an addict. In such a sickly atmosphere, one can hardly expect that momentary attention be paid to a point already noted. The point is that accolades of change always imply something unchanging.

Better minds have always known that. Newman praised change only because he knew that there was a faithfulness to type across doctrinal development, if it was true development and not a deformation. Being convinced that there were realities worth conserving Edmund Burke could argue, without contradicting himself, that concessions were to be made to rebel Americans: "Nothing in progression can rest on its original plan. We might as well think of rocking a grown man in the cradle of an infant."[5]

Being convinced as if it were a dogma that all men are created equal, Lincoln could urge the emancipation of slaves and deplore some "dogmas of the past" as being "quite inadequate to the stormy present," and insist on the duty "to think anew and act anew" and "disenthrall ourselves" in the process.[6]

But at a time when being in the thrall of what is novel is taken for the only sign of sanity, one can expect hardly an echo to the claim that it is not possible to sing the praises of change without paying homage, however unobtrusive, to permanence. Unobtrusive as that permanence may appear, it should seem obvious to any mind moderately keen on logic. Heraclitus failed to note that his claim, all is change, predicated the permanence of change. It did not dawn on Parmenides that he effected a change in claiming that nothing ever changes. Yet, contrary to the view perpetuated in histories of philosophy, those two sages did not contradict one another. They merely opposed one logically faulty formula to another no less defective.

The contradiction between the two was only apparent, and therefore the task of reconciling it could not be avoided. Democritus seems to have been exercised by this task. If atoms were the ultimate and permanent reality, change would then have consisted in their rearrangements and regrouping. This posed purely technical problems, which Democritus did not resolve to any satisfaction. It was sheer fantasy to say that atoms had hooks whereby to attach themselves to one another. He complicated such problems by postulating the existence of atoms of all conceivable sizes, including ·atoms infinitely large. There was further the problem of the undoubtedly obvious sense of personal permanence or identity. It is well to recall that Socrates' friends argued against personal permanence (immortality) with a reference to the atomists. If the Socratic reaction was an effort to save the sense of purpose, it was in terms of saving the sense of permanence in a welter of change.

Plato and Aristotle, who carried on Socrates' program, both held that the vindication of permanence in the teeth of change was a principal task for philosophy. Plato's eternally permanent ideas could not, however, be convincingly related to the level of ever-changing physical reality. In taking his starting point from the sensible world subject to change all the time, Aristotle knew that he also had to postulate something unchanging. This he did by proposing the idea of various substantial forms, akin in a sense to Plato's eternal ideas. But unlike such ideas, these substantial forms were postulated to come forth from something that was a substance, that is, something that "stands under" (*sub-stat*) the layer of existence that could be observed. On that level, by definition unobservable, lay also the prime matter, an entity totally void of any form, being sheer potency.

The effort of Aristotle brought out much better than that of Plato the mental dynamics which controls one's effort to cope with the problem of change, or the effort of seeing something permanent in what is changing. The dynamics demanded a conscious reliance on making an inference to the reality of something still physical though not observable. In other words, if one wanted to overcome patently extremist positions, such as the ones advocated by Parmenides and Heraclitus, one had to be ready to postulate entities, and not to forget at the same time that the urgency of making such a postulate did not give its object physical characteristics that could be identified in any specific way.

Forgetfulness, in different degrees, of this point has become a hallmark of Aristotelianism—old, medieval and new. Following the success of Bohr's atom model, some neo-scholastics heedlessly took the atomic nucleus for the prime matter and the orbital electrons for that substantial form which generated the accidents appropriate to it. But the nucleus, which had the potential of pulverizing entire cities, could easily discredit inept philosophical speculations as well. Had Aristotelians guarded themselves against that forgetfulness they might have forestalled the misunderstandings of friends as well as foes as to what the doctrine of transubstantiation could or could not mean even in modern times.

The Bohr atom seemed to bring a signal victory for atomism after it had been eclipsed by various fluids for over several centuries. But even the vast refinements brought to the Bohr atom did not answer the philosophical question about change as inseparable from some permanence. After the splitting of the nucleus into protons and neutrons, and these into a variety of quarks, and these again into gluons or what-not, the truly fundamental particles appear to be as elusive as ever. From the atom downward, those particles certainly failed to resemble particles, and certainly not hard round balls. Yet science, which is the art of counting the quantitative complexities of real matter, would find nothing so congenial as some truly ultimate bits of matter that in turn would serve as the natural units of measure and counting.

Whether this would mean a return to the atomists' explanation of change as a reconfiguration of basic units of matter is a question far less important than the question of what is the nature of those bits of matter. Modern physics showed that all matter, including all bits of it, is fully convertible into energy. Whereas physicists can measure energy and channel it in various ways (so many instances of change), they find no answer in science to the question: what is energy? Nor can they find an answer in science to the related question: what is a field? If they take the field for something physical, they run the risk of ushering in through the back door the once discredited ether, with its strange properties.

In other words, even in physics one has to be careful about the extent to which one can assign specific physical properties to some presumably physical entities. But this is not to be taken as a suggestion that the philosopher should turn to science for the solution of philosophical problems. The problem of change is a philosophical problem before it becomes a scientific one, and philosophical questions admit only philosophical answers.

The answer lies with the necessity of relying on inferences whose targets are not tangible. Such inferences do not begin with the inference, say that there is a mind, a universe, a God. These, as will be seen, remain the supreme inferences in philosophy about intangible realities. Such realities are, however, the objects of inferences even on lower levels. Inferences to intangible realities are indispensable long before one comes to those three, which Kant grudgingly called the three chief subjects of traditional metaphysics. To come to grips with the reality of most ordinary changes one has to infer that something remains identical in the subject that undergoes the change. Otherwise any rational judgment which cannot but refer to things changing, becomes riveted on the moment, with no validity across that time which is marked and measured by change.

That something is best called mere potency, a term less apt to create misunderstanding than the term prime matter. To ascribe any physical characteristic to potency or to prime matter is to turn it into an accident with nothing standing beneath as a substance, which, as noted above, always stands under. The philosopher may take some comfort from the fact that the physicist also has to infer the existence of entities, which it is better not to endow with observable properties. Otherwise he will reify mere mathematical constructs, such as fields and forces. In so doing he would merely drown himself in treacherous streams of which the mythical ether drift provided a memorable instance.

Undoubtedly it was the problem posed by change that led the inference, in the hands of Aristotle, to postulating entities known as substances. Oversight of the philosophical origin of the notion of substance led to identifying it with various "substances" and chemical concoctions, discrediting thereby that origin and creating confusion in chemical science. Confusion about what substance was meant to be reaches its height when a prominent paleontologist commends another for having been "thoroughly committed to the Darwinian view that variety is all and essence is an illusion."[7]

In doing so the paleontologist unwittingly calls attention to what is truly repulsive about Darwinism being taken for philosophy. It is not the perspective that in visiting the cage of some primates man may confront his very ancestors. It is the perspective of a grey flux of change with nothing stable in it. It is the perspective of a pseudoscientific destabilization of one's own personal identity. Darwin was repeatedly guilty of advocating something equivalent to that destabilization, although he was not philosophical enough to do it with full consistency. At any rate, to knock over a notion of substance which is a mere parody of substance properly understood, is merely to knock over a straw man, hardly a goal worth pursuing.

No scientist, no scientific method can abolish a philosophical conclusion that refers to an entity unobservable by definition, which straw men are certainly not. For whether the scientist likes it or not, philosophical problems keep asserting themselves, and so does especially the problem posed by any and all change, the very problem that evokes the perspective of substance. Scientists and philosophers may wish to take refuge in materialism. They may, however, be rightly asked to consider that materialism rests on the belief in the substantiality of matter.

If they are willing to face up to that challenge, they may not resist the task of facing up to a substance far more obvious than what can ever be suspected to lurk under any material change. The substance in question is usually denoted as soul or mind, or more concretely, that sense of personal identity that endures across a welter of physical, biological, neurological, and societal changes. Reluctance to face up to that reality can hardly be taken for a hallmark of intellectual consistency. Despisers of the reality of soul are hardly ever as consistent as were the most notable among existentialists. If these earned fame it was because of their grim consistency which some of them, such as Sartre and Camus, also articulated with rare literally skill.

Sartre's claim that "man is a useless passion" remains eminently quotable, but it is the philosophical consistency that motivated it which should seem truly memorable. He was consistent in dismissing the idea of substance, or permanence in any form whatsoever, so that change could be reduced to mere events and celebrated in an all the more uninhibited manner. Sartre is certainly to be credited for having insisted through thick and thin that one must deny substance or essence in its conceivably most perfect form, God, so that man as a substance might also be out of the way.

The gist of Sartre's philosophy lies in his claim that there are no essences "because there is no God to have a conception of it."[8] Therefore he was consistent in characterizing human futility as man's totally mistaken urge to posit such an infinite essence or substance. In doing so, man merely tries to divinize himself by believing that he can escape the grip of change: "To be man

means to reach toward being God. Or if you prefer, man fundamentally is a desire to be God."[9] And since this is a totally
mistaken desire, nothing of lasting value or reality remains for
man. He is lost forever in a senseless flow of change: "All human
activities are doomed to failure. Thus it amounts to the same thing
whether one gets drunk alone or is a leader of nations."[10]

Camus, in the long run, achieved a better perspective. But he
did not do it in terms of his own brand of existential philosophy,
which began with scorn for man's longing for clarity. Such a
longing, it may be proper to note, propelled Plato and Aristotle.
Camus did not have the perspicacity of these two. He overlooked
the fact that it was clarity which he tried to achieve by scorning
it. He declared such a longing to be irrational and the urge to
confront it to be absurd because it leads to suicide, either physically
or intellectually. It was in that sense that he claimed suicide to be
the only serious question in philosophy.[11] He recoiled from
saying that only such were therefore truly consistent who were
existentialists in the sense of taking themselves out of existence. He
deplored those, such as Husserl, who tried to resolve the absurdity
of human existence. For Camus they were guilty of intellectual
suicide. The only way of coping with absurdity was to ignore all
principles and standards as absurd reminders of permanence.

Being caught up in the Resistance taught Camus to respect
some principles and values. He did not, however, come to
consider the question of why there was any worth in sacrificing
one's life for others, an act very different from suicide. Was not
the very notion of worth something that transcended the moment?
And, speaking concretely, was there not something, a nature, in
man that transcended his momentary reality? Considering nature
would have evoked its synonym, substance, and something else.
Camus would have recoiled and muttered with King Lear: That
way lieth madness.

Madness hardly ever comes at once. When it comes, it first
may appear as a state of euphoria. Few intellectual enterprises may
be as exhilarating as that of taking a full count of the phenomena.
Their range is practically inexhaustible, not only because phenomena are countless but also because so are the moments of change.

Every change ushers in a new phenomenon. If there are philosophers whose task is never completed, they are the phenomenologists. They may be overjoyed over this fact, but here too an extreme is apt to provoke its opposite. In this case overjoicing may give way to a disillusion with the task of philosophy itself.

A systematic avoidance of questions of ontology, for such is the gist of the phenomenological method, can but produce a thirst for answers which are ontological in nature. Those who think that phenomenology can be cultivated at no detriment to a proper interest in ontology, should pause. The rush to phenomenology in recent Catholic philosophy and theology, which supposedly stand or fall with ontology, has already produced a state where big literary phrases increasingly crowd out elementary attention to questions of ontology, among them the question about substance. The word transubstantiation has indeed become a foster child among those who nowadays cast their Catholic lot with rhetorical reliance on the act of faith. As a psychological experience, the act of faith has, of course, endless phenomenological aspects, but its substantiality fades away in the measure in which one focuses on its aspects. This need not be necessarily so, but even phenomenologists are human. Phenomenology, whatever else it may be, amounts to a denial of balance with respect to questions of ontology, of which the question about substance is paramount. In fact even the most cautious cultivation of phenomenology induces such an imbalance.

There is no way of stilling the thirst for answers which phenomenology, let alone existentialism, triggers, without having a recourse to the word substance. It is the only remedy to the dizziness which cavorting in change is bound to produce. If one is to characterize modern philosophy, it is a revolt against substance. It started with intoxication. One should only recall the scene painted by Rabelais where philosophers, making merry in a tavern, ask for tankards filled with various substantial forms.

In a sober mood Descartes eliminated substances by insisting on clarity which quantities certainly provide but without penetrating the surface. Spinoza left only one substance, his infinite deity, which could not even explain why there were particular finite

things. This hardly augured well for the future of idealism. Kant
tried to repair the faults of idealism by systematically discrediting
the three chief essences: the universe, the soul, and God. He did
so under the pretext of tying truth to the sensory. Logic forced
him to manhandle all other existents, be they called things or
substances or essences. His systematic attack on God, soul, and
universe, forced him to ride roughshod over the world of change,
the world of science. He straitjacketed science in the mind's
categories, which, since he held them to be valid a priori, made
all change, on which alone can science feed itself, most doubtful.
This pseudo-rationalist attack on science was completed by Hegel,
about whom and his coterie Gauss, the prince of mathematicians
and no mean physicist, rightly complained that reading their
writings made his hair stand on end.

Science can, of course, do without the notion of substance
insofar as science wants to be science and nothing else. All its
counts are about quantitative changes, and all the more so as in
measuring and counting them it produces further such changes.
But those counts must refer to something, be it a molecule, an
atom, a quark, or a field, or else they will hang in mid-air. In fact
when a physicist rebuffs the philosopher's challenge to look into
the foundations of physics, his words may become a boomerang.
It may very well be that all of Samuel Alexander's talk about a
nisus as the reason for all change in the universe was, as Rutherford put it, but "hot air, nothing but hot air."[12] Yet it would
take a better argued sense of realism than the one available in all
of Rutherford's writings in order to justify his instinct for taking
protons and neutrons, which he was the first to postulate, for
tangibly real things. And nothing in Rutherford's writings could
be used as a refutation of those physicists who take protons and
neutrons, together with all elementary particles, for mere wave
packets. Yet, unless protons, and neutrons are real things, they
cannot not undergo change and thereby be registered by man as
rightful objects of his knowledge.

Protons and neutrons are not, of course, things in the sense in
which things are real on the macroscopic level. But they are
something, aren't they? This was the type of question that

prompted Plato and Aristotle to infer the reality of entities, however unobservable, that endure while changes go on. The question may not seem exciting in an age captivated by the kind of excitement which search for novelty for novelty's sake provides. Even less exciting may seem the answer that alone can resolve the question. But sanity demands that one's resolve should never weaken to keep posing the question, to trace out the answer, and to remain committed to it, no matter what. This kind of resolve wells up from a factor which may be best called the principle of unlimited curiosity. In everyday parlance it has always been known as the chief driving force of the human mind, our next topic.

---

[1] Omnia mutantur et nos mutabimur in illis.

[2] J. H. Newman, *An Essay on the Development of Christian Doctrine* (Doubleday Image Books, 1960), p. 63.

[3] The article was written by A. Sokal, a physicist at New York University and appeared in the Spring 1996 issue of *Social Text*. It took almost a year before some readers of that periodical began to suspect the hoax, which had completely taken in the Editorial Board.

[4] Janet H. Murray, *Hamlet on the Holodeck: The Future of Narrative in Cyberspace* (New York: The Free Press, 1997).

[5] E. Burke, "Letter to the Sheriffs of Bristol" (1777), in *The Works of Edmund Burke* (Boston: John West, 1807), vol. 2, p. 117.

[6] Message to Congress, Dec. 1, 1862, in *The Collected Works of Abraham Lincoln*, ed. R. P. Basler (New Brunswick, N.J.: Rutgers University Press, 1953), vol. 5, p. 537.

[7] See S. J. Gould's review of *Simple Curiosity: Letters from George Gaylord Simpson to His Family 1921-1970*, ed. L. F. Laporte (Berkeley: University of California Press, 1988) in *The New York Times Book Review*, Feb. 14, 1988, p. 15.

[8] J.-P. Sartre, *Existentialism and Humanism*, P. Mairet (London: Methuen, 1948), p. 28.

[9] J.-P. Sartre, *Being and Nothingness*, tr. H. E. Barnes (New York: The Philosophical Library, 1956), p. 566.

[10] Sartre, *Being and Nothingness*, p. 627.

[11] A. Camus, *The Myth of Sisyphus*, tr. J. O'Brien (New York: Alfred Knopf, 1955), p. 3.

[12] "Well, what have you been talking all your life, Alexander? Just hot air! Nothing but hot air."

8

Mind

All that has been said in the preceding chapters about the message, which is carried by a means, should at least strongly suggest that there are huge differences between the means and the message. The means, usually a book, is a very tangible object, whereas the message is an intangible object for understanding on the side of the sender as well as of the receiver. The intangibility of the message is further enhanced by its being sent *freely* and *for a purpose*. That the message is meant *to cause* understanding is very different from the manner in which tangible things bump into one another and exercise thereby a form of causality. Further, the range of the message may refer to things far beyond anyone's reach. It may, indeed refer to that sum of tangible objects, the *universe*, which is perhaps a reality far greater than the sum of things within the ken of all known cosmological models. Again, the kind of *clarity* which is at play in all such acts of understanding is far broader than the comparatively very narrow type of clarity on hand when one registers extension and measures it, which is but counting the sum of unit extensions. In no such way can the message itself be "sized" up.

The message is an act of understanding something, an act so fundamental that it cannot be explained in terms of anything else. Further, to try to understand understanding in terms of under-standing is equivalent to going around in a circle, while under-standing the process all the time. One can, however, profitably ponder why one should "under-stand" or "stand under" something, in order to understand it. To "stand under" suggests that the act of understanding an object or an event or a process is to get "under it" in a sense very different from a physical relation with respect to a thing, or event, or process. The act of understanding is a meta-physical act at least in this rudimentary, though still thoroughly metaphysical sense.

Acts of understanding are furthermore very different from mere physical acts or events, although in a sense very similar to them. Like physical acts, acts of understanding are acts, that is, isolated events. Both kinds of acts are tied to a special point, a combination of the here and the now, in space and in time. In the case of physical events, there is an innumerable and far ranging variety of such points. In the case of acts of understanding, the here is always tied to a lump of grey matter called the brain and each now is a conscious moment.

Once the word conscious is written as con-scious, it immediately reveals a suggestive power similar to the one already observed in connection with the word understanding. Just as far more is implied in the word under-standing than meets the eye, the invariably conscious character of the act of understanding reveals far more than what can be noticed by mere physical eyes. The now's of physical events constitute a sequence, a chain, very different from the manner in which the now's of the acts of understanding do. In the former the different now's remain strictly different, whereas in the latter they coalesce into that most immediate unitary experience which is consciousness. It is a unique experience also in that the one experiencing it is assured thereby of a personal identity across vast ranges of space and long periods of time. The spatial case was best illustrated in our time by astronauts who journeyed to the Moon and came back as the same individuals. As to time, one does not need to spend years in orbit, it is enough to grow old in any corner of the good old earth and find that long decades leave intact one's personal identity.

No wonder that the experience of consciousness has always been a thorn in the side of empiricists of all hues, who are resolved not to see in it anything extraordinary. If some of them marveled now and then at such an experience so different from anything else empirical, they certainly failed to say so. Still, consciousness never ceased to bother their philosophical conscience. It was, of course, easier to dispute consciousness in its manifestation as moral conscience than to try to discredit consciousness in a direct way. Consciousness was, however, always threatened whenever one scoffed at moral conscience. Fortunately, no serious men of jurisprudence and no responsible legislatures ever heeded Jeremy Bentham who wrote in his treatise on morals: "Conscience is a thing of fictitious existence, supposed to occupy a seat in the brain."[1] They knew the broader meaning of the proverb, "it is always term-time in the court of conscience." For unless moral conscience, so inseparable from consciousness, is not a figment of one's fancy, no sitting of Court can have justification whatever.

Direct or frontal attacks on consciousness cannot, of course, be made without getting involved in plain contradictions. A case in point is William James' declaration that consciousness is but "a name for a nonentity." He did not make this declaration in the fit of youthful extremism, but in ripe old age, when, of course, rigid resistance to the obvious may also assert itself. James, as is well known, claimed to have been for long very hesitant to part with consciousness as an entity. But in the closing years of his life he found "the hour ripe for it to be openly and universally discarded." He could only pity those hanging on to consciousness as ones "clinging to a mere echo, the faint rumor left behind by the disappearing 'soul' upon the air of philosophy."[2]

There was a touch of pontificating in all this and largely obeyed by the confraternity of psychologists who, if pressed, would not have objected to James' high-handed philosophizing that consciousness had "no right to take place among first principles." There were for him no first principles but only one "primal stuff in the world," which he called "pure experience."[3] Once this step of "radical empiricism" was taken, no explanation was needed except the claim that one had this or that experience. Psychiatry in turn became the culinary analysis of experiences. As to the science of psychology proper, there was plenty of justification to write two generations later: "Psychology having first bargained away its soul, and then gone out of its mind, seems now, as it faces an untimely end, to have lost all consciousness."[4]

Consciousness cannot be consciously denied, and not even ignored. Consciousness is at least an awareness of one's existence, a form of knowledge. Nor is it possible to know things in a way other than in one's manner of knowing the self, that is, consciously. This is why the mind, which to some extent is synonymous with consciousness, is like nature, of which the Romans of old realized that it will keep returning even after it had been chased away with a pitchfork. Surgical scalpels, microtomes, and laser rays have not been more successful in exorcising the mind even when it was contemptuously spoken of as a mere soul.

Neurosurgeons, who based their rejection of the mind on their failure to locate the mind while dissecting the brain, merely proved that it is possible not to see beyond one's nose. There would never have arisen the art and science known as brain surgery if man were not a nosey being and incorrigibly so. But there is a profound difference between a dog's way of pursuing a scent and a man's pursuit of targets that keep alive his curiosity. This is why the topic of the mind's creativity and the art of discovery refuses to be cubbyholed in empiricist and rationalist schemas.

No further apologies will be made in this chapter for taking one's mental experiences, or varieties of knowledge, for a justification to reopen the question, which is, in a sense, the central issue in all search for truth. The problem is usually referred to as the brain-mind relationship. To pose the problem in such a form may, however, amount to a distraction from making the kind of step first which alone can be the first step in shedding light on that relationship. For what is to be considered first are the characteristics of mental operations, or acts of knowledge. Only when at least some such major characteristics have been registered can one consider the question of whether those characteristics are such as to impose on any lover of truth the duty to ask whether there is a mind as distinct from the body regardless of its total dependence on the body for its operations.

Some of those characteristics have already been listed. Unlike bodies, thoughts are not extended. Unlike bodies that move necessarily, mental operations are often performed with an explicit sense of freedom and for a purpose at that. Again, the causation whereby one prompts understanding in another is radically different from the manner in which bodies impinge on one another. Bodies can be lumped together by physical forces to an astonishing degree. Yet even in that early stage of cosmic evolution when the matter of all stars of all galaxies was confined within a space not larger than the trillionth of a pinhead, whatever there remained in the form of basic constituents of matter, they did not interpenetrate. On the contrary, acts of knowledge fuse into one another, without the slightest indication that such a fusion involves measures of space.

Among all such mental acts the one experienced as the *now* deserves to be considered at some length. One reason for this is the monumental admission of failure on the part of no less a physicist than Einstein to try to do justice by physics to the *now*. Einstein's admission is all the more significant, because a leading logical positivist, Carnap, elicited it. Carnap hardly expected a sort of rebuff, when he traveled in 1935 to Princeton, in order to obtain from Einstein an endorsement, however indirect, on behalf of logical positivism as the genuine interpretation of the exact sciences and especially of the theory of relativity. Then as later it escaped Carnap and all logical positivists, that the theory of relativity is the most absolutist of all physical theories, and therefore a curiously non-positivist mental product. During the conversation the question of the *now* came up. Carnap, who sought an explanation of it in terms of physics could take no comfort from the fact that Einstein declared the conscious experience of the *now* to be purely subjective just because he did not see how could it be handled by physics.[5]

The physics in question was that special and general theory of relativity which so many have taken for a proof for the fusion of space and time. While the physics of relativity made possible the fusion of matter into energy, it could not, according to its chief formulator, account for that fusion of space and time which is the experience of the *now*. Those, and they are not few, who try to appear Einsteinian by larding their philosophical, and what is far worse, their theological discourse with brave invocations of space-time, play a most risky game. For what is left for the philosopher if his mind is no longer an objective reality, but a fusion of geometrical abstractions? And what at all can the theologian offer if there is no soul to receive it? Can a man chalk up any profit if he grabs all the space-time with its equally abstract world lines, but by the same stroke of Einsteinian logic he loses his grip on his very soul? Can a soul be worth fighting for except as an objective reality?

To declare the *now* to be something purely subjective may have dispensed logical positivists from the duty of facing up to the *now*, this most extraordinary and most obvious of all human experiences. But the experience did not thereby become nonexistent as William James would have it as well as all those who fall back on the word subjective to achieve the same objective. And since one's logical positivism logically makes one a physicalist, Carnap should have at least pondered that the second law of motion, action equals reaction, applies in all attacks on conscience. For just as doubts cast on moral conscience become doubts on consciousness, the declaration of consciousness as being subjective rules out of court moral conscience as well. The reason is simple: purely subjective experiences are not admissible in courts of law. Therefore all criminals might claim that the fact of their having been conscious at the moment of breaking the law, makes them exempt from legal prosecution. Some prominent interpreters of American constitutional law, so eager to impress Congressional committees with their references to supple bends in the gravitational space-time manifold, have yet to perceive this ominous consequence.

In addition to the *now* there is also the conscious knowledge of *nothing*. Why is it, one may ask that man, who is so utterly dependent on sensory impressions, can form the idea of nothing? After all whenever one consciously thinks of the nothing, something very positive and material goes on in the brain. Possibly, one day brain research may specify and pinpoint all the physical reactions that take place in all the neurons in the brain whenever the idea of nothing arises in one's consciousness. There may be on hand one day a full description of those processes, with all the energy transitions in all molecules fully displayed. An earnest inquirer after truth will certainly marvel at the enormous disparity between that display, which is very much something and the knowledge that has the nothing for its object. And what if one day brain research would succeed in writing out all the energy levels that correspond to consciousness itself? The display may demand long reams of computer printout or huge walls to be written on. The act of consciousness will only appear between the lines, poking gentle fun at the effort to render it in the category of extension, be it that of space or of time or of any combination of these into some esoteric space-time.

The printout or the writing itself gives away the effort by showing it to be an exercise of putting the cart before the horse. Once more a disreputable game is on hand whereby a step that in no way can be the first is paraded as the first step. For every printout, every piece of writing witnesses that unique mental ability which is to symbolize. Man is a symbol-making animal, and the only such animal known. That man started making tools for use in most varied physical circumstances was certainly a stunning act of generalization, so different from purely material processes. Generalization is a form of abstraction, which puts man far above the empirical level. But the extent of generalization involved in making tools, however primitive, should seem insignificant when compared with what is involved in making words, which, as far as we know, always occur in the kind of intellectual observations called phrases.

Further, words always function as parts of phrases, which are sweeping intellectual generalizations even when they refer to strictly particular empirical details. All this appears especially baffling when seen from Darwin's evolutionary perspective, in which material needs and use precede all developments, including the development of intellectual faculties. Already Wallace pointed out to Darwin that his explanation of the evolution of the mind was equivalent to putting the cart before the horse. If the ever larger brain is the product of an ever more intense intellectual exercise, the intellect, the mind cannot be assumed to be present in advance, so that its action may develop the larger brain. The only answer Darwin could give was an imperious No!, which he wrote on the margin of a reprint of an essay which Wallace sent him. This reply may have satisfied Darwin's resolve to fight tooth and nail anything indicative of something non-material in man, but it left the problem fully intact, in fact only growing in strength. Suffice it to think of Chomsky's admission, in reference to most elementary forms of syntax, that neural networks must have been ready in man's brain before man could have developed that incredibly strange faculty which is language, always the art of uttering sentences.

Whatever the futility of searching for the origin of language, it should be clear that language is not a vocal imitation of physical sounds or feelings or impressions. Were such the case, the human race would not speak a stunning variety of tongues, which contain an incredible variety of verbal expressions for bodily experiences that are universally the same for all humans. Every word bespeaks an ability which is to abstract and to do so in a sense far superior to, say, the act of abstracting from the appearance of a wide variety of apples the ideal form of that fruit.

Further, as has already been noted earlier, language lives in phrases as so many judgments, many of which have no counterpart whatever in material processes. One may perhaps be tempted to see in statements about change a mere reflection of material changes constantly in evidence. But where is the material equivalent to the judgment that changes do take place even when one does not observe them? Or should one dispute the truth of that statement just because that material equivalent cannot be pinpointed? Should one, for the same reason, see a mere fallacy in the judgment that things do exist independently of our observing them?

But one would look for a material equivalent even with respect to the intellectual content of the plainest statements of facts. Such a statement is, for instance, the assertion that a block *is* there. Does that assertion turn the mind into a block? Or to use more technical terms, does the assertion establish a one-to-one correspondence between the block and the knower? Indeed is that correspondence amenable to being expressed in terms of logic? Is not therefore the mind, the knower, much more than a depository of logical relations, although it has to be eminently logical all the time? Questions like these should give much food for thought for those who in their enthusiasm for empiricism fail to see that it can turn some unwary minds into sophisticated blockheads.

Empirical evidence, if handled judiciously, that is, with a mind freed from the shackles of empiricism, provides in every written or spoken word a proof of the mind. Now that computers have brought the Chinese into direct and pressing contact with modernity, it would be especially unreasonable to see any rhyme and reason in the view of Ernst Mach who extolled ideographic writing as being most consonant with sensationism, which he took, of course, for the valid philosophy. Ernst Mach, who ended up a Buddhist, should at least have pondered why, though armed with that most "philosophical" sensationist tool or ideographs, the Chinese of old failed to construct the tool, science, which they now feverishly apply in order to pull abreast with the West.

Since Champollion deciphered the Rosetta stone, it is clear that the Egyptian hieroglyphics were a form of phonetic language. It is not yet clear how that language transformed itself into the Phoenician and then the Greek alphabet that keeps only some vague traces of pictorial representation, such as the letter beta, which goes back to the Hebrew letter ב, which is called *beth*, because it gives some idea of a house. But the real challenge is to explain how the Egyptians, or whatever race before them, achieved what is certainly an intellectual feat and not the impinging of one particular object's image on one's perception. What they did was to take the first sound in a given word that refers to an object and to denote that sound whenever it comes up in speech with the figure of the same object. It would not be commodious to write the expression, "The Tale of a Tub," by drawing in succession a *t*able, a *h*are, an *e*gret, a *t*able, an *a*pple, a *l*izard, an *e*gret, an *o*wl, a *f*rog, an *a*pple, a *t*able, an *u*dder, and a *b*room—but, however picturesque, the procedure would still amount to phonetic writing. It would correspond to that magnificent feat of abstraction which is to use pictures for sounds, and then a series of pictures used as generalized symbols of spoken words. More shortly on this feat of abstraction which implies not one but three steps in it.

Phonetic writing is, of course, only a sample of symbol-making, the very means on which rests man's ability to form and send messages that can be understood. Why the same ability, hardly a mere biological ability, exists in countless other individuals is a question which cannot be answered if one takes a mere verbalization for an explanation. Verbalizations are equivalent to covering up old puzzles with a novel label.

That the mind is a secretion of the brain may seem a crude enough view, but at least it can be refuted. T. H. Huxley's claim, that the mind is a mere epiphenomenon, is certainly not refutable, because it is a simple refusal to consider the problem: why are intellectual acts, be they called epiphenomena of the brain, so strikingly different from it? Among the latter-day variants of Huxley's claim the phrase, "identity theory," gained academic respectability. This in spite of the fact that identity is a word that designates above all similarity, if it designates anything at all. Yet if there is dissimilarity, it is between the chemically specified processes in the brain and the intellectual acts corresponding to them. How this dissimilarity came to be taken so lightly, is still to be explored by historians of ideas. The result may not amount to more than to an illustration of the fact that one's eyes quickly accommodate themselves to darkness, a process which Burke memorably generalized: "Custom reconciles us to everything."[6] On the moral level this would amount to being slowly reconciled to committing the same criminal act again and again. Philosophy too has its moral component, since as a love of truth it can also turn into a hatred of it.

The same custom received further impetus with the view of computers as so many anticipations of intelligence available as artifacts. As all artifacts, computers too are a sum of atoms. It is known that in the best computer available today, the typical element on a chip makes connection with ten other elements, a number three orders of magnitude smaller than is the estimated number of connections that tie one neuron to another in the brain. But it is not known at all, it is a mere belief, that if that number in a computer is increased by three orders of magnitude, one will have on hand a thinking machine.[7] What, however, can be known (it had been pointed out in 1927 and by an unabashed materialist) is a frightful conundrum: If one's mental processes are equivalent to the actions of atoms, one can have no reason to assume that one's beliefs are true. Those beliefs may be sound chemically, but not intellectually. Hence there remains no reason for even supposing that one's brain (or one's computer) is composed of atoms.[8]

It is in that sense that the idea of artificial intelligence is most profoundly artificial. Without the mind, computers are so much scraps of metal and heaps of silicon. Some of those who make the best computers know this all too well. Thus, in the much celebrated triumph in May 1997 of Deep Blue over Mr Kasparov, it was the constructors and programmers of Deep Blue who emphasized that it was a mere robot. Champions of artificial intelligence hastened, of course, to charge that this was merely a lame move on the part of IBM lest it appear a promoter of artificial intelligence.[9] Actually what the victory of Deep Blue showed was that the human mind is least human when asked to perform a very large number of robot-like operations in a few seconds, let alone in a mere fraction of a second.

Indeed, ever since man first made the abacus he did so in order to relieve his mind of the burden of performing the same operations again and again. Such was the reason why the logarithm was invented, and later on mechanical calculating machines, and still later calculators operating with punchcards. While their constructors, such as Pascal and Babbage, would have been the last to impute thinking to those devices, much smaller minds quickly did. And when instead of metal cogwheels and iron rods, electron tubes began to do the switching with incredible speed, the fad was on to talking about artificial intelligence. The fad then claimed (and was given) academic respectability when the speed and efficiency were greatly increased by semiconductors and etched circuits.

Turing's test then claimed the best minds to refute it, although it consisted in the arbitrary narrowing of intellectual acts to operations with numbers and purely logical relations. No attention was paid when the question was asked about the true nature of programming the idea of nothing into a computer. In such an intellectual atmosphere one could not expect that serious attention should be paid to the task of programming such words as *is* and *are* and *should*, let alone whether an already existing program could program itself to do such task *meaningfully*. Most defenders of meaning, that is, of human intelligence gave away the game by allowing that the computer can do non-creative mental operations, but not truly creative ones. The implicitly conceded that the computer *understood* non-creative mental operations, as if the simplest arithmetic rules did not represent a most creative act of the human mind.

Once it was conceded, however tacitly, that the computer understood elementary additions, there remained no logical way to deny thinking ability to computers and to conjure up a glorious, superhuman future for them. The orgy of speculations about computers loving one another and siring one another is at best a symptom of the extent to which the minds of some humans could be desensitized to truth. At its rawest the orgy is a symptom of a rude abuse of the intellect which may best be called its bestialization. There is nothing really new in that brazen abuse. Almost two thousand years ago Galen exposed those who in the name of atoms degraded the mind to a heap of atoms. His argument was that it was the mind that in the first place saw atoms that could not be seen with physical eyes at all.

At that time it would, of course, have been premature to speak of discoveries. Only the flood of discoveries made by man during the last hundred years or so awakened philosophers of science to the inanity of Bacon's claim that discoveries are the fruit of induction, and done in an mechanical manner so that, to paraphrase Bacon, even a fool can use the method in a foolproof way. But even far better forms of logic than Bacon could dream of proved to be inadequate to explain scientific discoveries. Bacon was indirectly refuted when Einstein declared that there was no logical way to discovery.[10] Yet Einstein would have been the last to claim that what did not appear logical was not rational.

In view of all this, it may not appear presumptuous let alone illogical to ponder the possibility that a mind is responsible for all those marvelous intellectual acts. To evaluate this possibility one may profitably think of progress in philosophy as an advance across a field full of crevices. The history of philosophy has been useful at least in the sense of revealing the edges of chasms both right and left, that is, in the directions of idealism and of empiricism. Many fell over the precipice by taking tangible matter lightly. The history of Platonism proved at least that whatever its use for angels, it failed to give humans a reliable handle over flesh and blood reality. A priorism, a hallmark of idealism, invariably proved itself a dubiously heuristic tool. Those who narrowed their vision to the strictly material found it difficult to do justice to matter, which, contrary to materialists, is full of arcane properties, which only the mind can fathom.

To keep oneself at safe remove from precipices lurking on the right and on the left is itself an exercise which combines mind and matter. Not, of course, a mind, which à la Descartes can do nothing more with matter than touch the brain machine at the pineal gland. Such a mind was a ghost, a far cry from that mind which depends in all its operations most intimately on the brain. Still mental operations are so many refutations of the notion that they merely reflect matter. Wittgenstein nowhere missed the mark more than in claiming that clear ideas are so many pictures. His having had a training in aeronautical engineering may have had something to do with his being mesmerized with a narrow type of clarity. The most penetrating acts of the intellect that shed most clarity are not pictures of material processes, but words about them. In fact, words, such as however, as, but, nevertheless, in order, because and so forth cannot, even by the wildest stretch of imagination be taken for such pictures. Therefore the need will remain pressing to postulate a substratum, the mind, for such acts and explain satisfactorily the fact that means can deliver messages.

To assent to making such a postulate or rather an inference, has at least this much to its credit. It amounts to a clear and honest recognition that intellectual operations pose a problem and that it is intellectual cowardice to treat such a problem by covering it by vain phrases, such as identity relation, epiphenomenon, parallelism and so forth. The latest of these cover-ups has grown into a new branch of academic discipline, called cognitive psychology. While it represents an advance over a psychology lost in fathoming the subconscious and dark urges, its cultivators have so far made no honest effort to face up to the reality of the mind.

Their failure or reluctance contrasts sadly with Augustine's favorite dictum and advice, "intellectum vero valde ama," greatly love the intellect.[11] This advice, coming as it does from one who in his *Confessions* and in his writings on the Trinity displayed unparalleled penetration into the psychology of cognition, should seem preferable to Darwin's blurting out: "A dog might as well speculate on Newton's mind."[12] The advice does not assure ready grasp of what the mind is, but at least leaves the door open for an eventual success. Nor does the advice mean that one should follow Augustine in his Platonism, although he preceded by more than a thousand years Descartes in making the inference, *cogito ergo sum*, without becoming a Cartesian. It is possible to love the intellect in a way which is radically empiricist, though much more radically than William James proposed. One wonders what James, who was mesmerized by Kant, would have thought if informed that according to Thomas Aquinas even the categories of the mind are distilled from sensory experience.[13] This is why Thomas had never written anything contrary to the proposition that the mind is a reality which is known only through inference and therefore can never be taken for an object of direct knowledge. To recognize the reality of the mind is a mental exercise whereby one takes words, all of them universals, for more than mere words. One takes them, and rightly so, for carriers of universally valid truths that can be corrected only by falling back on truths carried by universals.

Only such philosophers, or scientists for that matter, who take words such as species, genera, energy, field, etc., for more than mere words, will have eyes to appreciate what it means to make cognizance of anything. In every such act they grasp what is universal, though it remains but an inference since only the particular is directly observed. Therefore they will not have difficulty in seeing that their grasp of the mind is not a direct knowledge but an inferential one, yet a truthful piece of knowledge for all that. While one all the time experiences consciousness, one does not have the experience of having a mind and yet still possesses one. The proof of this is any message sent by a means, so immensely different from the message itself.

Herein lie the limits to all sane speculations about the nature of the mind, about its various powers as distinct from its various actions, to say nothing of its ability to do what matter can never do: to be at safe remove from eventual disintegration, because all acts of the mind are integration whereas all sensory acts are divisions. Perennial endurance is therefore a legitimate prospect for an entity that, as will be seen, can achieve reasoned assurance about that absolute integrity and cohesion which is God. But precisely because the mind is so intimately tied to matter, it is only appropriate to consider first what is, next to its recognition of God, its greatest integrative achievement: its reasoned assurance about that totality of things material or the universe.

---

[1] J. Bentham, *Deontology; or, the Science of Morality* (London: Longmans, Rees, Orme, Browne, Green and Longmans, 1834), vol. 1, p. 137.

[2] W. James, *Essays in Radical Empiricism* (new impression; New York: Longmans, Green and Co., 1922), pp. 2-3.

[3] Ibid., p. 4.

[4] Sir Cyril Burt, "The Concept of Consciousness," *British Journal for Psychology* 53 (1962), p. 229.

[5] See Carnap's intellectual autobiography in P. A. Schilpp (ed.), *The Philosophy of Rudolf Carnap* (La Salle, IL.: Open Court, 1963), pp. 37-38.

[6] E. Burke, *On the Sublime and Beautiful*, Pt. IV, par. xviii.

[7] And certainly not a verity as claimed by John H. Holland of the University of Michigan. See *Business Week*, June 23, 1997, p. 84.

[8] This is a paraphrase of a passage of J. B. S. Haldane in his *Possible Worlds and Other Essays* (London: Chatto and Windus, 1927), p. 209.

[9] *The New York Times*, May 9, 1997, p. A1.

[10] This is implied in his words that "there is no way from experience to the setting up of a theory." See his "Autobiographical Notes," in P. A. Schilpp (ed.) *Albert Einstein. Philosopher-Scientist* (New York: Harper Torchbooks, 1959), vol. 1, p. 89.

[11] Epistula 120:13.

[12] Letter of May 22, 1860 to Asa Gray, in *The Life and Letters of Charles Darwin*, ed. F. Darwin (London: J. Murray, 1887), vol. 2, p. 312.

[13] *Quaest. disp. de Anima*, art. 5.

9

Universe

Even early in this century it was but a teasing generalization to say, as did Whitehead, that the history of Western philosophy is a series of footnotes to Plato. Today Plato would find congenial no more than a few footnotes in any typical philosophical treatise. Only on rare occasions would he find there something vaguely similar to the prayer which he made Socrates address in *Phaedrus* to "dear Pan and all ye other gods that dwell in this place."[1] The prayer is a petition for the favor of genuine self-improvement. This should be a most philosophical objective as long as philosophy is taken for the love of wisdom and not for logic chopping which rightly evokes the enterprise called deconstructionism. There is a big difference between cutting wood and merely chopping it.

Tellingly, the prayer was addressed to Pan, the god of Nature, or of the All (*to pan*), that is, the Universe, which the Greeks of old also called *kosmos*. Earnest desire for self-improvement and profound respect for the universe went hand in hand for much of the history of philosophy. That philosophical discourse is no longer intent on that worthy aim, at least not in an unabashed manner, is paralleled by the rapid disappearance of the universe from philosophy. Actually, instead of a parallel, one should speak of a correlation. By far the most striking diagnosis of that correlation is Chesterton's dictum, greatly cherished by William James, that in sizing up a prospective lodger a landlady first should inquire not about his income but about his view of the universe.

There is more depth in that single dictum than in the half a thousand or so pages of Whitehead's *Process and Reality*, often referred to as the last philosophical cosmology, a book published in 1929. Leaving aside the meager measure of self-improvement which the reader of that book may derive from it, he certainly would look in vain there for a single chapter on the universe. Perhaps this was the reason why Whitehead did not include the word "cosmos" in the title of the book which for this reason alone should never have been taken for a treatise in cosmology, let alone for the last great treatise of that kind. It should rather have been taken for a treatise in pantheism, minus *to pan* or the cosmos.

At any rate, by 1929 nobody was reading Herbert Spencer's *Synthetic Philosophy*, which deserves to be called the last philosophical cosmology because its author spoke of the cosmos, or at least of its evolution from its allegedly homogeneous primordial state to its present inhomogeneity or specificity. The pathetic character of that cosmogonical tale was best put by H. G. Wells who minced no words: "He [Spencer] believed that individuality (heterogeneity) was and is an evolutionary product from an original homogeneity, begotten by folding and multiplying and dividing and twisting it, and still fundamentally *it*," or something utterly nondescript and indescribable.[2] Nothing better can be said about Hegel's cosmogony as the process of the self-unfolding of the Absolute. There, instead of the material universe one merely finds Hegel's universe of ideas, all of them vague and slippery items indeed.[3]

The discourse of modern philosophers became patently less and less credible in the measure in which they slighted the tangible universe. Locke did not seem to have thought of this boomerang as he suggested to philosophers not to extend their vistas farther than the limits of the solar system. Then Hume decried cosmologies as so many cobwebs spun in spiders' bellies, which was certainly true of Descartes' cosmology. Shortly afterwards Kant claimed to have demonstrated that the notion of the universe was an invalid notion, in fact, the illegitimate product of the metaphysical cravings of the mind, itself a similarly bastard offspring of cogitation. Most philosophers followed suit head over heels. They should have instead pondered the result of Kant's having tried his hand at scientific cosmology. He did so in his *Universal Natural History and Theory of the Heavens* (1756). Nothing shows more succinctly the dubious character of Kant, the philosopher, than his efforts postdating the *Critique of Pure Reason* by a decade or so, to appear a forerunner of Herschel's discoveries of countless galaxies.

The only logical thing for Kant to do would have been to disavow either his "scientific" cosmology or the *Critique*, or preferably both. As far as the universe was concerned the claims of one work contradicted the claims of the other. Here was a truly Kantian antinomy which he failed to recognize, let alone to digest. In that respect most Neo-Kantians still follow the master with blind devotion, partly by leaving the subject of the universe aside. That E. Cassirer, the leading Neo-Kantian in this century, failed to discuss at some length Kant's ideas on the universe indicates as much a logic characteristic of the true thrust of Kantian philosophy as of modern philosophy. The latter, in its empiricist branch, had no more interest in the universe. The universe was certainly no part of Dewey's quest for certainty.

This is not to suggest that cosmology, or the presumed study of the universe, has totally vanished from public discourse. On the contrary, possibly never before has so much been said and published about the universe as in these very last decades. Only it is not the philosophers who do this, but the scientists. They have indeed hijacked the universe. This is, however, almost as bad as if all central banks had been taken over by counterfeiters of money. The fruits of that hijacking can be seen on almost all better-grade coffee tables. It became most stylish to cover them with lavishly illustrated albums about supernovae, black holes, and galaxies, some of which are now photographed in their very birthpangs. Only a philosophically serious (indeed logically cogent) paragraph is missing in all those albums about the universe. This is no less true of the technically forbidding volumes on scientific cosmology. The most one finds there about the universe is the remark that it is, by definition, everything.

People with impeccable scientific training are engaged in promoting this philosophically most dubious, but commercially very lucrative enterprise of which the late Carl Sagan's *Cosmos* is an egregious example. This fallout from science illustrates the saying about the chip off the old block and does it in a most philosophical sense. The block itself is now almost a century old. After some tentative anticipations in the hands of Riemann, Zöllner, and Schwarzschild that block suddenly emerged as robustly formed as once Pallas Athena sprang forth, fully armed, from Zeus' head. The year was 1917 when Einstein published the fifth of his memoirs on the general theory of relativity.

The special theory of relativity was called special because it applied only to bodies moving at constant velocity with respect to one another. A very special or restricted perspective indeed, because, strictly speaking, all real motions, that is, motions of real bodies, are either accelerated or decelerated. And this is certainly true of bodies subject to gravitation, which means all bodies as far as science has any knowledge of them. It was therefore logical that the general theory of relativity should be capped by a consideration of all accelerated reference systems, or, more concretely, by a discussion of the gravitational interaction of all bodies.

The expression "all bodies" may mean, if taken strictly, cosmos or universe. And since all bodies gravitate, their totality, insofar as they gravitate, deserves to be called cosmology, or a study of the totality of consistently interacting things, a totality known as cosmos, that is, the Universe writ large. Herein lies the rub both for philosophy and most immediately for science, and for many a scientist. Einstein, who took that fifth memoir of his as something that dealt with the Universe, also took his account of it for a support of his pantheistic beliefs. Otherwise he would not have been so upset when De Sitter pointed out already in 1917 that the cosmos as described in that fifth memoir was not stable. At the slightest perturbation that cosmos either expands or contracts. This was hardly good news for pantheism, which has at least that much common with theism: In both, the Ultimate— there God, here the Universe—is assumed to be unchanged and unchangeable. A god that expands or contracts, let alone if it does both in perpetual alternations, cuts no better figure than an accordion worked to death.

But the philosophically primary aspect (or rather defect) of the new scientifically articulated cosmology lay not in its religious connotations, whatever they might be. That aspect relates to questions such as these: How can a scientific cosmologist be sure that his model of the cosmos is truly about the strict totality of consistently interacting bits of matter? Can scientific cosmology contain the proof of the existence of such a totality? And if the scientific method cannot provide the answer, can philosophy, aided or unaided by science, do it?

The fact is that apart from a few occasions dating back to the 1920s and 1930s, scientific cosmologists did not even care to consider whether their cosmological models, most of them elaborations on Einstein's model, corresponded or not to that strict totality. Much less did they care to face up to the question: "Is there a Universe?" Instead, they took an increasingly flippant attitude towards the universe, that most encompassing of all physical realities.

Reference has already been made, in the chapter on causality, to the steady-state theorists' bland postulate that matter arises out of nothing all the time and that it does so spontaneously, without a Creator. Within a quarter of a century, scientific cosmologists began to speak of their art as one that enables them, in theory at least, to create entire universes literally out of nothing. They are now conjuring up, as so many magicians, embryo-universes in uncounted numbers, as implied in an inflationary cosmology, regardless of whether they can be observed or not. They make a rather pale figure of the God of old, who was believed to have the ability of creating a universe or anything else only in virtue of his infinite dominion over existence itself. For them a basement laboratory in another galaxy may do the trick. In claiming, on the basis of inflationary cosmology, that the universe has become the last free lunch, they certainly reveal inflated egos.[4]

One cannot help being reminded of Robert Louis Stevenson's biting remark about those who "swallow the universe like a pill."[5] All this was duly anticipated when, in 1931, De Sitter voiced his utter skepticism about the reality called universe. He took the universe for a mere hypothesis in which even contradictory features are to be tolerated.[6] This view set the tone, half a century later, of an authoritative account of scientific cosmology, whose very title, *The Invented Universe*, gives the gist of all its chapters.[7] About the same time scientific cosmologists claimed that their art gives them an experimental grasp over the question about the transition from non-being to being, previously held to be the exclusive domain of metaphysics.[8]

We have come indeed a long way from the counsel that brings to a close one of the earliest classics of relativistic cosmology. One cannot recommend highly enough the words that "It is appropriate to approach the problems of cosmology with feelings of respect for their importance, of awe for their vastness, and of exultation for the temerity of the human mind in attempting to solve them." On the other hand one has to put in a strong *caveat* about what follows, namely that those problems "must be treated, however, by the detailed, critical and dispassionate methods of the scientist."[9]

The reason for this *caveat* is very simple. Insofar as the scientist uses his scientific method, he has no right to talk of the Universe, or the strict totality of consistently interacting things. It may be that his model *de facto* covers that totality, but science can never be sure about that. Much less can science answer the question, "Is there indeed a universe?" Only those can invest science or scientific cosmology with the ability to answer this question who dispense it from the obligation to submit the truth of its conclusions to observation or experiments. It is not, however, possible for scientists or for their instruments to go outside the universe in order to observe it and provide thereby an experimental verification of it.

This should have been patently true within the context of that pompous vagary of science which is the so-called infinite Newtonian universe, a fiction of science, bordering on science fiction, postdating Newton by about a century. Newton himself, let it be noted, held fast all his life to the idea of a finite universe, regardless of his disagreement with Bentley about what later became known as the gravitational paradox of an infinite universe. Clearly, nobody could fancy travelling through Euclidean infinity, let alone beyond it so as to provide for an infinite universe that touchstone of scientific truth which is observation. At any rate, from almost the very appearance of the idea of an infinite universe it was pointed out that such a universe was saddled by the gravitational paradox and, given certain assumptions, even by an optical counterpart of it.[10]

Immanuel Kant, even though he was a rank amateur in matters scientific, and not an expert as he tried to pose, could have easily understood those paradoxes. Clear formulations of them had been widely available by 1755 when he made a most preposterous claim. He asserted nothing less than that he could do what Newton could not, namely, give a detailed account of the evolution of the solar system, with no recourse to God, and with the full parade of mathematics, if necessary. Kant never sounded more sophomoric.

Those paradoxes, which he ignored, certainly showed that the idea of an infinite universe was scientifically contradictory, but the science of the day did not show this to be the case about a finite universe. Kant kept mum about all this, possibly because he realized that it spelt the deathknell on the first antinomy, or his claim that the mind could not decide whether the universe was infinite or finite and that therefore the idea of the universe was not a valid notion. Most importantly he might have perceived that this outcome would have struck at the very root of his philosophical strategy, which was to destroy metaphysics by science, or at least by the veneer of it.

Yet when a Neo-Kantian, Clifford, who was also a first-rate scientist, concluded in 1872 that Riemannian cosmology (an anticipation of Einstein's) restored philosophical respectability to the universe, he clearly overshot the mark. Modern scientific cosmology certainly makes laughable Kant's first antinomy, which, together with the other antinomies, also suffers from illogicalities, a point aired long ago and by some first-rate experts on Kant's *Critique of Pure Reason*. Whether the universe is finite or infinite, modern scientific cosmology, in all its forms, leaves intact the inability of science to observe the Universe as a whole. This impossibility comes vividly through in cosmological models based on that fifth memoir of Einstein, in which a finite number of bits of mass (be they galaxies) are cast in a four-dimensional manifold or spherical space. That space is the totality of permissible paths of motion, all of them curved in the sense of being re-entrant.

Such a space is not something physically real and certainly not something that generates real matter including energy. Space in that context is a purely mathematical abstraction. It is another matter that scientific cosmologists soon began to invest that space with recondite physical characteristics, in brazen disregard of the lesson they had to draw about the ether. Here, too, Einstein's dictum, that the man of science is a poor philosopher, proved true. Whether philosophers can attribute something more to space is, in this respect, totally irrelevant. If they do and if that something is measurable, they have to take the consequences, which is simply this: over anything measurable, insofar as it is measurable, science has the ultimate word.

Science, as was noted above, cannot provide a demonstration that there is a Universe. Can philosophy do it? The first step towards an affirmative answer is to affirm reality as was demanded in the first chapter of this treatise on truth. Such affirmation alone justifies the means which is entrusted with any message, philosophical or scientific, about the cosmos. By reality plain physical reality is meant in any form, however trivial, be it an E-mail from one cosmologist to another. By consisting of bits, or ferro-silicon domains, magnetized in one of two possible directions, an E-mail is certainly a bit of matter, whatever else it may be.

As was emphasized at the outset of this treatise, all bits of matter are known primarily through their extension. Matter, insofar as it is extended (one may safely leave aside the point-masses of Boscovich and their even less logical modern versions) is measurable. The act of measuring is the application of a unit extension, or length. Whether that unit is one's foot or a platinum bar, or the He-Ne laser line at 632 991.339 x 10^{-12}m, or the astronomical unit (the Earth-Sun distance), makes no essential difference. A measure is a measure and is always the evaluation of this or that aspect of matter in terms of numbers. Measuring in turn is a form of counting.

Numbers are therefore applicable wherever there is matter, that is, throughout the totality of matter which is the Universe. It is that universal measurability of matter which gives universal validity to scientific laws. One does philosophy in assuming that matter behaves everywhere in the same way. This assumption becomes science only when numerical properties can be assigned to that behavior. The philosophical assumption that matter gravitates in the same way everywhere in the universe as it does on the earth or in the solar system began to become science only when Herschel measured some characteristics of the motion of double stars.

The recognition that matter is always and everywhere measurable, that to measure is to count, and that science in its bare essentials is a correlation of data counted, transpired in some details engraved on the plaque fastened to Pioneer X. Those figures showed geometrical patterns (a form of measuring and counting in terms of extension) and sequences of dots, the art of counting in binary arithmetic. It was rightly assumed that intelligent beings elsewhere in the universe can have science only by measuring bits of matter. Compared with this universality of numbers, rather illogical was it to have the figures of a man and a woman engraved on that plaque. Evolutionary science simply forbids the assumption that biological forces would have produced beings even remotely similar to hominids elsewhere in the universe. They would rather resemble bicephalic, tetramanous hexapods, as put by a paleontologist with tongue in cheek.

The intrinsic countability of matter guarantees the basic coherence of all matter in a totality or Universe. Regardless of man's inability to see with his physical eyes or with his instrumental extension the universe as a whole, his mental eyes, for whom numbers are a chief object, can obtain some general idea of that cohesive totality which is the universe. To grasp something about the specific nature of the countability of matter throughout the universe man needs an ever vaster system of measurements and their correlations. In other words he needs science.

This is not to suggest that science, which becomes as purely science is it becomes mathematical, would ever assure man about the specific structure of the universe, that is, about the basic correlation of pieces of matter taken in their totality. This lack of assurance is valid both for fundamental particle physics and for scientific cosmology, which appear to have more and more in common. The very reason which makes futile the efforts aimed at constructing a necessarily true system of fundamental particles, holds for cosmology as well. Both are a set of highly mathematical propositions and therefore subject to the validity of Gödel's incompleteness theorems. Those theorems state that no non-trivial set of arithmetic propositions can have its proof of consistency within itself. This means that a necessarily true scientific account of the universe is a pipe dream.

A priori thinking does not cease to be misleading just because it is dressed in esoteric mathematics. This is a lesson still to be digested by eminent men of science who dream about a final theory. One cannot help indeed being amazed on finding first-rate books on scientific cosmology (or fundamental particle physics) whose authors do not seem to know of Gödel's theorems two full generations after their publication.

Even apart from Gödel's theorems, philosophical logic demands an approach to reality which is the very opposite to an a priori approach. For if the very first step of knowing reality is a response to it, and if philosophical exercise must methodically repeat that first step in order to improve and progress, one's approach to the universe must retain that character. The question, "Is there a universe?" can indeed be answered, provided the cart is never put before the horse. The answer begins with the registering of reality, which always connotes a size and therefore a measurability or counting. The intrinsic connotation of matter with extension and measurability assures cohesion or coherence to our knowledge of matter wherever it may be, whether already within the ken of scientific observations or not.

This coherence implies the unity of the universe and its uniqueness. Apart from this it should be obvious that there is something contradictory in references to several universes. If there is an interaction among such universes, they form one single universe. If not, they are mutually unknowable, and certainly so scientifically. In a more philosophical vein the same can be rearticulated in terms of that first step insisted upon in this treatise throughout. That first step is the acting of matter on the mind, not, of course, as light rays impinge on a photographic plate. As particular things activate the mind, the mind registers in them the universal, without putting the particular into the straitjacket of a priori categories. All our words, let this not be forgotten, are universals, and even proper names are not altogether excepted from this rule.

The close similarity of two words, universals and universe, should suggest that a philosophical talk about the universe is possible only in the measure in which respect for the topic called universals is retained. To the extent to which that topic fell in disrepute among philosophers, they lost interest in the largest and most comprehensive of all universals, which is the Universe.

This loss means a number of things. For scientific cosmologists it means the problem whether they are right in using the term "cosmos" at all. Would not consistency demand from them to replace the word cosmology with some new word, say supergalactology? In doing so they would at least admit that science as such does not entitle one to speak of the Universe. At least one prominent astronomer recognized this problem after reading my book, *Is There a Universe?* Most others would continue in blissful disregard of the fact that cosmology is a most philosophical, indeed metaphysical discourse.[11]

The question, "How do you know there is a universe?" calls for better replies than, for instance, "I know it by intuition," or "it can be known by inspection." Philosophy alone can answer the question, but only if used in that logical manner in which no one tries to begin with the second step the march through one's own courtyard, let alone through cosmic spaces toward the Universe. If one does not have a taste for philosophy, one perhaps may avail oneself of an existential variety of it. It implies, however, that one should imitate in full Margaret Fuller, this champion of the education of women and a fearsome conversationalist who loved to impose on others her acceptance and rejection of a wide variety of ideas. It is not recorded what she expected other participants of a party to do when she flippantly remarked; "I accept the Universe." Carlyle, who was present, interrupted: "Gad you'd better." This silenced her for the rest of the evening, a rare outcome indeed.[12] Those scientists and philosophers who flippantly refer to the universe should also fall silent, now and then. For the idea of the universe is so great, as John Henry Newman once put it, that "only the thought of its Maker is greater."[13]

This was no incidental remark. Its context is one of the intellectually most respectable contexts produced in modern times. I mean Newman's series of lectures, *The Idea of a University*. The visible deterioration of most universities into battlegrounds of social activism, as their curricula are being beefed up by an ever larger number of "remedial" courses (at times not even dressed up in something more respectable), has much to do with the deterioration of their departments of philosophy into craftshops of deconstruction. This could in part happen because by the time this latest fad in intellectual self-extermination got under way, there was no need to deconstruct the universe, of which at most the idea was retained.

Such a universe can be disassembled all the more easily because it contains no reality that can hang together. The texts of idealist philosophy offer no information about the idea of that most encompassing physical reality, which is the Universe. If they do, as in the case of Hegel, they make a mockery of that idea. Whether the science of cosmology, which has been the hottest branch of science for the past two or three decades, will awaken philosophers to the reality of the Universe as a topic to which they alone have a birthright, remains to be seen. Hijacked goods have been invariably difficult to recover even when there was a dogged resolve to reclaim them.

Once that reclamation becomes successful, philosophy may become once more that love of wisdom indicative of the soul's longing for genuine self-improvement which for Socrates meant to be fair within, never to fight the spirit within, to consider rich those who are wise, and to be satisfied with the meager amount of money enough for a temperate man. All such wishes should appear to have firm ground, whenever one takes a look at the universe as modern science reveals more and more of it. Everywhere it appears stunningly specific. Gone are the days of Laplace's nebular hypothesis, which took for its starting point a nebulous state of matter about which science knew only that it was nebulous indeed. Today, the farther one looks into the past of the universe, the more brilliantly specific it appears, as the finest of all jewels. As such it provokes, as any finely cut gem, the question: Why such and not something else?

To ask and ponder this question, which points for answers beyond the Universe, writ large, displays the best abilities of the human mind. Such a mind should be seen to connote serious interest in self-improvement, with or without the help of cosmological considerations. Self-improvement cannot be truly such unless it is also ethical. In view of the flippancy that makes all too frequent appearances in the dicta of scientific cosmologists, there seems indeed a great need for that type of improvement. Those who claim to have the ability to create entire universes literally out of nothing, should be treated cautiously as they approach the safe-deposit sectors of their local banks. They are at least to be reminded that braggadocios do not change their character by being coated scientifically. Braggadocios are not a form of exultation, let alone of awe and reverence. They exude a distinctly unethical fragrance, the bad odor of contempt for moral accountability.

Moral accountability is valid only if beyond the *is* there is also a *should*. In an age in which scientific packaging is so important, it may be useful to recall that in relatively better days even some prominent scientists, Poincaré was one of them, insisted on the peculiar character of the verb *should*. Ethics should, however, stand on its own philosophical legs and not on stilts that some ethicists vainly hope to borrow from science. They should rather keep in mind Einstein's admission that he had never found in science ethical guidance. Once established in its own right, and not pseudoscientific props, ethics may provide a proper atmosphere for treating the foremost object available for any treatise on truth. That object is the Ultimate in being and intelligibility, deserving above all the kind of reverence which one rightfully expects to go with ethics.

[1] *Phaedrus* 279b.

[2] H. G. Wells, *First and Last Things. Confession of Faith and Rule of Life* (London: Watts, 1929), p. 30.

[3] I have in mind J. M. E. McTaggart's *Studies in Hegelian Cosmology* (Cambridge: University Press, 1901).

[4] Most emphatic in this respect is A. Guth, who now enlarged some earlier remarks of his into a chapter, "The Ultimate Free Lunch," which opens his book, *The Inflationary Universe: The Quest for a New Theory of Cosmic Origins* (Reading, MA: Addison-Wesley, 1997).

[5] R. L. Stevenson, "Crabbed Age and Youth," in *Essays by Robert Louis Stevenson* (New York: Charles Scribner's and Sons, 1918), p. 136.

[6] W. De Sitter, *Kosmos* (Cambridge, Mass.: Harvard University Press, 1932), pp. 133-34.

[7] Clearly, P. Kerszberg, the author of a book with that title (Oxford: Clarendon Press, 1989), should not have left the topic of the difference between the universe of the philosopher and that of the scientist, to the very last chapter.

[8] Thus Fang Li Zhi and Li Shu Xian in their *Creation of the Universe*, tr. T. Kiang (Singapore: World Scientific, 1989), p. 147.

[9] R. C. Tolman, *Relativity, Thermodynamics and Cosmology* (1934; Oxford: Clarendon Press, 1966), p. 488.

[10] As discussed in detail in my *The Paradox of Olbers' Paradox: A Case History of Scientific Thought* (New York: Herder & Herder, 1969).

[11] The book is the expanded text of my Forwood Lectures given at the University of Liverpool in 1992, published by its Press in 1993.

[12] See D. A. Wilson and D. W. MacArthur, *Carlyle in Old Age (1865-1881)* (London: K. Paul, Trench, Trubner, 1934), p. 177.

[13] J. H. Newman, *The Idea of a University Defined and Illustrated* (London: Longmans, Green and Co., 1888), p. 462.

10

Ethics

Changes made by man have an ethical component that no circumlocution can dissipate. One may argue that all ethical systems did less to palliate man's lot than the invention of anesthetics.[1] Still that lot remains a battleground between good and evil that no anesthetics can desensitize. One may take for a mere myth the Bible's report about Adam and Eve having known good and evil. Even so the fact remains that a distinct ethical perception dominates the myths of all major and minor cultures. As to modern culture, the very best in its literature is invariably a tale with some moral.

It is not possible to restrict the ethical component of man's existence to the broad vistas of ancient myths or of literature, classical or modern. The most trivial deeds of daily life carry an ethical stamp. This in spite of the fact that countless changes effected by man may seem morally as neutral as the means whereby he brings them about. Yet in the long run those changes can accumulate into huge moral warning signs. Primitive axes could deplete forests to an alarming degree long before chainsaws began to do the same to rainforests. The sense of ethical responsibility, which ecological problems triggered in our times, can at times be demanded from generations that long preceded us.

The problem of rainforests posed a question not so much of whether mankind would or would not destroy itself, as of whether it was morally imperative to prevent a marked deterioration of life. The problem, a message, translated itself into the question of what kind of means were people to utilize and in what quantities. That the use of carbonfluorides should be restricted came to the fore through the message symbolized by an ozone hole noticed over the Antarctic. The mixing of lead into gasoline was found harmful for lungs and therefore banned. Smoking is being prohibited in public spaces to prevent non-smokers from contracting lung cancer by merely being indirect smokers. Certain industries, such as the ones specializing in asbestos, accepted financial obligation to compensate for damages, though they staunchly disclaimed ethical responsibility.

Quite a difference from what happened among physicists responsible for the making of the atom bomb. As Oppenheimer memorably put it: "In some sort of crude sense which no vulgarity, no humor, no overstatement can quite extinguish, the physicists have known sin; and this is a knowledge which they cannot lose."[2] The statement should seem memorable also for the effort to avoid appearing just plainly ethical. Molecular biologists still have to find their moment of truth. Some, such as James Watson of double helix fame, are outright defiant. One can only shudder on recalling Watson's bold declaration made only a few years ago that only the genes need to be known, because any other information is useless.[3] Certainly so, if a scientist can claim that his own cloning would satisfy rightful curiosity and is not denounced as one guilty of prostituting the means of science in the most obscene way possible.

The fact is that means whose use should seem outright unethical have not only been retained but continuously perfected. The most emphatic ecclesiastical condemnation of firearms in 1347 failed to stop their being turned into frighteningly lethal weapons. There was at least one justification on hand: the making and improvement of firearms could not be limited to one group, to one nation, and therefore the principle of self-defense was quickly invoked. In the case of nuclear testing, reliance on this principle thoroughly undercut the idea of unilateral nuclear disarmament. What actually will happen about the destruction of biological and chemical weapons only the future will tell.

The means have their own power to force into the fore an ethical message. In order to do so they need not be unconditionally and maddeningly harmful. Compared with the scientific sophistication of the weapons of modern whaling ships, the harpoons of Captain Ahab of *Moby Dick* could seem mere playthings. Yet these apparently innocent tools were the very means whereby Captain Ahab found himself caught in a pursuit whose madness finally dawned on him as he muttered: "All my means are sane, my motive and my object mad."[4] Yet it was ultimately not that object and motive that let the big white whale conquer Captain Ahab, but an urge within him which he should have but did not control.

Or did he have an obligation, conveyed by the word "should," which, incidentally no trick in logic can derive from "is" and its variants in the indicative tense. To derive the "should" from a latter-day variant of Bentham's "felicific calculus" can satisfy only those who take their armchair comfort for normalcy. The principle of "the greatest good for the largest possible number" is so blatantly pragmatic that cruel dictators could readily invoke it.

Such champions of a pragmatic logic would not note that Captain Ahab himself settled with pragmatism by not calling a spade a spade. Had he done so, he would have deplored his pursuit not as mad, but as something outright evil, that is, morally wrong. Yet he must have known that he was pushing himself and his entire crew into self-destruction. Was this merely madness or was it a sin? By trying to cover up with a psychiatric label something essentially unethical, that is, sinful, Captain Ahab anticipated modern man's desperate footwork to obliterate the categories of moral good and moral evil so that he might escape the profoundly moral predicament of human existence, steeped, to put it bluntly, in sin. To know this it is not necessary to take Professor Coles' course at Harvard, dubbed "Sin 31." It is enough to practice daily the increasingly forgotten art of examining one's conscience, not, of course, in relation to ten mere counsels, but to the Ten Commandments.

Recourse to the categories of economics will not help in escapism from sin. Fundamentally unethical aspects of marxism and capitalism are exposed alike through a strange contrast between them. Expropriation of private possession is an unquestionable virtue for marxists, whereas capitalists put private property on a pedestal. These opposite policies resulted in marxism's being the exploitation of man by man, while capitalism, so some wits suggested, was the same in reverse order. In both cases virtue was made of vice, the ethical component being sublimated into indexes of production or of profit. In both the means are perverted into ends, the essence common to all forms of sin.

No logical escape hatch is offered from man's ethical predicament by specious rhetoric. It is hardly logical to deprive all but one, the Seventh, of the Ten Commandments from a strictly ethical content. The illogicality rests with the cohesion among those Commandments. Thus for, instance, it is hardly possible to sin against the Seventh, which forbids thefts, without also short-changing truth, which is forbidden by the Eighth. Also, thefts begin with coveting, which is forbidden by the Ninth and the Tenth. Since the Ninth forbids the coveting of one's neighbor's wife (or secretary or babysitter) the step to the Sixth should seem a very short one indeed. Yet the Sixth is no longer taken for even a mere counsel, although the brazen flouting of it now threatens the biological survival of modern affluent society. The latter now emancipates children from parental authority, the gist of the Fourth, which bases the duty of obedience on existential dependence. Clearly, then, it is atavistic in this society to refer to the thrust of the first three Commandments, which refer to a reality infinitely above any societal factor.

For the first time in history man is experimenting with one-parent families, taken for a normal alternative to old-fashioned monogamous unions. Same-sex unions are receiving legal protection to the extent of their being granted the right of adoption. Advocates of polygamy have begun to raise their voice, and they need no other arguments than the ones used with success on behalf of same-sex unions. Such quantum jumps in sociological experimentation demand, of course, huge jumps in logic for their justification.

Illogicalities of at times colossal measure indeed set the tone of ethical messages that alone are acceptable in public discourse nowadays. The messages rest on the seemingly complete victory of capitalism, which in turn may be taken for the full implementation of the political theory of John Locke. It was he who almost three hundred years ago defined the *raison d'être* of the State as its being the guardian of private property and of its free accumulation. To be sure, Locke did not mean that anyone could freely hurt anyone else's interest in accumulating private property. But as one holding the innate goodness of actual man, Locke had better ignore why man's pursuit of private property could readily degenerate into its inordinate hoarding at the grave detriment of others' legitimate interests. In substance, his theory raised the means to the rank of a message. With that sleight of hand Locke was forced to justify another, which consisted in his assumption (part of Locke's ethical message) that man would naturally handle the means in an ethically proper manner.

Locke's doctrine of the innate goodness of man as he actually exists certainly conflicted with the basic tenets of the Reformation, though not with its "reformation" as politically implemented in the Glorious Revolution of 1688. The latter was not so much a revolution as the final seal on the legal status of the new propertied classes. Originally financed from the plundering of monasteries, leaders of these classes had an all too clear idea of profit-taking which the new mercantile economy offered. By bringing about the Glorious Revolution they wanted to have a safe legal approval for the ethics of the new economy so that its questionable aspects need not be aired.

This initiated, through Locke's good services, the process by which the categories of the ethically good and ethically evil became transformed into the categories of legally permissible and legally prohibited. And since these legal prohibitions are the reflection of how citizens vote, the revisability of what is legal brings along the radical relativization of the ethical. This did not happen overnight, but the true nature of the process has now become too obvious in the legislative battles in America. Efforts to elect a president who would in turn appoint "liberal" judges are fueled by the conviction that any sort of permissiveness can be given an ethical halo provided it is declared constitutional.

One can bemoan the fact that the Ten Commandments have turned in public perception into the Ten Counsels, or something much less, but the process is undeniable and logical. If man, as he actually exists, is believed to do the good by natural inclination, there remains no barrier against viewing any and all inclination of man as something naturally good and thereby entitled to legal protection. The latter, as is well known, is ultimately a function of counting the votes cast at regularly repeated elections. Nothing forbids, therefore, that any of the self-evident truths on which the constitution of the State as envisaged by Locke rests may be openly changed into what they increasingly are in practice: purely transitory agreements with no unconditionally ethical character.

Not being enough of a prophet of moral fiber, Locke could not foresee this development. But a prophet of a very different kind fully warned and did so three thousand years before Locke came to the scene. Whatever one's opinion of the Ten Commandments, let alone of their superior origin, one must at least be impressed by a warning given simultaneously with their promulgation. The warning, which begins with a stricture against spreading false reports, puts to shame most litigations in our lower and higher Courts, where technicalities count for more than plain truth. Then, after a similar stricture against bearing false witness, Moses declares: "Neither shall you allege the example of the many as an excuse for doing wrong, nor shall you, when testifying in a lawsuit, side with the many in perverting justice" (Ex 23:2). These strictures strike at the very root of modern jurisprudence where to an increasingly alarming degree the majority opinion amounts to a justification with a moral character, which is such in name only.

This stricture, "in name only," need not be taken for a moral prejudice. One does not prejudge the question of morality by considering the elementary fact that majority vote is but a sum of votes, however heedlessly cast, a sum which is always a numerical figure. Numbers, however, are mere ideas, though Plato and latter-day admirers of the Platonic heaven may contend otherwise. Numbers do not exist as do entities to which non-numerical concepts refer. Therefore about numbers, and about numbers alone, one cannot say that they are morally good just because they exist. Hence there is nothing morally good in the fact that since a statistically significant part of society pursues this or that behavioral pattern (say polygamy), the pattern is therefore good.

The expression "statistically significant" leads one to the Gaussian curve. About two percent of the area lying under that curve towards either of its extremities is usually taken to be negligible. Thus political parties that gain no more than four percent of the total vote are denied the right to be represented in Parliament. Similar is the arbitration between various forms of societal or individual behavior. All depends on the number of people who behave this or that way. Hence the enormous effort of some groups, whose behavior until recently was considered grievously deviant in the moral sense, to make it appear that their numbers rescue them, so the argument goes, from the limbo of statistical insignificance. If statistically significant, however, their behavioral pattern deserves, continues the argument, legal recognition, which then is taken for moral approval. The means, numbers (or statistics), are made to parade as messages, and indeed the pseudo-ethical kind of messages, that will not cut into human flesh and blood, but rather pamper it.

This identification of mere numbers with ethical principles or with their absence is the magic wand used by ethicists, whatever their efforts to appear ethical in the old sense. Obviously those efforts demand extraordinary manipulation of words. The oracles of Delphi should seem poor seconds to modern ethicists in the skill of churning out ambivalent statements. Indeed they prove themselves to be the latter-day version of haruspices of old, those past-masters of ambiguous counsels obtained from the investigation of a material which has nothing to do with the problems on hand. Ultimately, they expect ever larger numbers of the public to come around to a view, or medical procedure, which only a few years earlier appeared abhorrent to most and for which they want to construct an "ethical" seal.

Those ethicists can certainly count on the media to bring about this shift in numbers and make thereby the most revolting acts and procedures appear to have "redeeming" value. The final report of the Presidential commission on the cloning of humans made no secret of this tactic. The reshaping of the majority view, which in olden days would have taken five generations if not five centuries or five millennia, is expected to take place, in this case, within a mere five years. Therefore the Commission argued that the cloning of humans should be outlawed only for five years. The Founding Fathers certainly expected to lay more lasting foundations.

One may argue that the Founding Fathers merely represented a majority view. Therefore, whether they liked it or not, they could not logically claim that certain truths they held to be self-evident would remain at safe remove from any future challenges. Theirs was a pre-Darwinian illusion, so the argument goes, about something unchanging and unchangeable in human nature. With that illusion having been "scientifically" exposed for what it really was, there remains nothing intrinsically sacred or intrinsically moral. Therefore, the only mechanism to secure societal calm is to leave matters to the majority vote obtained at regular intervals. The calm is deceptive. In the political process, suffice it to think of the presidential election campaigns, there is no farewell to arms.

Whatever the "scientific" seal on the Darwinian message, be it dressed up as sociobiology, it certainly cannot cope with the human mind, which the Founding Fathers held in the highest esteem. That mind bears witness, of course, to absolute moral values, but to see this the Founding Fathers should have placed themselves on better philosophical grounds than the ones which the Enlightenment and Scottish commonsense philosophy could provide. They could not find those solid grounds in Locke or in any of the books they were familiar with.

The grounds are those of realism where philosophy begins with objects and continues with the recognition of other mutually irreducible facets of man's messages to others, such as his acting freely and for a purpose. Such messages, both words and acts,

make man recognize that he interacts with beings of the same
nature as he is. He perceives his utter dependence on others as
well as their dependence on him. Herein lies the wellspring of
man's sense of social justice, often called the sense of the golden
rule. The fact that those messages carry truth about realities that
exist even when man does not think of them and that can be
corrected or refuted only by propositions taken for truths,
eliminates the specter of relativism. Therefore on such grounds
one can rightly nurture the conviction that there are ethical
tenets, such as the golden rule with an absolute value.

On these solid grounds one can alone turn into philosophical
messages a number of propositions that derive from self-reflection
and can powerfully witness to man's ethical nature. One's sense of
self identity, one's moral consciousness, one's sense of love, one's
ability to sacrifice one's interest on behalf of others all rest on
those grounds, and they especially do so as messages conveyed
to others. Severed from those grounds ethics becomes purely
subjective and relative. The radical relativism of all moral tenets
then inescapably follows.

Modern society divests itself at a maddening rate of all of its
inherited ethical heritage as so much cumbersome ballast in
order to sail headlong into the waters of radical secularism. There
it hopes to find the fulfillment of its Utopian pursuit of the big
white whale of heaven on earth, or the condition of instant
gratification. It forgets that Utopia will come only when men will
grow wings. Until then a society that does not believe in angels
has no right to expect its policemen, to say nothing of its politi-
cians and media moguls, to behave like angels.

Pauses in that headlong rush are momentary and sporadic.
There is an outrage when a professional boxer bites off the ear of
his opponent, though not to the extent of reconsidering the
ethical status of professional boxing. Sexual molestation of children
is still generally decried, though not to the extent of prohibiting
TV and Internet from carrying messages that threaten the sexual
sanity of children. Ever more numerous are the moral gurus who
profess deep concern about the diminution of the sense of sin
while they do their best to exorcise that very sense. In the process
the means is perverted into a dubious message as illustrated by

the book, *Whatever Happened to Sin?* Morality is claimed to be served, while the sense of moral responsibility is dulled so that sinful acts may not cause psychic trauma if they do not cause physical discomfort. Sophisticated cover-ups for the voice of moral conscience are being marketed with great success.

Direct killing is still considered a crime, if not a sin, but the killing of viable fetuses is held moral if it secures the mother's health as something very different from a direct threat to her life. All is done to spread technical know-how about population control, but at the same time moral status is given to in vitro fertilization, sperm banks, surrogate motherhood, to mention only a few of the new ways of producing more humans. The justification is to assure mental comfort to those who cannot have or do not want to have babies in the normal way. Human fetuses are sold and bought as a kind of medicinal meat, in total disregard of the fact that human beings with "inalienable rights" and "personal dignity" must first exist in the fetal stage. Ethicists prefer to ignore the question of whether those rights and that dignity can be conferred on a lump of flesh just because it successfully leaves the uterus.

Western man has indeed gone a long way in trying to base his ethical predicament on purely subjective grounds, be they called critically established practical reasons, as, for instance, the voice of moral conscience as celebrated by Kant. Contemplation of the starry sky did not generate firm belief in a divine lawgiver, nor did respectful listening to that voice generate firm commitment to it. No wonder. The sage of Königsberg denied to both that Lawgiver and that voice the status of objective truth. Even if one considers far better philosophies than that of Kant, one may still say that ethical philosophy has never generated a firm ethical stance. Yet the fallacy of Confucius' reasoning, "When things are investigated, then true knowledge is achieved, when true knowledge is achieved, then the will becomes sincere,"[5] passed until recently for the basis of public education. The turmoils of the latter are an inevitable consequence of the now widespread contempt there for claims about truth, and even for the view that truth may perhaps be known. Everything has become relative there, except for this absolute truth.

Yet a firm ethical stance needs inspiration other than abstract considerations, however sound. Einstein did not specify the source of ethical probity when he remarked that he had obtained no ethical values from his scientific work,[6] whose value was enormous, to say the least. He had to mean much more than sheer veracity with respect to data of observation, when he said that it is the character that makes the scientist.[7] He did not offer anything specific when he warned that it was "easier to denature plutonium than it is to denature the evil spirit of man."[8] At any rate his private life, caught in lustful liaisons,[9] was the very refutation of the contention that science can serve as the source of ethical probity, let alone of heroism, which he certainly failed to display vis-à-vis Hitler.

In fact, science, when left to itself, invites the opposite to moral probity. On the basis of science alone, mankind is but another animal species, locked in a grim struggle for survival. And even within the species itself, the self-sacrifice of the individual, in fact even some altruism on his part, is difficult to justify. Darwin proved himself more outspoken in this respect than many Darwinists, old and new. The following passage, coming as it does from his autobiographical notes, bespeaks a deep uneasiness on the part of a distinguished man of science: "A man who has no assured and no present belief in the existence of a personal God or a future existence with retribution and rewards, can have for his rule of life, as far as I can see, only to follow those impulses and instincts which are the strongest or which seem to him the best ones."[10]

Such is a clear illustration of the logic at work when man's ethical predicament is evaluated in a framework that excludes considerations of that ontological and moral absolute, which is God. Disregard of that moral absolute is sufficient to justify those behaviorists who with J. B. Watson do not feel utter revulsion over the fact that their methods enable them to turn any baby "into a thief, a gunman, or a dope fiend."[11] The moral abyss opened up by such vistas is a roundabout vote on behalf of the view that, on the basis of various ethical considerations one can indeed make a valid inference to the existence of Absolute Holiness. The frightful spectrum of immorality looming large from that abyss should energize those who are loath to consider that inference or drag their feet to surrender to its existential portent. The changes for the worse are intimated in the possibilities hinted at by Darwin and Watson. The changes for the better have been displayed by saints. A Voltaire made a hollow boast in saying that he was not born to celebrate the saints.[12] Yet theirs remains a unique existential message, riveted in the reality of God, of which they proved themselves the palpable means of intimation. If saints do anything they certainly show the shortcomings of the philosophical message even when it is emphatically about that Truth which is God.

[1] W. E. H. Lecky, *History of European Morals from Augustus to Charlemagne* (New York: D. Appleton, 1869), vol. 1, p. 91.

[2] A statement which Oppenheimer originally made at M.I.T. in 1947. See J. R. Oppenheimer, *The Open Mind* (New York: Simon, 1955), p. 88.

[3] Reported by *The Trenton Times* (Feb. 25, 1995, p. 1) from Watson's Einstein Memorial Lecture given in Princeton a day earlier.

[4] H. Melville, *Moby Dick* (New York: Modern Library, 1926), p. 185.

[5] Tahsue Liki, ch. xlii, in *The Wisdom of Confucius*, ed. and tr. by Lin Yutang (New York: Modern Library, 1938), p. 140.

[6] In a conversation with Manfred Clynes, during the winter of 1952-53. See P. Michelmore, *Einstein: Profile of the Man* (New York: Dodd, 1962), p. 251.

[7] Quoted in C. A. Coulson, *Science and Christian Belief* (Chapel Hill: University of North Carolina Press, 1955), p. 64.

[8] In an interview with Michael Amrine, *The New York Times Magazine*, June 23, 1946, pp. 42 and 44.

[9] As documented in R. Highfield and P. Carter, *The Private Lives of Albert Einstein* (London: Faber and Faber, 1993).

[10] *The Autobiography of Charles Darwin 1809-1882*, ed. Nora Barlow (New York: W. W. Norton, 1969), p. 94.

[11] J. B. Watson, *The Ways of Behaviorism* (New York: Harper and Brothers, 1928), pp. 35-36.

[12] "Je ne suis pas né pour célébrer les saints."

11

God

The means must be real so that a message may be really delivered to real people—such was the starting point of these reflections on truth. The most obvious and most elementary facet of a means is its limitedness. Being always strictly limited, the means functions therefore not merely as a vehicle of a message, but a message in its own right. The message is about the need to provide satisfactory reason for the very existence of the means, a limited entity. The reason can only be a being with unlimited perfection. Such reasoning is valid even in its apparent triviality. It is driven by what may be called the principle of unlimited curiosity.

Being a very limited reality, the means, or any object for that matter, should provoke the curiosity about why such a reality does exist at all. The problem of explaining why any limited perfection exists at all does not cease to be a problem just because it does not appeal to palates that have lost their tastebuds for ontology or metaphysics. The existence of any limited perfection (all perfections available to direct knowledge are extremely limited) cries out for an explanation of its ontological limitedness which is something far deeper than the limitedness of shape. The latter is merely a pointer towards the former. The explanation can only be found in a being which is self-explaining in the sense that it possesses all perfection in an absolutely perfect way, and above all the perfection to exist and do so without any limitation. This is the reality, the existence absolute, the only meaning to be properly associated with the word "God."

Such a meaning is not something way beyond the grasp of anyone interested in reasoning and reflecting. In fact, however unprofessional they may be in philosophy or theology or in both, they can grasp that meaning with a felicitous phrase, but only to fumble it in the same breath. A case in point is R. Buckminster Fuller of geodesic architecture fame, who wrote: "God, to me, it seems, is a verb not a noun, proper or improper."[1] That God is a verb had, of course, been stated with no hesitation whatever in the Book of Exodus. There (3:14) God is reported as having identified himself as the One who Is, without discouraging anyone to think that the One who most emphatically exists (a verb) is truly One (a noun). Philosophically sensitive theologians would add that there is in God no real separation between existence and essence.

Fuller most likely coined his partly felicitous phrase with a subconscious reliance on that foremost biblical name of God. Memories of biblical phrases might have also prompted him to think of God as One, who, as befits a verb *par excellence,* must be the ground of any act, small and vast, including the great cosmic process. But for all of God's innermost involvement in all acts, God is not any of those acts and not even all of them. He is the ground of them all, who in no sense needs them. Were he any of them, he would be also a noun, which he is not as distinct from his existence. It should indeed seem telling that consideration of God as a pure existence maintained itself within a historically continuous body, the Church, that has not ceased claiming that it was sent by God to mediate him to man. Had Fuller thought of this, he may not have presented his perception of God as a verb and not a noun as a way of distancing himself from what he called "secondhand gods." He also could have easily learned that none of the great mystics had ever thought that his or her unutterable communing with God was mediated by ecclesiastics. In that sense too, God, to recall Tennyson's facetious remark, is certainly not an "endless clergyman."

The foregoing argument of the existence of God antedates Thomas Aquinas, who gave it a pregnant formulation in his fourth way. Nor is there anything new in the fact that the argument does not automatically generate conviction. That the presentation of a proof is not necessarily a feat of convincing is a truth as old as the hills. To formulate a proof is to practice a method, whereas to convince someone is an exercise that deserves to be called art. The latter should not be wasted on anyone insensitive to it. By the same token no time should be wasted on anyone who at least is not slightly perplexed by limited existence which is the most universal form of experience.

A mere reference to existence, to the perfection which is to be, which in turn is very different from just to happen, may not strike a sympathetic chord at all in an age that has just got tired of existentialists. Most of these were not interested in an existence that transcends the moment, in spite of their heavy reliance on means whose permanence, however limited, refuted their claims that existence was momentary. Actually, they could not even claim that their books existed when they were reading them, because the moment of reading a book never extends beyond reading a word in it. In a post-existentialist age that wallows in deconstructionism, it is no longer attractive to hold high the primary facet of each and every means, which is the fact that it *does* exist, whatever its limitedness. Contempt for the question of existence is the tacit presupposition of deconstructionism.

As to the phenomenologists, they took their stance, it is enough to think of Husserl, in a thematic renunciation of any concern for existence. They wanted to be totally free for the intellectual delight of savoring endlessly the inexhaustible riches of phenomena, with no further questions to be asked. Phenomenologists proved to be the butterflies of philosophy, though with a difference. Their work could resemble a happy canvassing of flowery meadows whose colors were made even more brilliant by the sunshine of springtide. But unlike real butterflies, they did not seem to realize that there is in flowers a lifestem of existence and that spring and summer are not forever. Fall and winter will inevitably prompt questions of existence that cast long shadows indeed.

As to those phenomenologists who tried to be such with no systematic disregard for questions of existence, they certainly proved what is also a law of life. Undue preoccupation with secondary facets of life inevitably dulls appreciation for the question about life or existence itself. Philosophers, too, are very limited beings in this respect as well. All those who professed concern for ontology while trying to be phenomenologists could not help thwart in their readers whatever appreciation they had for ontology, or the study of existence.

Distaste for ontology has been further fueled by the sway of science, which is having the impact of a cultural juggernaut. The impact is all the more deceptive because, unlike the huge juggernauts of old, etched circuits are the marvels of miniaturization. But precisely because they are almost imperceptibly small they distract from the fact that they are not different from any other means and objects of science. They all are very limited. Indeed the more scientific they are the more precise is their limitedness. Science thrives on the limitedness of all things material and on their readiness to reveal more and more of the precision which marks their limitedness.

Such minds should not, however, be misled by appearances. As was argued before, empirical reality first reveals itself by its quantitative properties, by its size in particular. Now such quantitative properties can readily be traced, especially with the help of science, to the quantitative properties of other things and so on, but never *ad infinitum*. Recourse to regress to infinity is not an explanation, but only its facile postponement. Further, very superficial is the mind which lets quantities, or the sequence of their particular sets, distract from what quantities are supposed to reveal, namely, the very reality of the thing endowed with quantitative properties.

About all such things science poses a question—why such and not something else?—but it does not pose it with a philosophical or metaphysical thrust. Although the quantitative magnitude of things is, as was argued early in this book, the most immediate pointer to their existence, science has an interest only in the markings indicated by its pointer needles. The concern of science is to make the workings of those needles ever more precise quantitatively, but not to ponder their existence. The latter it takes for granted. Science is not interested in the fact that the metaphysical lurks beneath anything physical, which is limited inasmuch as it is physical. Science is not metaphysics, and its exclusive concern for quantities can only dull the sensitivity for metaphysics.

Still a metaphysician can derive much help from what science does as it traces the quantitative measure of things to measures that are more universally applicable, though still very limited. Such a limited facet is the blueness of the sky which science has traced to the equally limited property of nitrogen and oxygen molecules to scatter more effectively the shorter wavelengths in the visible spectrum. That metals do rust, that glass is transparent, that fire dies out when deprived of air, that water begins to freeze on the top, that blood is red, that sugar tastes sweet, are just a few examples of a limitedness which science has successfully traced to equally limited, that is, specific properties of molecules. Any chapter in any textbook on science provides a plethora of illustrations of this strategy of science.

This strategy of science can provide much ammunition to the metaphysician who is eager to reargue in an age of science the cosmological argument. This argument must not, of course, be confused with that distortion of it, so deceptively attractive in Kant's time and even now in circles that want to hide their anti-religiously fueled distaste for metaphysics with easy recourse to science. They certainly make much of the fact that Science has become in modern times one of the three S's of effective packaging of all useful and especially useless merchandise. To present the cosmological argument as if it were an argument from design is a fallacy in logic which Kant rightly exploited in order to dismiss the former without considering the latter on its own merit. For his dubious purposes, which was to cast doubt on the rightfulness of inferring the existence of God as one of the three objects of traditional metaphysics, it was enough to take a potshot at very dubious formulations of the cosmological argument. Had Kant seriously tried to demolish the design argument, so different from its parodies, he would have had to face up to the kind of metaphysics that would have exposed the fallacies of his own pseudometaphysical strategy as well as of his misconstruction of the cosmological argument.

The metaphysician interested in the cosmological argument should pay much attention to the fact that science must of necessity feed on the specificities of things and that it cannot feed on anything else. If one keeps in mind that any specificity stands for inhomogeneity, one can see that Eddington evoked, however unwittingly, this lifeline of science as he noted that "the realities of physics are inhomogeneities, happenings, change." All happenings, all changes connote quantitative specificities which science can investigate and which it alone can do properly. Science does this by tracing a set of quantitative specificities to other such sets. And provided one has in mind physical sameness, one may agree with Eddington in saying that "undifferentiated sameness and nothingness cannot be distinguished philosophically."[2] For the sameness which is metaphysical and is so in an unlimited manner is nothing less than God himself. Long before Greek philosophers noted anything of this, the Prophets and Psalmists found the distinctive character of God in the fact that he neither changes nor does have that end which is the most radical of all changes and most destructive of sameness.

There is no need to mix this philosophical consideration into what science does, which is to trace one set of quantitative specificities to other such sets. Thus, for instance, science traced some chemical changes to elements, then it traced the elements to their atomic constituents, doing careful measurements all the time. Although some scientists were ready to take a particular stage of investigation for the final stage, the search went on. Science did not side with Mendeleev who took the elements of his famous Periodic Table for so many ultimate entities, irreducible to one another. Science did not approve of even the faintest suggestion of something definitively primordial and final when such names as proton and omega were coined for some subatomic particles. As to the so-called fundamental particles, science finds that none of them are fundamental.

The immediate scientific reason for this is not something philosophical, a sense which the word "fundamental" may above all connote. The reason is simply that whatever is quantitative offers itself to further quantitative analysis. Quantities are infinite in the sense that their division and multiplication can go on endlessly. In that sense science, and science alone, shall never run short of research projects. The search on the scale of the very large shows the same. Whatever the intrinsic merits of the inflationary model in which the observable universe is just one of countless other universes, this latter set of universes will, as a quantitative set, spark the search for sets even more encompassing, whether the inflated egos of some cosmologists like this or not.

This search has its perhaps most graphic illustration in the efforts to penetrate further and further back into the cosmic past. In going from the study of transitions characteristic of the first three seconds to those that occurred during first few nanoseconds, science goes from quantitative statements to other such statements. In the process science comes up with a view of the totality of matter which, in a sense, is increasingly more specific because the quantitative properties stand out ever more sharply in their increasing comprehensiveness.

This feature of modern scientific cosmology was stunningly anticipated by Chesterton when he compared the universe to a jewel.[3] The contrast cannot be greater with Laplacian cosmogenesis which dominated much of 19th-century thinking, or rather sank it into signal confusion. The primordial nebulous state which Laplace took a for starting point gave the assurance to many that the present state of inhomogeneity could somehow arise from some primordial homogeneity. Illogical as this cosmogony was, its scientific veneer made it also an effective antimetaphysics.

To see this, it should be enough to consider that it is the specificity of things that prompts efforts to trace them to something else. The idea of an allegedly homogeneous primordial state will not give anything to the mind to gain hold of. In fact, the vision of such a state will lull the intellect into believing that no questions need be asked about it. It is taken for something which is self-explanatory. This antimetaphysical wishful thinking is, of course, greatly helped by the fact that the mind's alertness is as much dulled by the phantom of such a universal homogeneity as the brain would be atrophied if one's head is stuck in a thick fog. All this, and possibly a phase in the life of Laplace, who like an accomplished chameleon thrived in the most different political regimes, may lie behind his famous remark that he does not need the hypothesis called God.

As a physicist he certainly did not need such hypothesis. The equations of physics, once in place, work splendidly with no reference to God. There is no end to making the equations of physics ever more comprehensive in their quantitative grasp. Openness to that hypothesis (God) is, however, demanded as long as the mind searches for an explanation that relates to the existence of things and not merely to their quantitative properties. Any specific set of such properties can be traced to another, with no need to worry about the trap of a regress to infinity. The latter is a trap for heedless metaphysicians and not for sensible physicists who are intent on doing physics and not philosophy. In that sense physics represents a chain to which ever more links can be added because in the process there is no need to ask the question: Why such a chain and not something else?

The question cannot be diluted by efforts that aim at constructing cosmologies with no boundary conditions. As long as those cosmologies must be tested with observations of the actual physical reality, they must contain specificities, such as the values of physical constants and various quantum rules. These express the fact that physical existence is restricted to a certain set of quantitative values. It matters not whether the actual cosmological model is about the true totality of things or not. Those who, rather naively, take this or that cosmological model for the true representation of cosmic totality, need not even refresh their metaphysical sensitivity to realize the true bearing of the question: why such and not something else? Those with less naivete may be supposed to have enough of that sensitivity to make do with a few super-galaxies, no less limited intrinsically than is a telephone pole or any stick or any stone.

There is no escape from taking that question in its metaphysical seriousness by resorting to dreams about final theories. That escape hatch has been closed by Gödel's theorems, which still have to sink into scientific consciousness, and especially into the consciousness of some leaders in fundamental particle physics and cosmology. According to those theorems no non-trivial set of arithmetic propositions can have its proof consistency within itself. Yet any theory of fundamental particles and cosmology should be highly mathematical. Consequently, it cannot claim to itself that touchstone of finality which is built-in consistency. Apart from this it should seem a form of hubris to think that just because a particular theory can successfully cope with all known experimental data, no unexpected data would ever arise on the horizon. As to the trick whereby the answer about the specificity of a given universe is relegated to the specificity of another, though totally unknown universe, one should not waste time on it, nor on its tricksters full of scientific wizardry.

Nor should one see any logic in Whitehead's claim that the universe as we see it shows only one set of specificities but through its eternal existence will take on all such conceivable sets. The claim is wholly gratuitous, with no support whatever in facts. Why, Whitehead, a mathematical physicist, in addition to being a pure mathematician and a logician, could, in 1927, ignore questions about entropy is difficult to fathom. This is not to suggest that the law of entropy can be turned into a proof of the createdness of the universe. Such a proof would shift the argument from ontology to temporality. There is, however, no way of showing scientifically that a given state of matter was preceded by nothingness. This remark is also valid with respect to the often heard idea that the Big Bang puts one on the threshold of creation. When scientists say this, they display philosophical muddleheadedness. When theologians say the same, they disclose a failure of theological nerve, which originates all too often in their distrust of philosophy or their inability to handle it, or in both. Remedy is then sought in invoking a science about which they usually know precious little, including its specific method.

The ultimate source of the specificity of physical reality must be sought in a consideration which is strictly philosophical or metaphysical. The consideration does not become scientific just because science could be used with great effectiveness to pile up data about the specificity of all things in space and time. The philosopher must use those data in a way which is very different from the way scientists use them. For the scientist, quantities are but quantities, and he can forever live happily in his quantitative heaven as long as he does not confuse his very earth, or material universe, with heaven, while that universe supplies him with endless quantitative data. For the philosopher, quantities are chief pointers to the reality of things, and since quantities mean limitation, they are also pointers to the limitedness of things as they exist.

One has therefore to fall back on philosophy if one is to ask the question—Why such and not something else?—of *existing* things, whether individually or in their totality which is the universe. What is to be explained is why such and such a set of limited existents does exist at all. In other words, the act that assures existence to a set of limitations is not a choice among a great many other sets already existing, but an act which gives existence to one specific set of limitations. The act is not creative in the trivial sense of redesigning the shape of this or that already existing material entity (be it that logical impossibility which is Plato's unformed matter). The act is creative in the sense of lifting something from non-existence into existence. It is not an act of a demiourgos, but of a being that alone can be truly creator, because it has that full power over existence it alone can have.

Therefore the act of creation is a creation out of nothing. Not that the nothing should be thought of as something subtly reified. The nothing merely means the total absence of reality. Therefore the power that creates must include within itself reality itself, with all its conceivable perfection, simultaneously and without limits or imperfections. It has to be totally different from any finite object. It has to be infinitely perfect in every sense. It must therefore possess all conceivable perfections in an infinite degree with no trace of that imperfection which is limitation in any sense. The inference that carries the mind to assert the existence of such a being is therefore composed of three steps. It begins with assertion, continues with negation, and ends with a superlative reaffirmation.

The last step, however positive, is therefore not equivalent to an intuitive knowledge of the infinite perfection, but is prompted from reflections on entities that are radically limited. Such are the human perfections of being conscious, personal, and being free. All these attributes in man denote radical limitations in him. Still, insofar as they denote perfections these must be assumed to be present in that Being, together with infinite goodness and holiness as inseparable from infinitely perfect existence. Further, it follows from the perfection of such an Existent that no need in it is fulfilled by his act of creating. Such an act merely indicates a free overflow of his infinite goodness. For if creation is not free, it degenerates into a process of emanation which has to be necessary, as it is in any pantheistic outlook. Within such an outlook "the universe is only a fault in the purity of Non-Being."[4] As the free act of an infinitely good Being, creation has to be an act of totally selfless giving, that act of a totally unselfish love. Such a being, Existence itself in its absolutely perfect form, is called God.

This argument from specifics to their source which is infinitely non-specific insofar as specificity implies limitations, can, of course, be variously articulated. Here the line of thought from physical specificity was pursued both for epistemological and cultural reasons. Epistemology, rooted as it should be in the recognition of reality, should make much of the priority of quantitative specificity that primarily reveals the existence of things. Consideration of such specificity, so proper to scientific inquiry, should also commend itself in this modern culture where science is ubiquitous. There are, of course, other variants of specificities that may be used for constructing other proofs of the existence of God than the one outlined here, which is the cosmological argument enriched with considerations provided by science. The argument is, however, in no way a scientific proof of the existence of God. God, who by definition is even less extended than a mathematical point, cannot be the object of scientific discourse, reasoning, and proof. Otherwise he would be the fruit of a glorious exercise in tautologies, as all equations of physics are in ultimate analysis.

The foregoing argument should appeal to scientifically tuned minds as it may energize their often dormant philosophical acumen. Minds with genuinely philosophical sensitivity may find in a mere stick, a very limited being, a powerful pointer to the existence of God, an argument that can be sized up with hardly any need for discursive steps in reasoning. In either case, it is, however, important to realize that one has on hand a very special kind of argument, or proof. The proof is inferential in the highest degree.

In most proofs the object to be demonstrated or proven is available to the senses. Even in most inferences that object is at least indirectly verifiable. But already in demonstrating the existence of the material universe, one is faced with a proof whose target is forever inferential, though fully material. One cannot go outside the Universe to verify its physical existence by observation. When it comes to demonstrating the existence of the mind (soul), the demonstration is not only radically inferential, but also has for its object something which is no longer material but strictly spiritual. In respect to demonstrating the existence of God, the inference demands a yielding in an even higher degree to the demands of reason, which is satisfied only with a fully satisfactory answer.

In other words, the real issue is about the measure of satisfaction which is to be granted. Insistence on an unlimited measure of satisfaction can be vindicated partly by considering the logical consequences of the refusal to grant that unlimited measure. Can truth really be spoken of if there is no absolute, infinite Truth? Is not the rejection of such a Truth an invitation to mere pragmatism? Can reasoning be salvaged if there is no ultimate reason? Can anything be more than relative if the Absolute is not recognized? Can wholesale skepticism be avoided if there is nothing absolutely valid? Is not man left with nothing but blind necessity if one declines to see something compelling in the inference to the existence of the One who created freely not only the Universe but also man's very free will?

The inference that there has to be a God, that it is compelling to postulate his existence, does not turn God into a necessary being. The postulate is not necessary in the sense of mechanical unavoidability, but in the sense of being compelling as long as the hunger for ultimate explanation is to be satisfied. In claiming that "no necessary being can explain existence,"[5] Sartre had in mind a Being that was necessary without being infinitely free at the same time, and not essentially free whether to create or not to create anything. The being called God is infinitely different from and superior to its Sartrean parody, which was a parody because, in line with all parodies, it could not exude love. Love which is necessary is but a compulsion.

Once that infinite, necessary Being, God, is seen in this light, it is possible to shed some light on the only real argument against his existence. The argument usually takes the form of the objection: It is impossible to assume that an infinitely good God should allow suffering in any form, let alone in the incredibly vast range in which suffering is on hand in uncountable cases and forms.

All such cases and forms relate to man's suffering. Suffering is inseparable from man. Were not man on hand, not a trace of suffering could be associated with purely physical processes, such as volcanos, hurricanes, earthquakes, tidal waves and, last but not least, bombardments of the earth by comets. The universe appears to be a "violent" universe only because man can become the target of its "violence."

Plants do not seem to suffer, while animals do, although the latter do not appear to suffer consciously regardless of the often plainly excruciating character of their suffering. Too many animal species feed on other animals, a gruesome fact which no sentimentality can gloss over. This was the reason which Darwin singled out, in his later years, for his having become an agnostic. He should have therefore come to repent the perverse delight he had taken in his younger years in shooting as many birds as he could.[6] Not a trace of such a compunction is found in his early Notebooks which, however, contain not a few virulent denunciations of metaphysics as well as of the uniqueness of man.[7] If man by his consciousness is not unique among animals, then all humans should become vegetarians, because consumption of animal flesh can be justified only if animals are not conscious of their suffering in the sense in which men are.

Whatever man's physical sufferings, they should pale into insignificance before the moral suffering that man can inflict on other men and on himself as well. No one who argues on behalf of the existence of God can be taken seriously unless he appreciates words such as these: "I'm glad I don't believe in god. When I look at the misery of the world and its bitterness I think that no belief can be more ignoble."[8] Still, in the long run, seriousness is on the side of the argument that God must exist.

For in order to be glad, one must have consciousness, which in turn is inseparable from the sense of being free. In fact the foregoing objection against belief in God makes sense only if it is done freely. With freedom comes, however, the possibility of abusing it, and all too often by violent acts. Such acts have, however, a far more important reference point than mere human beings. If there is a God, and there is one, man's responsibility for the use of his freedom relates primarily to God. The use of freedom therefore carries with it an eternal responsibility.

It is a fact of anthropological history that man has always felt the urge to propitiate God by offering various forms of sacrifices, including the burning of first fruits and of the best parts of sacrificial animals. The Greek and Roman hecatombs are well known. Josephus is rather reliable in reporting about the hundreds of thousands of lambs killed in the Temple on the eve of the Passover in his time. Indisputable are the reports of the Spanish conquistadors of Mexico City about the tens of thousands of humans whose hearts were ripped out in order to placate the gods.

The cessation of such practices is largely coincident with the coming of Christianity. The meaning of that change is all the more challenging because Christian faith was synonymous with the highest conceivable sacrifice ever, a sacrifice done in utter freedom and in full surrender to the will of God the Father by his incarnate Son. About Incarnation, Trinity, grace, resurrection, heaven and hell a philosopher can only raise the question of whether these notions imply logical contradictions or not. And if all those notions appear to him nonsense, he should still have a predilection for the kind of nonsense which is logical rather than illogical.[9]

This advice should have stood particularly in good stead a Condorcet, so boastful of reason and so contemptuous of Christianity. "We owe to the Schoolmen," Condorcet wrote, "more precise notions concerning the ideas that can be entertained about the supreme Being and his attributes; the distinction between the first cause and the universe which it is supposed to govern; the distinction between spirit and matter; the different meanings that can be given to the word *liberty*; what is meant by *creation*; the manner of distinguishing the various operations of the human mind; and the correct way of classifying such ideas as it can form of real objects and their properties."[10]

The Scholastics would not have worked out those very important metaphysical notions had they not been believing Christians, a point which, however crucial, Condorcet would have found excruciating to mention, let alone to emphasize. Yet he should have done so, because facts demanded it. For it was a fact that Christian philosophers made their all-important contributions to philosophy through pondering the injunctions of St Paul and St Peter. The former urged them, and of all places in the Letter to the Romans (12:1), to see to it that their religious homage is a rational service. Instructed by St Peter (1 Pet 3:15), they did their best to be ready to answer any reasonable objection that could be made against their hope.

What Christian philosophers did, constitutes intellectual history. History also shows that signal contributions of Christian philosophers lose their vigor, once separated from the matrix that inspired them. This is why so many series of Gifford Lectures, now amounting to almost two hundred, given over more than a hundred years, taste like stale water that time and again does not even flow towards God, however vaguely defined.[11] Drinking such water hardly energizes one to assume the posture of worship. Natural theology retained freshness and robustness only so long as it recognized its indebtedness to some outstanding facts that show God to have entered history in some special way. Those facts are known as miracles, or facts that exceed all known natural powers.

The question of their factuality is independent of the supernatural purpose they were meant to serve. Therefore miracles are a legitimate object of philosophical investigation insofar as such an investigation puts proper premium on facts or objects, all of which, even if miraculous, have a claim to be registered on open minds.

[1] From his poetical essay, "No More Secondhand God," written on April 9, 1940. See his *No More Secondhand God and Other Writings* (Carbondale, Ill.: Southern Illinois University Press, 1963), p. 28.

[2] A. S. Eddington, *The Expanding Universe* (Cambridge: Cambridge University Press, 1933), p. 57.

[3] G. K. Chesterton, *Orthodoxy* (London: John Lane, 1909), p. 115.

[4] P. Valéry, "Ebauche d'un serpent," in P. Valéry, *Charmes,* commentés par Alain (Paris: Gallimard, 1926), p. 179. In the poem Valéry is lead from declaring the problem of evil to be insoluble to denying the existence of the universe itself.

[5] J.-P. Sartre, *Nausea,* tr. L. Alexander (New York: New Directions Publishing Company, 1959), p. 176.

[6] See *The Autobiography of Charles Darwin. 1809-1902,* ed. N. Barlow (New York: W. W. Norton, 1958), p. 44.

[7] For details, see my *Angels, Apes and Men* (La Salle, IL: Sherwood Sugden, 1983), pp. 52-53.

[8] S. Maugham, *A Writer's Notebook,* in *The Partial View* (London: W. Heinemann, 1954), p. 48.

[9] It was on this ground that James Joyce declined the advice to abandon Catholicism, which he did not practice, and become a Protestant. See his *A Portrait of the Artist as a Young Man* (1916; Penguin Books, 1977), pp. 243-44.

[10] Condorcet, *Sketch for a Historical Picture of the Progress of the Human Mind,* tr. J, Barraclaugh (New York: The Noonday Press, 1955), p. 95.

[11] See my book, *Lord Gifford and His Lectures: A Centenary Retrospect* (1985; 2nd revised and enlarged edition, 1995).

12

Miracles

"Of the adequacy of the cause, if present, there can be no doubt."[1] So did J. S. Mill state what no logician can deny, namely, that if God exists, the possibility of miracles follows. The God in question has, of course, to be infinitely more than Plato's demiourgos. The latter, to recall the etymology of the word, is a public contractor, albeit on a cosmic scale. He merely executes the cosmic blueprint which is not of his making, if it is of the making of anyone at all. Plato's infinite Good, superior as it may be to the demiourgos, is not a creator. The cosmos, as celebrated by Plato, is as eternal and necessary as the Good, and so are its laws. They cannot be broken for any reason whatsoever.

Miracles, if they are truly interferences with the laws of nature, are part of a conceptual heritage very different in many ways from the one the Greeks of old bequeathed to us. Miracles are an integral part of the message known as biblical revelation that begins with Abraham and culminates with Jesus Christ. For the Synagogue miracles ceased with the prophets (with Daniel in particular). The Church, however, kept claiming that the miracles of its Founder continued within it as a chief means of proving the credibility of its proclamation about Him.

In the biblical context miracles serve that moral purpose which consists in the redemption of man. The moral thrust of miracles is their pivotal aspect, which discussants of miracles, whether theists, agnostics, or atheists, can ignore only at the risk of impairing their vision even with respect to what involves physics or biology about miracles. All this is stated here as an observation about a certain logic involved in miracles as Christians understand them. Miracles are an issue raised by Christians alone, and only by a class of them, usually branded as "conservatives." There is a logical connection between the Christian message as these "conservatives" understand it and miracles as the indispensable means of its credibility. The connection has been articulately conserved by such a chain of Christians as formed by Origen, Augustine, Thomas, Pascal, Newman, and Maritain, a chain noteworthy not only for its intellectual eminence but also for its moral qualities.

So-called "liberal" Christians have for some time turned their back on miracles as unworthy of a Christianity that has come of age. By this they mean the age of science. Biblical miracles have been the principal target of their demythologization of the Gospel story in particular. What they mean by demythologization consists in the naturalization of biblical reports about miracles, a procedure in which they make much of science. Only some keener eyes noticed that Bultmann, the chief of demythologizers, invoked not science but scientism when he declared that the coming of electromagnetism had once and for all discredited belief in miracles.[2]

Bultmann, of course, did not care about Church-miracles and not even about the logic that connects them with biblical miracles. Yet on the basis of pure logic alone, these two sets of miracles should seem to stand or fall together. No rational defense of biblical miracles has ever proved feasible whenever it implied a rejection of Church miracles. Here too the waving of the Bible has turned out to be an inept handwaving. But those who waved the Bible still had the Bible in their hands. In the hands of the demythologizers the Bible was deprived even of its being an accurate reading of human nature. They expected the readers of their re-interpretation of biblical narratives to ignore what should be most obvious, namely, that man, a potential angel, can act the beast, to recall a phrase of Pascal. The tragedy should seem compounded by the fact that genocides and democides have skyrocketed in this most scientific century of ours.[3]

Such is indeed the dark background against which alone can one assign a broad rationale to miracles. They have never been meant for entertainment, for intellectual titillation, for the amusement of Academies of Science. They were always for the healing of a deeply wounded human nature. Only by focusing on that predicament of man can one unfold the full meaning of the "adequate cause" of miracles, to recall Mill's phrase. For that cause, in order to be adequate, has to be a God who is both above and inside the visible world. The God of the deists, who never worked a miracle, was not truly inside that world or nature. He was a Creator *manqué*, who watched his work from the distance of some dubiously splendid isolation. Only a truly Creator God, who is infinitely above nature can also be most intimately within it, a point which remained wholly lost to the Greek poet whom Paul quoted on the Areopagus as the One in whom we live, move and are.[4]

Such a perfect being had to care, as emphasized by that fine logician of the 19th century, John Henry Newman, in his *Grammar of Assent*. As a great work in logic, the *Grammar* exudes respect for facts, culminating as it does in a portrayal of the historically unexplainable triumph of the Christian Church over established paganism, a triumph in which Church miracles played a crucial part. Those miracles were part of the means whereby God came to the rescue to a mankind caught, as Newman put it, in some aboriginal calamity.[5] Anyone disdainful of the notion of original sin should take care lest he start dreaming about man as a being who naturally does good and therefore is in no need of miraculous promptings. Any issue of any daily newspaper should be enough to discredit those dreams.

Many of those who dispute the factuality of miracles are, as so many children of the Enlightenment, notoriously tight lipped about the facts indicative of that calamity. This is why they discourse most inadequately about that "adequate cause." Particularly telling is the case of David Hume, this classic debunker of miracles. In his famed essay "Of Miracles," Hume defines that adequate cause most inadequately. He takes that cause for a mere reflection of the uniformity of laws of nature who as such must therefore "behave" in strict uniformity. Since miracles would be so many departures from that uniformity, they cannot be brought about by a God who must obey his own laws.[6]

It wholly escaped Hume that the cosmological argument rests not on the laws themselves, but on their being a reflection of a most specific state of empirical reality. Perhaps he could have sought an excuse for his oversight with a reference to most of the natural theology current in his ambience. He still had no right to ignore Leibniz's penetrating question, "Why things must exist so and not otherwise?"[7] It is this question that gives special credibility to the cosmological argument within the scientific context as science reveals an ever more stunning measure of specificity about the universe both in space and time.[8]

The laws of nature cry out for a Creator, who was able to choose one particular set of laws out of an infinitely large number of such sets, all possible but not yet real, and embody it in an actual specific world which He created. In such a perspective, the uniformity of laws ceases to be an argument against miracles. In that perspective, and there alone, the breaking of the laws of nature will not have the anthropomorphic connotation of tinkering with them. Actually, it is the critics of miracles who will be pushed into anthropomorphism and about the very factor, science, which they invoke against miracles. The fact is that Hume himself was led to pour sarcasm on cosmology, indeed on the notion of the physical universe in terms of the very logic whereby he tried to debunk the cosmological argument. It was not for the last time that a misconstruction of the cosmological argument led to a deconstruction of the universe as well.[9] This is worth noting because even today some champions of Hume, who regard his debunking of miracles as the last word in the matter, fail to take note of this most revealing connection.[10]

Hume, of course, makes a valid point, still a preamble to discussing the factuality of miracles, when he states that "The *Christian Religion* not only was at first attended with miracles, but even at this day cannot be believed by any reasonable person without one." Again, he is right in excoriating those who want to retain miracles on the basis of faith alone, without satisfying the just demands of reason about them: "Whoever is moved by *Faith* [alone] to assent to it, is conscious of a continued miracle in his own person, which subverts all the principles of his understanding, and gives him a determination to believe what is most contrary to custom and experience."[11]

Such was the parting shot in Hume's essay "Of Miracles," which he delivered in full confidence that he had disposed both of the possibility and of the factuality of miracles. He had signally failed in respect to the former. Well, he did not try to be a strict logician. As one who disposed of causality in favor of mere customs and habit, he had the right to lay a claim at most to a kind of a "modal" logic, or a cavorting in specious concession to the moods of one's reasoning.

As to the question of factuality, one should insist on it all the more in the case of one whose first major book fell dead from the printing press, as he himself put it, but who firmly established himself with his second and much shorter book. It was called *Enquiry concerning Human Understanding*. Classic have indeed become its concluding words in which Hume urged that only such books should be saved from being thrown on the pyre that contain facts and mathematics. Concerning the latter he spoke only by hearsay, apart from some elementary courses he had taken at the Edinburgh Academy in his mid-teens. This, of course, would not have been a debilitating factor in the case of a mathematical genius, which Hume certainly was not. Facts were no less a demanding issue in respect of a Hume who prided himself on being a "scientific" historian of the England of the 17th century, a qualification that no one accords him any longer. Hume nowhere proved himself to be more cavalier with facts as in his essay "Of Miracles."

In that essay he did not consider a single miracle in any detail. Obviously he tried to score cheap points when he reported with glee the disputes which some miraculous events that took place at the tomb of the Abbé Paris, a Jansenist, had occasioned in Catholic France. Hume thought he could get around the factuality of miracles by claiming that not a single miracle has ever been attested by a sufficient number of trustworthy witnesses; that reports about something extraordinary always gain hold on human imagination at the detriment of common sense; that miracles always abound in barbarous nations, but never occur in civilized lands; that miracles claimed by opposing religions are destructive of all miracles.

Still, all this depended on the claim that since no miracles have ever been attested, not one would ever occur, although Hume did not seriously review reports about a single one. His confidence anticipated that of Adler, the psychotherapist, who in the presence of young Popper dismissed a report about a new case as one that had to be exactly similar to the thousand cases he had already seen. Popper expressed his astonishment with the question: "But what if the thousandth and one case happens to be different?" a question that has resounded ever since and also fell upon too many deaf ears, and certainly so in respect to miracles.[12]

Hume's overweening approach to the factuality of miracles stands out very badly against a fact of which Hume could not be unaware. As one who in Paris lived in the circle of *philosophes*, he could not be unfamiliar with the encomium which Voltaire heaped on Benedict XIV as the chief glory of the world of the learned.[13] Whatever the sincerity of Voltaire, who may have tried to obtain some benefice thereby, the pope had enjoyed great reputation for his learning already as Prospero Lambertini. He did so precisely in his capacity as the "devil's advocate," or the official whose duty is to sift spurious miracles from credible ones. His scholarly reputation rested largely on a work which came out first in four massive volumes between 1734 and 1738. In the ten years that passed between the publication of the last volume and that of Hume's essay "Of Miracles," there had to be plenty of opportunity for Hume to take note of what was contained in that volume about the factuality of miracles and about the most careful sifting of the trustworthy from the false.

That fourth volume, that would have done credit to any professional historian of medicine, witnessed a profound interest in medical science. The same interest prompted Lambertini, who became pope in 1748, to found in 1752 the Academy of Medicine of Bologna as a complement to its famed Faculty of Medicine. Compared with Lambertini's earnestness and erudition, Hume's handling of miracles evokes one who merely tries to score some cheap points. Most importantly, Lambertini had a philosophical basis on which to argue the possibility and factuality of miracles, biblical or other. As to Hume, his philosophy barred him from arguing against them, unless the invocation of customs and habits passes for philosophy. The latter, which Hume took more for a sophisticated amusement than for a quest for truth, can be such only if it implies an unstinting respect for facts.

To see this difference, one need only recall that Lambertini's favorite book was the *Summa theologiae* of Thomas Aquinas. Lambertini often quotes Thomas on crucial points, such as when he refutes Spinoza's claim that a truly infinite God cannot work miracles. An infinitely perfect being who is not free, replies Lambertini with Thomas, who had anticipated Spinoza's objection, is very short on perfection. Underlying such an argumentation is an unconditional respect for primary items concerning knowledge. One of these is the reality of the free will of the human being who knows. Whereas it was not Lambertini's purpose to set forth in detail an epistemological theory of the manner in which one knows a fact to be a miracle, his fondness for Thomas' way of arguing indicates the principal points he would have made. As one whose mind was riveted on facts taken, rightly or wrongly, for miracles, Lambertini would have clearly upheld the primacy of facts or objects as something that caused the mind to know. In other words, Lambertini would have argued the priority of the means over the message, the only way to argue consistently the case of knowing anything, including miracles.

That fourth volume contains also a detail that might have given to Hume a salutary glimpse of contemptuous handling of those who cared for facts even they passed for miracles. He claimed that they never investigated miracles as would have been the duty of people respectful of the intellect and especially of their great responsibility as advocates of a revealed religion. The story, which might have made Hume blush, came in the context

of Lambertini's dealing with cures in which the psychic element
dominated over the physical. He modestly presented the story as
if he had learned about it from a book which the Jesuit Guillaume
Daubenton published in Paris in 1716 on the occasion of the
beatification of François Regis (1597-1640), the Jesuit apostle of
the Vivarais area in France in the mid-1600s.[14] As the postulator of
the cause Daubenton had to spend some time in Rome and be in
frequent consultation with the "Devil's advocate," or Promoter of
Faith, an office which Lambertini filled from 1708 till 1727.

The story was carried far and wide in the many reimpressions
of Daubenton's book, which was in even greater demand following the canonization of François Regis in 1737 and came out in
English translation in London the following year.[15] Hume
therefore did not have to read Lambertini's forbiddingly learned
tomes in order to get wind of the story about a young English
aristocrat who on his Grand Tour in Europe arrived in Rome. He
must have arrived there a year or two before the beatification that
stirred, as Daubenton noted, considerable interest in miracles as
approved by Rome. Daubenton also drew attention to the
disparity between some hundred or so miraculous cures that had
been presented during the previous decades to the Vatican in
support of the canonization of saints, of which only one was
accepted.[16]

Through the good services of a prelate in Rome, so goes
Daubenton's account of the story, the young English aristocrat,
doubtful of "popish" miracles, obtained a dossier on cures that
have been submitted for recognition as miracles. After having
perused the dossier our Englishman told the prelate: "The
evidence set forth for believing in those events was remarkable and
complete. If everything proclaimed by the Church of Rome were
as certainly true, and were based on such authentic and well-
examined foundations, we should see no reason why we should
not assent to it all, thus exploding all those jokes and mockeries by
which your miracles are called in question." One can only imagine
the shock of the young aristocrat, on hearing the prelate reply:
"But you must know that of all these miracles which seem to you
to be so firmly established, not one has been approved by the

Sacred Congregation of Rites, as it found the proofs to be insuffi-
cient."[17] The prelate was, in all evidence, Lambertini himself, still
the "devil's advocate."

Hume, who tried to cover his flippancy about factual cases
with sanctimonious warnings about intellectual responsibility for
facts, could not have seen that the shoe was on the other foot. His
philosophy, which had diluted respect for facts in general, pre-
empted the case for miraculous facts. In other words he failed to
see that any argument against miracles is only as strong as the
consistency with which one can dispute that facts can be known,
indeed that facts or objects are the very causes of knowledge. In
other words, he failed to see that his argument against miracles
was a classic case of a philosophical boomerang.

At any rate, Hume failed to prove that one can have certainty
about mental habits or customs, the kingpins of his philosophy. It
escaped him that facts, objects do not take an iron grip over the
mind. Certainty about reality is a facet very different from the
certainty of some logical relations. It can, however, become a
valuable habit, just as one can settle into the habit of thinking that
one only needs habits and customs in order to get along in life
and, *horribile dictu*, earn philosophical kudos for good measure.

Against Hume's and other forms of skeptical as well as
subjectivist philosophies it is largely irrelevant to engage in subtle
distinctions about the status of the laws of nature. It is more to the
point to probe into basic attitudes towards facts, such as concrete
cures. There is no point in going to Lourdes if one has the
mentality of Zola, who on arriving there declared that even if a
spectacular cure were to take place under his very eyes, he would
not accept it for a miracle. No wonder that he had to twist and
turn facts so that his explanation of cures as cases of self-suggestion
might appear credible. His book *Lourdes* is a proof of this.

There is no point in refuting the cures worked in Lourdes if
one does not care to study the archival depositions, the long
testimony of doctors, both believers and skeptics. There is no
ground for claiming respect for scientific evidence if one refuses
to go from one Arrondissement of Paris to another and see with
one's own eyes a group of beneficiaries of medically unexplainable

cures obtained in Lourdes.[18] It is not scientific to ignore sworn depositions made by doctors and take refuge in blithe references to psychosis. Again, it is not scientific to consider the case for Lourdes settled just because a certain sector of the press sees no merit in it. The media still has to prove itself a reliable arbiter in matters philosophical and even in plain matters of fact. Thus the media never reports about what it should know best, or the deliberations of daily editorial board meetings as to what will appear in the front page, what will be relegated to the gutter, and what will not be reported at all.

One need not be a first-rate tailor to register reliably a huge hole in a coat—the remark of a Belgian physician who repeatedly diagnosed Pieter De Rudder before and after his sudden healing on April 7, 1875. For what the healing filled was almost literally a huge hole that gaped in the form of a suppurating wound in the middle of De Rudder's right leg where the bone was crushed over several inches by a log felled by him on February 16, 1867. The sudden cure of the wound that previously resisted any treatment and the complete restoration of the bone constituted a big news,[19] though not for every one who could have been rightfully expected to take notice and study the facts. Renan, who had already stipulated that only a fact that had been declared by five Scientific Academies to be unexplainable should be taken for a miracle, certainly did not care to travel from Paris to Belgium.

Although one need not be a world-famous physician to register reliably miraculous cures, doctors of such fame have not been absent from among those who made depositions about medically unexplainable cures that took place under their very eyes in Lourdes. One of them was Alexis Carrel, arguably the greatest surgeon of this century. With three other doctors he witnessed the total flattening, in thirty or so minutes, of the enormously swollen abdomen of Marie Bailly, twenty-three, dying of tubercular peritonitis. During those thirty minutes, and even for the next twenty-four hours, nothing left her body. At that time, May 28, 1902, only members of the Société Médicale of Lyons knew that young Carrel, he was then 29, had only two weeks earlier reported to them about his method of suturing ruptured blood vessels that made history in surgery. Within a year Carrel was banished from the University of Lyons where his registering of the facts of the cure of Marie Bailly was taken for a crime against the intellect. He went to America where he perfected his method to the point that he could perform organ transplants in animals, for which he received the Nobel Prize in 1912.

By some strange twist of Fate, he happened to be a close observer of the condition of Marie Bailly already on the train that took her to Lourdes two days earlier. He was convinced that she had but a day or two to live. When Marie Bailly was about to be pushed on a stretcher from the hospital to the Grotto, Carrel vowed, in the presence of two other doctors standing by the stretcher that if she were to return alive from the Grotto he would become a monk. By the evening Marie Bailly was eating without vomiting, the next morning she got up on her own. On examining her on that morning, Carrel found an arm-length hard piece in her right abdominal area which disappeared by the evening. In still another day, Marie Bailly boarded the train, spent 24 hours on hard benches, arrived refreshed in Lyons, took the streetcar home, and had to prove to her family that she was indeed Marie Bailly.

Some of these details became widely known only when in 1949, four years after Carrel's death, his account of what he saw became printed under the title *Voyage de Lourdes*, quickly published also in English translation.[20] Had a young graduate from Oxford or Cambridge read that book, together with the archival depositions, he would have been tempted to do as that young English aristocrat did two and a half centuries earlier, and see in Marie Bailly's cure a well-attested miracle. Yet he would have been in for a big surprise, had he waited for another dozen years or so. In 1964 the International Medical Commission of Lourdes, the highest scientific forum of studying cures at Lourdes, decided against taking the cure of Marie Bailly for something unexplainable by medicine. The reason seems to have been that neither the depositions, nor the dossiers of the medical history of Marie Bailly, on whom surgeons in Lyons refused to operate three months earlier, contain a reference to the possibility of a neurotically induced pseudopregnancy.

Those who read Carrel's testimony as well as the archival evidence can only conclude that leaning over backward, lest one should make a mistake, can at times be greatly overdone. Yet this overcautious attitude compares most favorably with the attitude of the late Carl Sagan, a self-appointed spokesman of the scientific way of ascertaining any truth. He dismissed in a few lines all the miracles of Lourdes as being equivalent to cases of slow remission of cancer which statistically occur in one of every thousand cases.[21]

In saying this, Sagan, the scientist, cut a sorry figure indeed. It was not he, but another scientist of similar stature who tried a somewhat better way to discredit miracles. It was, of course, right for him to deplore the method which consists in comparing the rate of healing in those who pray or are prayed for, with the rate of improvement in those who do not pray and are not prayed for. Yet he quickly changed the subject when I raised the question of whether it was not far more important to study the medical report about any of the truly startling cures. One wonders what he would have said if confronted with one such specific cure. About its being medically unexplainable a Jewish doctor provided the chief testimony. Doctors may, of course, say something about the intensity of prayers that have been addressed to Edith Stein, a convert from Judaism and a victim of the Nazis, eventually beatified on the strength of that cure. But for a scientist it makes little difference as to whose help is invoked. A scientist can only be interested in observable facts. If he is not intrigued by some very obvious fact, he cuts a sorry figure.

Still sorrier is the case of any theologian who professes himself to be a Christian and at the same time tries to talk himself out of miracles, biblical and other, as something at variance with scientifically established laws of nature. What has already been said about the true meaning and bearing of the uncertainty principle makes it unnecessary to dwell on theologians who have found in it a resolution to their pseudo-problem. They want perhaps miracles but only such that do not constitute an overruling by God the laws of physics set by Him. One can, of course, only pity all those theologians and students of theology who have found persuasive Bultmann's howler that Maxwell's theory of electromagnetism discredited any claim about miracles once and for all. It is not so easy to expose the somersaults in logic of those who sought in the modern mathematical doctrine of chance or of stochastic variables a means whereby God can perform miracles without interfering with the laws of nature. These zealous gentlemen are as a rule either experts in statistical theory or in theology, but never in both. Most importantly, they have never impressed others with their philosophical cogency.

For ultimately the question of miracles is a philosophical question, before it becomes a question in theology. The logic of that question is in part the one which Mill's dictum, quoted at the start of this chapter, sums up. The logic should be widely known. Around the turn of this century, a prominent British physicist, Sir George Gabriel Stokes wrote in a prominent context: "Admit the existence of God and the possibility of miracles follows."[22] Later, the novelist W. Somerset Maugham, a professed agnostic, unfolded more of the same logic: "If you once grant the existence of God, I do not see why you should hesitate to believe in the Resurrection, and if you once grant the supernatural I do not see why you should put limits to it. The miracles of Catholicism are as well authenticated as those of the New Testament."[23]

Maugham also referred to still more in that logic, indeed to its real ground, without, however, being able to cope with it. He began with saying that "belief in God is not a matter of common sense, or logic, or argument, but of feeling."[24] But if there is logic in the claim that God cannot be known, at least through inference, the same logic would threaten all other inferences, indeed all knowledge, to become a mere sentiment, a mere habit, a mere custom, as Hume would have it. The question of miracles is indeed that primordial question of philosophy, which is about the way of knowing facts, objects, indeed anything. Those who dispose of miracles, especially by praising to the philosophical sky Hume's method of debunking them, should first come clean about their own ways of knowing anything with certainty. This they must do as long as they try to cure others of their readiness to hold some facts for miracles. Once they come clean or at least show a readiness for doing so, they may not perhaps reject out of hand the following advice, which is certainly in line with the basic and initial thrust of this book: to know any fact, even a fact that qualifies for a miracle, one first of all must keep one's eyes open; then the fact, the object, shall readily register itself in the receptive mind. Once there, it can serve as a reliable vehicle of messages, including their philosophical kind, and support a treatise which claims to be not about opinions but about truth.

[1] J. S. Mill, *A System of Logic, Ratiocinative and Inductive*, III, xxv, 2. In *The Collected Works of John Stuart Mill* (Toronto: University of Toronto Press, 1970), vol. 7, p. 623.

[2] See R. Bultmann, "New Testament and Mythology," in *Kerygma and Myth: A Theological Debate*, ed. H. W. Bartsch, tr. R. H. Fuller (London: S. P. C. K., 1957), p. 5.

[3] See report in *The New York Times* (Dec. 14, 1997, p. WK 7) about G. W. Scully's study, "Murder by the State," where the figure 170 million is given as the number of those who in this century were murdered by their own governments.

[4] In his speech on the Areopagus, Acts 17:28. The poet in question is the Stoic Aratus (c. 315-240 B.C.), author, among other things, of the astronomical poem *Phaenomena*.

[5] See the Doubleday Image Book edition, pp. 310 and 376. On Newman's emphatic reminders of that calamity, see my essay, "A Gentleman and Original Sin," *Downside Review*, July 1996, pp. 192-214.

[6] References are to the text in D. Hume, *Essays. Moral, Political, and Literary*, ed. T. H. Green and T. H. Grose (London: Longmans, Green and Co., 1875), vol. 2, pp. 88-108.

[7] In his *Principles of Nature and Grace* (1714), See *Leibniz Selections*, ed. P. P. Wiener (New York: Charles Scribner's Sons, 1951), p. 527.

[8] For further details see the preceding chapter and especially chapter 3 in my book, *God and the Cosmologists* (Edinburgh: Scottish Academic Press, 1990).

[9] See ch. 7, "Bricks without Mortar," in my Gifford Lectures, *The Road of Science and the Ways to God* (Chicago: University of Chicago Press, 1978).

[10] Thus A. Flew in his Introduction to Hume's *Of Miracles* (La Salle IL. Open Court, 1985).

[11] D. Hume, *Concerning Human Understanding and Essays*, vol. 2, p. 108.

[12] K. R. Popper *Conjectures and Refutations* (1962; Harper Torchbooks, 1968), p. 35.

[13] The encomium is in a hexameter, "Lambertinus hic est Romae decus et Pater orbis/ Qui mundum scriptis docuit, virtutibus ornat." Quoted from R. Haynes, *Philosopher King. The Humanist Pope. Benedict XIV* (London: Weidenfield and Nicolson, 1970), p. 180.

[14] *La vie du bienheureux Saint Jean François Regis apôtre de Velay . . .* (Paris: 1716). I have consulted the edition of 1841 (Lyon: Librairie Catholique), where the passage in question is given on p. 361.

[15] *The Life of St John Francis Regis* (printed by John Hoyles and sold by Thomas Meighan, in Drury Lane, London, 1738), viii + 368pp.

[16] See the edition of 1841, p. 360. Lambertini is mentioned on pp. 355 and 365.

[17] I am quoting Haynes' translation in *Philosopher King*, p. 32.

[18] The group was presented by Dr. Prosper G. Boissarie, the first director of the Bureau in connection with a lecture at the Musée de Luxembourg in Paris in 1895 as a reply to Zola's attacks on Lourdes. See P. G. Boissarie, *Zola, le roman et l'histoire. Conférence de Luxembourg* (Paris: Bonne Presse, 1895). See also Boissarie's massive report, *Les grandes guérisons de Lourdes* (Paris: Donniol, 1900), 560pp.

[19] For details of De Rudder's cure, see ch. XII in *Twenty Cures of Lourdes Medically Discussed* by F. de Grandmaison de Bruno (London: Sands 1920).

[20] This English translation, to which Charles Lindbergh wrote a rather irrelevant introduction, was republished by Real View Books in 1994, with a new Introduction written by me, in which I made a meticulous use of the Archival material in the Medical Bureau of Lourdes.

[21] C. Sagan, "Channeling or Faith Healing—Scam or Miracle?" *Parade Magazine*, Dec. 4, 1994, pp. 14-15.

[22] G. G. Stokes, *Natural Theology* (London: Adam and Charles Black, 1891), p. 24.

[23] S. Maugham, *A Writer's Notebook*, in *The Partial View* (London: W. Heinemann, 1954), p. 11.

[24] Ibid.

13

History

Miracles are interventions in the physical world, whether on a large or a small scale, so that man may exercise a better control over that inner world which is his very nature. Control that nature he must, or else it is ripped apart by a relentless struggle between some unmistakably higher aspirations and some patently lower instincts in him. Only by writing off all modern criminology can one dispute the reality of that conflict whose grim depths psychoanalysis has failed to fathom. External or political history too remains an unfathomable puzzle if that inner conflict is not recognized for what it is. That Paul of Tarsus saw the resolution of that conflict in terms of a salvation history has at least one facet to commend it. Salvation history, which miracles are meant to support, is an honest facing up to a grim struggle both within man and society, which only some dreamy-eyed utopians and brave social engineers would dare ignore.

Whether one takes a long view or a short view of it, salvation history remains perplexing, to say the least, though there may be at least one saving grace to its very notion, namely, its realism. The idea of the Kingdom of God includes the recognition that the wheat and the tares would grow side by side within it until the end of time. Opposed as it is to the "world," the Kingdom of God is not exempt of tragic features that are certainly the staple characteristic of ordinary history. The latter hardly justifies rosy prognostications, such as the one that took the end of World War I for the end of all wars. Within a mere two decades mankind was in the throes of another World War, compared with which the first may appear a relatively mild affair. The prospect of more than a thousand years and 33 billion dollars, which it would take, with the help of presently available technology, to defuse and remove the over a hundred million landmines "gracing" the globe, may give a pause to anyone with a touch of realism.[1]

Henry Ford's quip, "history is more or less bunk," reveals a frustrated puzzlement about history which holds in its grip all those whose concern for and wizardry with means defines their message of salvation. To let as many as possible enjoy the vistas of open spaces, as Ford put it to justify his mass production of cars,[2] may prove a very confining message even in the not too long run. Suffice to think of the impasse about implementing measures to prevent the further warming of the atmosphere by global proliferation of automobiles and all sorts of internal combustion engines. Wars once fought for the control of salt, and very recently for the control of great oil deposits, may soon yield to conflicts about the respective extent to which developed and undeveloped nations may pollute the environment. Open spaces are turning into increasingly opaque spaces, in no small part because of Ford's skill with production, on which rides the goddess of free market economy.

The myopic view on human history, within which the coming of age of the production line is taken for history's culmination, has not been successfully challenged by historians and certainly not by their Marxist kind. Those historians who sought a meaningful message in history by centering not on the physical means, but on ideas, did not prove more convincing. They merely produce, Toynbee is a case, variants on the message of Ranke, the greatest nineteenth-century historian, for whom history manifested God's very will. Whatever may have been the message of that will, its means of manifestation was the dialectic of the Hegelian World Spirit, which had already made Hegel run roughshod over the facts of history.

This non-theological facet should have given second thoughts to Ranke who in addition failed to specify the meaning of the key word in his famed methodological precept that the historian's task is to establish the actual manner in which events took place.[3]

For whether one translates Ranke's *eigentlich* as actually or properly or exactly, his precept does not provide an answer to the fact that historians can perform their task only if they are properly selective about the facts of history. Do they thereby distort history? Whether they do or not, they cannot help being selective. They have to be selective even when using, in obedience to Ranke, only those documents that originated during the phase which they are investigating. For if the phase chosen is long, the documents are too many to be accounted for. Therefore the historian is obliged to select some, which he therefore judges to be relevant and by the same stroke declares irrelevant the ones he omits. Conversely, if the phase chosen is too short, there may not be enough documents to justify a narrative.

The task of selection cannot be circumvented even if one assumes that selection is not a philosophical task. For to write history is to do philosophy. The very word "history" relates to the act of giving a philosophical account. Borrowed from the Greek, "history" is merely the noun form of the verb *historein*, or to give a reasoned account.[4] In the measure in which this was forgotten, the reasoned account of past events became a mere story, at times but a glorious fable and even a libelous script. On the level of professional history writing, the deterioration is conveyed in the remark, apparently humorous but in fact rather biting, that every historian gives his story and nothing more. On the level of power politics, that same symptom translates into the remark that history is written by the victors or rather by historians dutifully serving them. What these can do with history is best illustrated by a remark of Anthony Froude, the best stylist among all English historians, and certainly convinced of being part of a victory never to be reversed. He did not blush as he took the facts of Elizabethan and Victorian England's victorious history for the letters of the alphabet which by selection and rearrangement can be made to spell out anything.[5] Such historians always have their means to relay a message which becomes dated very quickly, unless the message is confused with the style.

Behind all such discomfitures of historiography there lies a habit, widespread enough, of handling in a cavalier way the justification of the philosophical presuppositions that support one's writing the history of this or that. Ranke proceeded that way when he assumed without further ado that Hegel's philosophy of history was essentially right. Those who had no taste for Hegel would fall back on the climate of opinion within which it was not possible to question the true status of the idea of progress as a basic presupposition. Although J. Bury exploded the idea of progress as one which begs the question, it retains its hold on the imagination of the educated and further weakens their philosophical sensitivity. The latter was not strengthened by the emphasis, put during the nineteenth century, on critical editions of ancient documents. Editorial accuracy is not equivalent to attention to the indispensable role which philosophy, indeed epistemology, must have in the historical method.

No wonder that a minor sensation was created by R. G. Collingwood's books, the first of which, published in 1924, had the intriguing title, *Speculum mentis*. It was followed by the explicitly thematic *Essay on Philosophic Method* (1933) and the widely read *The Idea of Nature* that appeared only posthumously, in 1946. One of the reasons why Collingwood did not succeed in energizing the philosophical acumen of his fellow historians was, of course, that he was an idealist in the extreme. All history had to be "the history of thought," if Collingwood was right in saying that "historical thinking is an activity . . . which is a function of self-consciousness, a form of thought possible only to a mind which knows itself to be thinking that way."[6] This definition of history, or rather historiography could only strengthen the view that in writing history the historian merely gives his story and nothing more.

In deploring the fact in 1931 that "historians reflected little upon the nature of things and even the nature of their own subject,"[7] H. Butterfield gave a diagnosis that could be given several decades later as well. In fact the sickness of eschewing philosophy should have seemed the more chronic the louder was the lip service given to its importance. This is what E. H. Carr did in his Trevelyan Lectures delivered at the University of Cambridge in 1961. He contrasted the historians' earlier state of innocence as free of philosophical concerns, with their present state of fall and sin. In the former state "historians walked in the Garden of Eden without a scrap of philosophy to cover them, naked and unashamed before the god of history." Yet even after their Fall, many historians, so Carr appraised the situation, "pretend to dispense with a philosophy of history," but in doing so they "are merely trying, vainly and self-consciously, like members of a nudist colony to recreate the Garden of Eden in their garden suburb."[8]

Yet Carr, too, met his comeuppance as do all those who try to construe a philosophy of history without coming clean on their philosophy. Philosophy is not equivalent to stating the major problems of epistemology and leaving it at that. But this is precisely what Carr did after hoisting a philosophical petard on his articulation of the method of history: "The predicament of the historian is a reflexion on the nature of man." This was, however, preceded by an enumeration, which to a moderately keen philosophical eye could seem like a chain of fuses. Starting from the dichotomy between facts and their interpretation, Carr rightly saw the connection of this with other apparent dichotomies, such as the one "between the particular and the general, the empirical and the theoretical, the objective and the subjective."[9] To these pairs of profoundly epistemological terms he later added the personal and social, the free and the determinist, which clearly landed him into those depths of epistemology where one is up to one's ears in metaphysics. But in the end, Carr found no more inviting depths than the unfathomable stream of change and no better reasoned policy about it than the advice that the historian should jump into the stream wholeheartedly. To make matters appear even more ironic, he described the act of cavorting in that stream as a participation in progress, a word whose various meanings he had already criticized without coming up with his own definition of it.[10]

This was a very dubious paeon of uncertainty, which Carr, tellingly enough, supported with a reference to modern science. This was all the more ironic because as one with undisguised sympathies toward the Soviet Union, Carr chided those Westerners who underestimated Soviet science and technology. He, however, showed no appreciation for the fact that science and technology in the West were decisive factors in the political situation that originated in the outcome of World War II. A brief recall of the role of radar, of the deciphering of the German secret code with the help of first-generation computers, of the nuclear bombs and of some less gruesome products of science should forcefully suggest that science was the means of history and that whoever had more science had more say in deciding the course of history and thereby specifying its message.

This view of science did not fail to receive further support as the twentieth century approached its completion. The Gulf War was a contestation between Western scientific know-how and that which the Soviet Union delivered to its proxy, Iraq. The latter was cast in the role of inflicting a defeat on America, similar to the one which Vietnam had already administered. The Soviet Union, with the reformer Gorbachev at its helm, would have thereby been assured a few decades of respite, hopefully enough to catch up with the United States in science and technology. There was indeed enormously much to catch up with, if it was true that in the mid-1970's not even every department in the Soviet Ministry of Defense had a computer. Already then the Soviet Chief of Staff, subsequently purged, admitted that the Cold War had been won by the Americans, because the next war would be decided by the speed which only computerized planning and weaponry could assure.[11]

If, however, science is *the* means of history, what is history's message? Does that message consist in the dictum that might is right, or that those still with the balance of power in their favor should unabashedly play the hypocrite, though "with a touch of self preservation"?[12] This stark view is hardly attenuated by a recourse to the idea of democracy and to its policy whereby the use of scientific-military power is deposited in governments by the people and for the people. For if democracy is merely the best of all bad forms of governments, and often even less, the use of power in the hands of those who have it is hardly promising. After all, people are not infallible. Indeed, their fallibility is proportional to the unavailability of proper information. The flow of information is, however, heavily controlled by the editorial policies of major channels of information, policies often steeped in openly selfish ideologies.

These policies are markedly pragmatist for all the professed respect of their spokesmen for principles, such as human dignity. Their standards match those of the final recommendation of the Presidential commission about the cloning of humans. According to that recommendation the Federal Government should not outlaw the cloning of humans for more than five years, because by then the thinking of society would get around to the idea of cloning.[13] Obviously the Commission, or at least its majority, thought that during that period the thinking of society would be sufficiently "educated" by those who control most channels of information. And since information is gathered and dished out with an ever heavier reliance on the tools of science, this constitutes a further proof that science is indeed the means of history. But if such is the case, what is the message?

Was the message capsulized well ahead of time in Aldous Huxley's *Brave New World*? In essence nothing different is offered in *The End of History* by F. Fukuyama, who sees the goal of history in a comfortable living that technology, supported by market economies, should make available all over the globe. But can the free market, feverishly driven as it may be by the latest in technology and science, achieve the goal that societies all over the globe may be equally prosperous? Is there any sign that the rich nations are building up the economy of the poor nations so that the latter may no longer be in a disadvantageous position toward the former? Do not rich nations take away with one hand much more than they give with the other? Do not they guard their scientific and technological breakthroughs more carefully than their troop numbers and their deployment? Is there not a dire warning for the future in the fact, now half a century old, that it was the West that set up the Iron Curtain, because otherwise the rush of peoples from the Eastern bloc to Western Europe would have made impossible the appropriate raising of living standards there? Have not more such curtains (in terms of economics) been raised elsewhere since then around the globe?

Honest answers to such questions can only make a confused situation look even more so. In such a situation it has often been helpful to take a look at origins. With respect to a history ever more powerfully fueled and controlled by science, the origin to be reviewed should be the origin of science and of that science which by giving control over nature, where everything moves, can alone move history. The question about the origin of that science is the most decisive question that can be raised with respect to scientific history and also the most ignored question by historians of science and even by those specializing in political history.

I mean historians both in the West and in the East. Suppose one tries to set the question of the origin of science from the viewpoint of the great non-Western powers, such as the Muslim world, or India, or China. After the great debacle of its great Leap Forward, China is now making tremendous leaps forward in catching up with the West scientifically and technologically. This is all too well known. Much less is discussed by the Chinese the question of why science did not originate in China of old. Why is it, one may ask, that the land which saw the first use of magnets and gunpowder, failed to give rise to a Galileo and a Newton? Is it really true that a feudal system long prevailing in China blocked the rise science there? Will such a sociological answer do with respect to a similar story in ancient India, which produced rustfree iron two thousand years before Bessemer and invented phonetic writing independently of Egypt? Is it true, as Nehru claimed, that science failed to develop in his native India because it did not remain faithful to its ancient creative spirit? Behind this claim, which did not contain any clear definition of that creative spirit, there lurked indeed a deep sense of national frustration.

But it is the Muslim world, now on its global crusading march, that should feel keenly the weight of its scientific backwardness. Why did it have to borrow only half a century ago the technological know-how from the West so that its vast oil fields might be exploited? This and similar questions should seem to weigh all the heavier on the Muslim mind because the Arabs had a far better start toward true science than the Chinese and Hindus of old. A better start, precisely because it was a start that could be refuted quantitatively. But this is what the Muslim scholars failed to perceive over that half a millennium during which they were in possession of the entire Greek philosophical and scientific corpus. The latter had its chief systematization in Aristotle's account of the physical world, as set forth especially in his *On the Heavens* and *Meteorologica*.

Both works lean heavily on philosophy, but not at all on observational statements which on a few occasions were set forth quantitatively. A most preposterous and at the same time most ignored of these quantitative propositions was Aristotle's claim that of two bodies the one with twice the mass of the other would fall from the same height in only one half the time taken by the other body.[14] This detail, already mentioned in this book, cannot be recalled often enough, together with its broader context, if its instructiveness is to be fully perceived. The proposition was patently contrary to plain evidence. One could refute Aristotle's claim by merely standing on a chair and perform the experiment.

Why then was Aristotle, one of the keenest minds ever and a most careful observer in biology, lured into such an absurdity? There must have been most powerful motivations on hand. To see them one should recall Socrates' agonizing search in the *Phaedo* for a human purpose that lasts beyond the grave. He felt he had convincingly found such a purpose if it could only be shown that all material bodies moved towards a terminus that was best for them. It was that terminus which Aristotle later presented in terms of the doctrine of natural places. But a physics which aimed at the saving of purpose, was not physics but philosophy. Insofar as that physics contained quantitative propositions, the latter could be tested, indeed refuted and help thereby reveal some wrong presuppositions at work beyond them.

The testing failed to come for a very long time, although no other proposition in physics could ever have been refuted more easily. The proposition was meekly repeated by Aristotle's commentators throughout all Hellenistic times. Yet the experimental refutation of that proposition could not by itself lead one to the heart of the matter. Tellingly, the fallacy of what is central in Aristotelian physics had already been rejected before Galileo came along, let alone the legend was hatched that he had dropped two balls, one a hundred times larger than the other, from the Tower of Pisa.

This strange reversal of steps further proved that quantitative considerations, though autonomous, must be preceded by philosophical ones within which they can live out their autonomy. Thus Galileo merely gave a quantitative form to the idea of the "uniformly difform," that is, accelerated motion, which he inherited from the late-Scholastic tradition. Nor did Galileo invent the idea of inertial motion. He took it from Copernicus, together with the idea that the inertial motion of the stars had to be circular. Copernicus, who himself relied on the idea of that motion to answer problems posed by the two motions he attributed to the earth, merely repeated a by-then two-hundred-year-old tradition.

This tradition was born around 1348, when John Buridan of the Sorbonne took a most original look at some passages of Aristotle's *On the Heavens.* Buridan's originality did not lie in taking exception to Aristotle's claim that the motion of the heavenly sphere is eternal because the world is uncreated. From the very moment when Aristotle's works began to be commented upon in medieval universities, theologian after theologian disagreed with Aristotle's eternalism. They were keenly alive to the definition of creation in time as given at Lateran IV in 1215, a definition which reiterated also the age-old Christian tenet about creation out of nothing. Both tenets were metaphysics at its best as well.

Buridan's originality lay in the fact that he went beyond the metaphysics of the beginning of the existence of bodies to the physics of the beginning of the motion of bodies already existing. In essence and almost verbatim he said that in the beginning, when God made the heavens and the earth, He gave a certain quantity of impetus to all celestial bodies, which quantity they keep because they move in a realm where there is no friction.

In stating this, Buridan in substance anticipated Newton's first law of motion. To be sure, he thought in terms of a circular inertial motion, the point which all too often is held against him by historians of science, who cannot stomach the matrix of Buridan's innovation. The matrix is the Christian tenet of creation out of nothing and in time, very different from the corresponding tenet one finds in the two other great monotheistic religions, the Jewish and the Muslim. For the Christian tenet is riveted on Christ, the only begotten Son in whom the Father created all.

The absence of such a riveting in the two other monotheistic religions may help explain why their intellectuals have invariably fallen victim to the ever present lure of pantheism. Long before Spinoza and Einstein, great Jewish intellectuals were pantheists. Avicenna and Averroes forecast a similar trend within the Muslim intellectual ambience. Hence it was not a Jewish or a Muslim scholar who performed Buridan's feat, the essence of which deserves a brief though close look.

Beneath the discovery of inertial motion there lay a concept of creation and Creator that is indispensable for the formation of an idea of nature, which, though fully a creature, is fully autonomous. The prosperity and sanity of science hang on that autonomy. But this kind of autonomy could not be conceived within a pantheistic framework. There the universe—it is enough to think of the role of Aristotle's Prime Mover—was in continuous quasi-physical contact with the First Cause. Worse, since the Prime Mover was not a creator, the universe could only be an emanation from it (as articulated in great detail by Plotinus), and therefore the universe necessarily had to be what it was. About such a universe nothing is so tempting as to figure out its workings on an a priori basis. And why not? If the universe and the mind are generated by the same emanation, it should seem natural to assume that an introspecting mind, being an organic part of the universe, should be able to fathom its laws. But then no need, or at least no acute need will be felt to investigate the physical universe on an a posteriori basis, that is, by performing experiments about it.

So much in a nutshell about the origin of that science which half a millennium later propels history to an extent that cannot be exaggerated. The origin is strictly theological, and in that profound sense in which *Christian* means something that has its origin in Christ. A recourse to that origin is all the more timely today, when pantheism has novel champions in those scientists who claim that scientific cosmology gives them the theoretical power to create entire universes literally out of nothing. They merely suspect the reason why Christianity resists them more resolutely and articulately than any other factor.

Christians themselves still have to do their homework on that score, although it should be enough for them to consider one facet of the etymology of the word *cosmos* or *universe*. In their Greek and Roman use the two words were respectively synonymous with *monogenes* and *unigenitus*. Of course, both these words also meant the only begotten son of a father. But both words also stated that the cosmos or universe were eminently the only begotten entities from the Ultimate entity, which was never really different from the cosmos or universe itself.

The inference should therefore seem obvious. Belief in the concrete Jesus Christ, the only begotten Son, is emphatically incompatible with pantheism of any sort. At the same time, nothing irritates a pantheist more than the specter of Christ, especially when that specter includes science as well, this new savior of the modern world. Hence the resistance by prominent historians and philosophers to the full truth of what Pierre Duhem unfolded in heroically written volumes about the medieval origins of modern science.[15] The very fact of those volumes is so much salt rubbed in the wounds of that modern mind that stakes its absolute autonomy on science. But modern man owes that science to that very being, Christ, whom he most wants to remove from his horizon. Therefore that modern man, who does not tire of finding difficulties with Christ and with a Church that alone preaches Him fully, finds in the origin of science something much more than a problem of intellectual history. But it hardly indicates an unconditional respect for the facts of that history that every effort is made in some circles to keep under cover the foregoing conceptual connection between Christ and the rise of science.

Yet the fact remains that belief in Christ has at least one fact to recommend itself to men of our times so dependent on science. That belief played a crucial role in making possible the only viable birth which science had in all human history. Strange as it may appear, science, this only-begotten deity of modern life and by far the most powerful propellent of modern history, would not be here without belief in Christ as the only begotten Son of God. One need not be a Christian, merely an honest thinker, to see the intimate historical and philosophical connection between what Christ is, according to faith, and the origin of science. One need not be a historian of science, in command of medieval stenography, to see the difference which the birth of science in the Christian West made not only to the West but also to the rest of the world as well. One, of course, has to protect one's eyes from the false glare of the press, academic and non-academic, that tries to draw attention away from all this.

One certainly must avoid taking a clue from those historians of science, who in order to take the sting out of the Christian origin of science fall back on a claim that should disqualify them as historians. The claim is that even if there had not been a Buridan, his historical breakthrough would have been formulated anyhow sooner or later. A brief recall of the stillbirths which science suffered in all great ancient cultures[16] shows that Buridan, or someone equivalent to him, could not have come soon enough. To claim that there would have been a Buridan sooner or later is to assume that it is history, an abstract entity, that makes men, and not concrete men and their no less concrete minds that make history.

One need only have an honest mind to see that the connection between Christ and science is one of those cases in which a mental recourse to the origin is very relevant in making a prognosis about the future. Nothing would be more treacherous than to take the present moment in history, suddenly free from the agonizing experiences of the Cold War, for something permanent. On the horizon there already loom large and much more dangerous confrontations. Can free market policies cope with them? Is a World Bank, even one far more powerful than the present one, the means of defusing those confrontations? Is there a rebuttal in terms of micro or macro economics to Christ's words that the poor will always be with you? And is there an answer, independent of Christ, to ensure that the poor, either kept in ignorance about Christ or taught to take him lightly, will not one day rise in a manner which will make their earlier rise, as engineered by Marx and Lenin, appear to be child's play?

Religion, by which both Marx and Lenin meant primarily faith in Christ, may be the opiate of the people, but it may also be their sole assurance of a lasting purpose even in dire poverty or in the face of prospects far more excruciating than the one embodied in Gulags and gas chambers. The idea of a classless society turned out already to be a dream. The dream of a universally prosperous society is not safe from a rude awakening whose first intimations may be heard from the stock markets of the Far East. Beyond the inevitability of a global ice age (preceded by a global hothouse engineered by a mankind unable to restrain its use of scientific means) there lies the question of whether the human race, now at least three million years old, has been a mere flotsam and jetsam on some murky cosmic and historical waters.

The answer is a dire yes, if no affirmative answer is given to the possibility that all humans are so many created beings, created in that strict sense which only a creation in Christ can assure. A mankind which does not consider itself created in that sense should, however, beware of scanning the sky for messages in terms of coded radio signals from other civilizations in cosmic spaces. For the originators of those signals can be then nothing more than glorified beasts. The fact that they reached us with signals will certainly prove that they have much more powerful technical means at their disposal than we humans have today and for a long time to come. Their message can, however, be no more than sheer selfishness of selfish genes.

Only if man can assure himself that he is a created being, can he have assurance that aliens from outer space are also created beings, so many children of a loving Father Almighty. But here too facts, or at least the estimate of facts, must come first, for all estimates of probabilities must rest on facts. They alone give a clue to the purely empirical and philosophical side of the question about the extent to which mankind may or may not be alone in an incredibly vast universe.

[1] See the report of W. E. Leary in *The New York Times,* Dec. 16, 1997, p. F1.

[2] See H. Ford, *My Life and Work,* in collaboration with S. Crowther (Garden City, N.Y.: Doubleday, Page and Co., 1926), pp. 189-190. For the full context of Ford's dictum on history, see *Henry Ford,* ed. J. B. Rae (Englewood-Cliffs, N.J.: 1969), pp. 53-54.

[3] The phrase is in Ranke's Foreword to his *Geschichte der romanischen und germanischen Völker von 1494 bis 1514: Zur Kritik der neurer Geschichtschreiber,* in *Sämmtliche Werke* (3rd ed.; Leipzig: Duncker und Humblot, 1885), vol. 33-34, p. vii.

[4] As made clear by the closeness of *historein* to *istemo* in *ep-istemo-logy.*

[5] An attitude so notorious as to be recalled in the article "Froude, Anthony," in *Dictionary of National Biography,* vol. XXII, p. 686. There it is also reported that Froude viewed Shakespeare's historical plays as the best historical record of the periods they deal with.

[6] R. G. Collingwood *The Idea of History* (Oxford: Clarendon Press, 1946), p. 289.

[7] H. Butterfield, *The Whig Interpretation of History* (London: George Bell and Sons, 1931), p. 67.

[8] E. H. Carr, *What Is History?* (New York: Vintage Books, 1961), p. 21.

[9] Ibid., p. 34.

[10] See ibid., pp. 176 and 208.

[11] As revealed fifteen years later by H. Gelb in his communication, "Who Won the Cold War?" to *The New York Times,* Aug. 20, 1992, p. A26.

[12] The advice of A. M. Rosenthal, former editor of *The New York Times,* in its October 3, 1997, issue (p. A15).

[13] See my article, "Cloning and Arguing," *Linacre Quarterly* 65 (Feb. 1998), pp. 5-18.

[14] *On the Heavens,* Book I, ch. vi. A history of commentaries on this passage is still to be written.

[15] For the story, see ch. 10, "The Historian," in my *Uneasy Genius: The Life and Work of Pierre Duhem* (Dordrecht: Nijhoff, 1984), and its sequel, *Reluctant Heroine: The Life and Work of Hélène Duhem* (Edinburgh: Scottish Academic Press, 1992), which contains much unpublished material, unavailable at the time when the former work was written.

[16] A story set forth in my *Science and Creation: From Eternal Cycles to an Oscillating Universe* (1974; 2nd enlarged edition, Edinburgh: Scottish Academic Press, 1989).

14

Alone?

It makes for an amusing spectacle when physicists and astronomers, who swear by Darwinism as the ultimate explanation of any and all events in the realm of the living, bank on its mechanism but ignore its message. This happens whenever they slight prominent Darwinists, who hold that it makes no sense to talk of extraterrestrials, let alone to look for them. Such a Darwinist is Ernst Mayr, easily the dean of Darwinists today in the United States, and the most prominent among taxonomists. According to him, SETI, or Search for Extraterrestrial Intelligence, "is a deplorable waste of taxpayers' money."[1] Another is Joshua Lederberg, the Nobel-laureate geneticist. After he had read my paper, "The Earth-Moon System and the Rise of Science," just before its delivery at the 1996 Plenary Meeting of the Pontifical Academy of Sciences,[2] he confided to me that he had never had any use for SETI.

In that paper I criticized SETI on two distinctly empirical grounds. One relates to the history of science on earth, the only such history we know. Astronomers and physicists supportive of SETI view the emergence of science as a more or less foregone conclusion. To their excuse, they find no warning against this cavalier approach to the history of science in the writings of most of its professional historians. Yet, as will be seen, some facts of that history are so obvious that no professional training is required to take proper note of them. The other ground of my criticism of SETI derives from the consideration of some features of the Earth-Moon system. They are so obvious as to leave those physicists and astronomers, who ignore them, with no excuse whatsoever. It should be an integral part of their professional expertise to keep those features vividly in mind and constantly remind of them any and all.

Behind their dogged resolve to ignore those features there must lie enormously strong motivations, none of them scientific. Such motivations aim at safeguarding a message which is very philosophical, though presented as something genuinely scientific. According to that message human intelligence is a mere epiphenomenon of biochemically highly diversified tissues, commonly called grey matter, ready to appear anywhere in the cosmos whenever the appropriate chemical conditions are on hand. This is their message. Their means is a brazen selectivity with the data of science and of its history.

Such a selectivity amounts to the manhandling of widely available truths. If the Earth-Moon factor is taken into account, it is not possible to reach the estimate that there are about ten thousand (10^4) planets in our galaxy with technologically advanced civilizations on them, capable of sending radio messages that can be detected from the Earth. But the Earth-Moon factor fails to appear in the Drake equation, proposed by the astronomer Frank Drake in 1961, which has since served as the basis of such estimates, whether in its original form or in its variants.

The equation, $N = R^* f_p n_e f_l f_i f_c L$, as given in Drake's book, *Is anyone out there?*, published in 1992,[3] can easily be restated in plain words. One begins to evaluate N, or the number of planets as specified above, by estimating R^* or the number of suitable stars, such as our Sun, in our galaxy. Obviously only a fraction of such stars will have planets around them, a fraction denoted by f_p. This fraction is further reduced by estimating n_e or the number of planets hospitable to life, such as our Earth. Again, only on a fraction of this number of planets will life actually emerge, a fraction denoted by f_l. This fraction is further reduced by the factor f_i, or the fraction of planets where life evolves into intelligent beings. Of this number only a fraction is left when one considers f_c or the number of planets with intelligent creatures capable of interstellar communication. A further reduction is necessitated by considering the factor L, which refers to the lifespan of such civilizations during which they are detectable.

A most obvious defect of this method is the absence there of an explicit, special reference to the Earth-Moon system, or a factor which may be denoted by f_{E-M}. The reason for this new factor is that the origin of the Moon is independent of the origin of the Earth. Indeed the Moon's origin is so chancy as to make the Earth-Moon system a freakish feature of the solar system. The Drake equation would then read as $N = R^* f_p n_e f_{E-M} f_l f_i f_c L$.

The position of the new factor in the equation is justified by the fact that the rise of life on Earth is greatly dependent on the Moon. The Moon produces the tidal basins about which it is generally assumed that, even if they were not the site of the origin of life on Earth, they played an indispensable role in the transition of life from sea to land. But the Moon is not at all a natural part of the Earth's development. The Moon came to be attached to the Earth by a most improbable event.

The now widely accepted scenario assumes a body, called X, of the size of Mars, to have had a glancing collision with the Earth. There are at least six independent parameters, all of them with a low degree of probability, at play in making the glancing collision result in a Moon orbiting the Earth. Such parameters are the mass of X, its velocity, the direction of its motion relative to the Earth's rotation, the plane of its orbit relative to the plane of the Earth's orbiting around the Sun, and the stage of the Earth's evolution itself. Finally the collision has to be a glancing one, that is, limited to a rather narrow outer shell of the Earth's body. This is demanded by the fact that the Moon's density equals that of the Earth's mantle.

If one assigns to each of these parameters a probability of one tenth, a rather conservative estimate, their combined probability is 10^{-6}, which would then reduce Drake's estimate to 10^{-2}, or from ten thousand to a mere one-hundredth. And if one assumes more realistically that the probability of at least four of those parameters is only 10^{-2}, the combined improbability of those six parameter is 10^{-10}, which in turn would reduce Drake's estimate from 10^4 to 10^{-6} or from ten thousand to one millionth. In other words, once the Earth-Moon factor is taken into account, the probability that there is at least one technologically advanced civilization in our galaxy is merely one in a million. This is very different from the expectation held high by Drake that there are at least ten thousand such civilizations in our galaxy.

No such estimates were made when about ten years ago attention was drawn in an obscure journal to the need to take into account the Earth-Moon system in evaluating the Drake equation. Yet it seems that publication even in a prominent journal would not have caused as much as a ripple, given the pseudophilosophical wishful thinking that dominates the circles supportive of SETI. They have willing allies among historians of science, who should have shouted their heads off as a reaction to the blight expectation which takes the evolution of science on earth for granted. It should have been enough for them to ask any and all to look at the Moon in order to purge themselves of that expectation. A moderately educated look at the Moon may help one to notice the enormously haphazard course of science from the Greeks of old to Newton. That course is even more counterfactual than the course of military or political history, a facet still to be taken seriously and explored in detail by historians of science. They may find that much less than the coming of democracy and free-market economy can the rise of science be taken for granted.

To get the first intimations of this it is enough to look at any globe and compare the big rivers shown there with one another. Of those rivers only one, the Nile, has a long and fairly straight course in the South-North direction, which touches on the ecliptic and ends at a point in the temperate zone where an important center of learning developed. Without the Nile, Eratosthenes could not have measured a sufficiently long distance on the Earth, a distance needed for his calculating its radius and circumference. No geologist in his right mind would claim that the Nile is a necessary feature of the Earth's surface and that therefore a replica of it must appear on those other earths eagerly looked for by the champions of SETI. Yet Eratosthenes' calculation remains the very basis of all astronomy and beyond it of all science.

To be sure, that calculation alone would not have by itself led even to Ptolemaic astronomy. It is on the road of science towards Ptolemy that the Moon played an indispensable role. Only because the Moon's apparent diameter is equal to the Sun's are there full lunar eclipses. These in turn were indispensable for Aristarchus of Samos to develop a most ingenious method to calculate the absolute sizes of the Moon and the Sun and the relative and absolute distances among the Earth, the Sun, and the Moon. His calculations are the basis of Ptolemaic astronomy, without which there would have been no Copernican turn. There is nothing preordained in all this, which should seem very chancy indeed, and hardly good news for those who stake their Weltanschauung on their rosy evaluation of the Drake equation.

Without the Moon, Newton would have lacked a much needed assurance about the correctness of his physics. Whatever the truth of the fall of an apple on young Newton's nose, the fall of the Moon in its orbit was indispensable for Newton to convince himself that the same law of acceleration worked indeed both in the heavens and on earth. The rate of the fall of the other planets was not yet known in Newton's time with sufficient accuracy to provide him with the kind of certainty that makes or unmakes exact science.

With Newton's *Principia* in place, there was in place a science which had a live birth and as such could be followed by a development which may appear almost a foregone conclusion. Almost but not entirely. From Newton to Einstein and beyond, all physics is the quantitative study of the quantitative aspects of motion. Nothing more, nothing less. In that sense, the post-Newtonian development of science may be taken for something inevitable. Still there remains the fact that this development was the work of geniuses. But can geniuses, such as Newton, Faraday, Maxwell, Planck, Einstein and others, be taken for granted? Einstein himself noted that if not he, others would have certainly come up with the special theory of relativity. He was not willing to concede the same about the general theory. Indeed if one link of the chain of those geniuses had not come about at the right place and time, there would have arisen a domino effect of disastrously cumulative delays. Historians of science might speculate about them with much profit both for themselves as well as for the champions of SETI.

Even a cursory recall of the chanciness of young Faraday's road to science may send the chill down the spines of sanguine appraisers of the Drake equation. And what if Maxwell had not been a younger contemporary of Faraday and a fellow Briton? What if Planck had followed the advice of Jolly and not chosen physics for a career? What if Einstein had started talking not at the age of six but at the age of sixteen or twenty-six or perhaps never? All this could have happened and should be taken into consideration when estimating the probability of the development of science on earth. For this is the only development of science on the basis of which one can speculate on its development elsewhere. Any other speculation is a facile game with the human intellect, scientific and other and certainly a rank abuse of the scientific method.

But the period of science history which should be most revealing in this respect relates to the three or so centuries preceding Newton. This consideration imposes itself as long as one takes exact science for the quantitative study of the quantitative aspects of moving bodies, and not for the interplay of some tortuous psychological and sociological factors. These, because of their inexactness, turn the prediction of the history of science into an even more unpredictable matter, themselves being rather indefinable.

It is otherwise with the truly exact components of exact science, that is, with their exact laws. Their original formulation can, for the most part, be readily pinpointed, which in turn makes for a more reliable estimate of how predictable was indeed the rise and further evolution of science. Of all those exact components none are so exact and fundamental as the three laws of motion. Once those three laws appeared together in Newton's *Principia*, which also contained on their basis a cohesive system of physics, the further development of science was assured even though its rate of growth remained largely unpredictable.

One might therefore take the *Principia* for the birth of exact science, but for the fact that of the three laws of motion Newton could take credit only for the third. He borrowed the second, that action equals reaction, from Descartes, without giving credit to him. As to the first law, Newton and his contemporaries no longer knew what Descartes still suspected, namely, that its origins went back to the Middle Ages. And since that first law, the law of inertial motion, grounds the two others, both historically and conceptually, it may be justified to locate the viable birth of science in the Middle Ages.

What has already been said in the previous chapter about that viable birth and the several monumental stillbirths of science in ancient times constitutes a factor that augurs badly for hopeful evaluations of the Drake equation. More such factors emerge if one considers the slow progress of science from Buridan to Newton. What if Buridan had postponed by two years his work of commenting on Aristotle's cosmology? He might have easily perished in the Black Death that claimed one-third of Europe and decimated Paris itself. What if the dueling sword that cut off Tycho Brahe's nose had struck an inch higher and deprived him of his eyes? He would not have put together a vast and incredibly precise set of observations of the position of Mars. Kepler then would not have written his book on Mars, which contained the conclusion that its orbit is elliptical. Nor would Kepler have formulated his two other laws of planetary motions, had Brahe's data not been available to him.

Before one draws the obvious inference that in this case there would have been no Newton and no subsequent and irresistible advance of physics, one may ponder with profit the role of Jeremiah Horrocks. A genius of an astronomer, who died at the age of 22 in 1641, Horrocks wrote the first readable account of Kepler's work and finished it in that very year. What if death had claimed him a year earlier? And what if Wallis, the famed mathematician, had not saved Horrocks' manuscripts and published them in 1664 and again in 1678? The book, *Astronomia kepleriana propugnata et defensa* came most handily for young

Newton just as he was thinking hard on a physics of motion, valid throughout the universe.

So much about the uncertainties of science on Earth. What is not at all uncertain is that, as set forth in the preceding chapter, the great breakthrough came in terms of, yes, orthodox christology. This point is most significant both in its intrinsic conceptual merit and also in reference to the endless glib remarks which champions of SETI make about the Incarnation. To many of them Jesus Christ is a planet-hopping savior, if they care to think of him at all.

Their casting Christ in such a contemptible role hardly betrays any depth in the thinking of SETI's ardent champions. They, of course, are wont to betray their shallowness in many other ways. Clearly, one can only be in despair of the human mind's abilities, if one expects from extraterrestrials the solution to our chief human vexations, some of which have been triggered by the growth of our science. I was exposed to one such preachment by an astronomer of the Arecibo radiotelescope while visiting there sometime in 1991. He must have derived extra satisfaction from seeing me wearing the Roman collar. I did not tell him a word about my being a physicist and a historian of science, in addition to being a theologian. Humility is good for the soul which needs better satisfaction than quick points scored on the spur of the moment. Anyway, no one proud of having a soul should regard arguments as so many easy means of vanquishing other souls. These can only be gained or lost.

Yes, souls, which are mere epiphenomena within the perspective of SETI. Why then are its champions so eager to find extraterrestrials? Are they perhaps unsure of a for-them crucial issue? Do they search because they assume that a positive outcome would prove that man is a mere flotsam and jetsam in unfathomable cosmic waters and as such is his own master, unaccountable to any superior force, such as God? Or are they lonely without daring to admit it? Are their hearts frightened, as was the heart of Pascal's *libertin*,[4] by the specter of immense empty spaces?

Those spaces may turn out to be as void of intelligent beings as appeared around 1935 when O. Lovejoy came out with his *The*

Great Chain of Being, a historical survey of all the previous illusions generated by heedless adherence to the principle called cosmic plenitude.[5] Were those, such as Immanuel Kant, who even determined the moral characteristics of denizens on all the other planets, from Mercury to Saturn,[6] reliable philosophers? Or is philosophical reliability equivalent to clichés of which the history of philosophy is as full as any other history? Such and similar lessons of intellectual history can be ignored only at great peril, lest it should prove once more the case that the only thing man learns from history is that he ignores all its great lessons.

On the basis of Darwinism, mankind should be most reluctant to acknowledge radio messages from outer space. On the basis of Darwinism (did not Darwin say that it might be better to leave to a dog to speculate about the mind of Newton?[7]) one cannot claim that intelligence is everywhere the same in the universe. Much less can one claim on the basis of Darwinism that genuine love would arise from the biochemical diversification of some tissues. On the basis of Darwinism one can have only one advice concerning extraterrestrials. The advice—go into hiding—was given by the Nobel laureate C. Yang in 1961, an advice still more sensible than all the philosophies dished out by advocates of SETI. Extraterrestrials, should they visit us, would take us for plain slaves, if not for mere protein reservoirs. No other conclusion is admissible on the basis of Darwinism, if it is taken at face value, and not with the trick of trying to eat one's cake and still having it.

Mental tricks are a roundabout proof of the fact that the human mind is infinitely more than matter or any of its configurations. Configurations, numbers never play tricks. Only minds can play tricks even to the point of trying to trick themselves. Such minds, to leave aside their far more exalted abilities, could come out (and in the case of each and every mind) only from a direct creative action, which only a truly Creator God can perform. Such a God would hardly produce a very large number of planets with exactly the same physical conditions prevailing throughout their entire lifespan (an incredibly tall order on a purely natural basis) so that the evolutionary process on them would lead to the emergence of higher organisms similar to us.

Those physical conditions would include the provision that all those other earths would be bombarded by huge comets and meteors as the Earth has been hit by them at regular and irregular intervals. The course of evolution, of life and even of history on the Earth was heavily dependent on those at times catastrophic impacts. Another factor, the role of undersea volcanos is just beginning to be seen in its true extent. Could one realistically assume the close duplication of all such very chancy factors elsewhere? Have not the drastic catastrophes triggered by those factors redirected time and again the course of biological evolution on our Earth? And what about the role of the Moon as a shield for the Earth against some giant comets and meteors? Was not one of these, whose impact on the far side of the Moon resulted in the huge Giordano Bruno crater, heading for the Earth in June 1178?[8] Would not such an impact, if it had hit the Earth somewhere in Western Europe, have wiped out the 12th-century Renaissance and put an end to the nascent universities?

The Creator and only the Creator, could have, of course, allowed the evolutionary process elsewhere to lead to different higher organisms that still could be endowed with mind. Only on that supposition can one see any rhyme or reason in Loren Eiseley's evocation of extraterrestrials, who with strange limbs, odd faces, and weird eyes direct their telescopes into outer space.[9] On that presupposition one can even imagine bimanous, tetrapodal hexapods possessing intelligence and science to boot.

For all we know, it should seem that we are alone, though not at all, if God is with us. Take away God, and the greatest plenitude will become loneliness incarnate. Such is the ultimate message of the means called science. Properly speaking, physical science has no right to deliver such a message, in fact any message, although physicists constantly deliver a great variety of them. For any message lands one in metaphysics, whose means is not a man-made instrument, but a mind open to the glaring evidence of objects before one's eyes. Eyes, however, must be kept open and protected from the ever-recurring danger of being blurred. This happens whenever the message becomes the means and the means the message.

Those who make this error cultivate the subjective, however unwittingly, and isolate themselves from objective reality. The inner overcrowding which subjectivism, contrary to its promise, keeps producing, will prove confining to them and indeed suffocating, with no offer of an exit. Subjectivism—be it called sensationism, empiricism, rationalism and idealism—is a blinder against noticing the Ariadne's thread leading out from self-imposed labyrinths. But those intent on constructing their message so as to account fully for the means by which they convey it, should find in the experiment the kind of exhilaration which stands for sanity of mind, balance of emotions, and abiding sense of purpose. In a more formal way they should find in the process of going from the means to the message, the very basis on which alone can a treatise be written about truth.

[1] E. Mayr, *Toward a New Philosophy of Biology* (Cambridge: Harvard University Press, 1988), p. 73.

[2] October 22-26, 1996. See vol. IV, pp. 279-290 in the provisional publication, *Commentarii* of that Plenary Session (Vatican City, 1997).

[3] See F. Drake and D. Sobel, *Is Anyone Out There? The Scientific Search for Extraterrestrial Intelligence* (New York: Delacorte Press, 1992), p. 52.

[4] Pascal, *Pensées*, tr. J. M. Cohen (Penguin Classics, 1961), p. 57 (#91).

[5] A. O. Lovejoy, *The Great Chain of Being: A Study of the History of an Idea* (1936; Harper Torchbooks, 1960).

[6] See my translation, with introduction and notes of Kant's *Universal Natural History and Theory of the Heavens* (Edinburgh: Scottish Academic Press, 1978).

[7] Letter of May 22, 1860, to A. Gray, in *The Life and Letters of Charles Darwin* ed. F. Darwin (London: John Murray, 1887), vol. 2, p. 312.

[8] O. Calame and J. D. Mulholland, "Lunar Crater Giordano Bruno: A. D. 1178 Impact Observations Consistent with Laser Ranging Reports," *Science* 199 (24 Feb. 1978), pp. 875-77.

[9] L. Eiseley, *The Immense Journey* (New York: Vintage Books, 1959), p. 162.

Index of Names

Index of Subjects

229

(continued from p. ii)

By the same author

Miracles and Physics

God and the Cosmologists
(Farmington Institute Lectures, Oxford, 1988)

The Only Chaos and Other Essays

The Purpose of It All
(Farmington Institute Lectures, Oxford, 1989)

Catholic Essays

Cosmos in Transition: Studies in the History of Cosmology

Olbers Studies

Scientist and Catholic: Pierre Duhem

Reluctant Heroine: The Life and Work of Hélène Duhem

Universe and Creed

Genesis 1 through the Ages

Is There a Universe?

Patterns or Principles and Other Essays

Bible and Science

Theology of Priestly Celibacy

* * *

Translations with introduction and notes:

The Ash Wednesday Supper (Giordano Bruno)

*Cosmological Letters on the Arrangement
of the World Edifice* (J.-H. Lambert)

Universal Natural History and Theory of the Heavens (I. Kant)

Note on the Author

Stanley L. Jaki, a Hungarian-born Catholic priest of the Benedictine Order, is Distinguished University Professor at Seton Hall University, South Orange, New Jersey. With doctorates in theology and physics, he has for the past forty years specialized in the history and philosophy of science. The author of almost forty books and over a hundred articles, he served as Gifford Lecturer at the University of Edinburgh and as Fremantle Lecturer at Balliol College, Oxford. He has lectured at major universities in the United States, Europe, and Australia. He is honorary member of the Pontifical Academy of Sciences, *membre correspondant* of the Académie Nationale des Sciences, Belles-Lettres et Arts of Bordeaux, and the recipient of the Lecomte du Nouy Prize for 1970 and of the Templeton Prize for 1987.